Volume XXXI: NUMBER TWO
2006

Contents

BOOK REVIEWS

Modern Psychoanalysis

The editors invite submissions of articles to MODERN PSYCHOANALYSIS. Manuscripts should be typed, double-spaced, on one side of 8½ ×11-inch white paper, or as a word-processing file on a CD-Rom or a 3½-inch disk. Hardcopy submissions should be in triplicate with a SASE. Footnotes and bibliographies must conform to the style of this journal. The editors should be informed, with the submission, if the article has appeared or has been submitted elsewhere.

MODERN PSYCHOANALYSIS, the journal of the Center for Modern Psychoanalytic Studies, 16 West 10th Street, New York, NY 10011, is published semiannually. Individual subscriptions are on a yearly basis: $53.00 per year. Institutions: $60.00. Write for foreign rates.

ISBN 978-0-9790972-5-6   YBK Publishers, Inc., 39 Crosby St., New York, NY 10013

MODERN PSYCHOANALYSIS is abstracted and indexed in *Psychoanalytic Abstracts* (Pa. A).

The Phyllis W. Meadow Award for Excellence in Psychoanalytic Writing

THE EDITORS and JENNIFER WADE

We are pleased and proud to publish these essays, honored as they are in the name of our late founder and longtime editor, as well as the personal reflections of the award's administrator, Jennifer Wade.

Of the award's stated reasons for being, one is especially meaningful to us: to encourage writing and publication by psychoanalytic thinkers and practitioners who might not otherwise have undertaken to be writers. Each of these four essays is the first by its author that the journal has had the opportunity to publish. Along with their own merits they represent to us an expansion of the great conversation in which this journal is privileged to participate. We welcome every such addition as an enrichment of the harmony of all those voices.

—The Editors

Shortly after Phyllis W. Meadow's death in 2005, I conceived the idea of a psychoanalytic writing award in her honor. It was, I am sure, a way out of mourning. I could move toward creation and away from loss. I could keep my supervisor of many years with me by initiating a project reflecting our shared interest in writers and what they write.

I liked the idea of rewarding psychoanalytic writers. A bit of internet research established that this was not a popular notion. I wanted a prize that would buy a vacation or (our winner's choice) a couch, real grati-

© 2006 CMPS/*Modern Psychoanalysis*, Vol. 31, No. 2

fication for a group living mostly on faint praise and their private-practice incomes. I wrote a rather pleading letter to a foundation president I know in California, suggesting they fund the prize. Victoria Seaver Dean of The Seaver Institute wrote back and said sure.

Dena Reed and Mimi Crowell, presidents, respectively, of the Boston Graduate School of Psychoanalysis (BGSP) and the Center for Modern Psychoanalytic Studies (CMPS), agreed to sponsor the award, and we established a committee of judges.

After announcing the competition far and wide, I realized the big problem with my plan. We were not simply going to hand a three-thousand-dollar check to the winner; we were going to be yet another source of rejection to the much larger group of authors brave enough to compete. A writer myself, I had somehow been blind to this reality. As psychoanalysts, you will recognize that I had displaced my own eagerness for recognition onto the potential winner, while also satisfying myself with the knowledge that this was a competition I could never lose. A bit of emotional work helped me remember that the carrot of a prize is nice, but it's there to encourage the deeper and more painful pleasure of writing a finished work and daring to send it out.

I reverted to my identification with the winners in the excitement of the award ceremony last summer in New York City. First-prize winner Claudia Luiz and the three authors receiving honorable mention, Stephen Guttman, Patrick Lee Miller, and Alina Schellekes, came with family and friends from as far as North Carolina, Tel Aviv, and Massachusetts. In the thrill of that night I thought it might be as much fun to give prizes as it is to write a single page of good prose.

Phyllis W. Meadow worked passionately as analyst, teacher, administrator, and writer to expand the understanding and influence of psychoanalysis. She was convinced that the future of the profession depended on the development of a literature that communicates its effectiveness. The key to this, she believed, was the publication of in-depth, single-case studies. A thesis-length version was a requirement for graduation from the three analytic institutes she founded. Throughout her career Meadow refined this assignment to better illuminate the science in the art of psychoanalysis. As founder and editor of this journal, Meadow cultivated scholarship that eschewed jargon and brought the reader into the consulting room. The author of many articles and books, including most recently *The New Psychoanalysis* (2003), Meadow expanded on the theory of technique first developed by Hyman Spotnitz to treat patients suffering from schizophrenia and other severe character disorders.

It's worth restating Meadow's instruction to focus on identifying the repetitions in the transference. The cure, she asserted, was not in the patient's remembering, but in the working through of his conflicts in relation to the analyst. Stay in the moment with the patient's love and hate and use the induced feelings to shape interventions. Meadow advised against interpreting the transference. As an editor she put it differently: let the drama of the interaction tell the story.

No wonder Meadow said writers make good analysts and writing makes analysts better. The drama of the consulting room has a potency that is the stuff of literature. We write not only to demonstrate the efficacy of the treatment, but also to nourish other analysts. Our work can be lonely and draining. We read not only to learn, but also to find inspiration.

I found it with Meadow. She had a way of making me feel as if anything were possible. Obstacles were not roadblocks but opportunities to get my hands dirty and enjoy the fight. To spend any time with her was to become involved in her most urgent projects of whatever sort—lobbying for state licensing of practitioners, strategizing toward establishing graduate degrees in psychoanalysis, negotiating with building contractors. Her attention to all these other matters when I was with her roused an abandoned, sibling-rivalry sort of feeling in me at first, but soon enough came to seem a kind of tithing to our larger enterprise. I found myself stitched into the fabric of the institute and of the profession. How could I help internalizing some of her ambition?

And so, I hope that the Phyllis W. Meadow Award for Excellence in Psychoanalytic Writing will inspire authors to bring a new level of creativity and intelligence to the literature of our profession. This competition is open not only to clinicians, but to anyone with psychoanalysis on his mind, very much including the patients we treat. I encourage authors to try something new. Go to the edge of their experience. First and foremost, aim for cohesion, clarity, and persuasiveness. Eloquent and substantiated articles on theory and practice not only contribute to the discipline of psychoanalysis, they exercise the muscles of emotional logic so basic to our work. Good psychoanalytic writing cultivates our capacity not only to understand, but also to receive whatever our patients offer and use it creatively.

In the four winning papers the reader is invited to visit two old stories and two new. First-prize author Claudia Luiz describes a long-term analysis with a preoedipal patient in "Pushing Through Boundaries of Inner Space: The Need for Analytic Transparency in the Treatment of a Juggler." With affecting humility Luiz, a Massachusetts psychoanalyst, shows how her patient's and her own struggle to be together meld to form the cure. Honorable Mention recipient Alina Schellekes writes of her work with an intensely fragile woman in "Writing As a Protective Shell: The Analysis of a Young Writer." Schellekes, an associate member of The Israeli Psychoanalytic Society, is chair of a new program focusing on the study of primitive mental states at the Tel Aviv University School of Psychotherapy.

Stephen R. Guttman and Patrick Lee Miller each received Honorable Mention for papers that address questions of psychoanalytic knowing. In his historical survey of the concept of hysteria Guttman enriches our understanding of this core concept and highlights the value of regularly refreshing our thinking about our theories and our patients. In "*Oedipus Rex* Revisited" Miller considers how much and in what way Oedipus knew of his origins and his fate. Miller, a professor of philosophy at Duquesne University in Pittsburgh, finds in Sophocles' work an admonition to analysts to respect what is beyond our capacity to know.

Phyllis W. Meadow is gone, but a piece of her lives within all of us who knew her. I share my piece with you. Thanks to The Seaver Institute and the many people from CMPS and BGSP who have given so much of themselves to this project.

—Jennifer Wade

REFERENCES

Meadow, P. W. (2003), *The New Psychoanalysis*. New York: Rowman & Littlefield.

31 Washington Square West, Ste. 6B
New York, NY 10011
jennwade@aol.com

Modern Psychoanalysis
Vol. XXXI, No. 2, 2006

Pushing Through Boundaries of Inner Space: The Need for Analytic Transparency in the Treatment of a Juggler

CLAUDIA LUIZ

This paper describes the evolution of a 17-year modern analysis of Mr. M, a juggler, during which resistances were successfully resolved without interpretation and with an almost complete absence of psychological exploration. The paper examines the concept of analytic transparency and demonstrates that the distinct way this psyche organized itself to manage and discharge tensions required taking an analytic stance that was unusually transparent.

In this paper I hope to clarify a concept I've termed analytic tranparency. I use the word "transparency" as an alternative to analytic "neutrality" to emphasize the difference between how I conceptualized this treatment as compared to that of other, more classically Freudian neurotic or hysterical personalities. While neurotic patients may appreciate the analyst's neutrality and objectivity, I believe that this patient had to feel he knew the analyst.[1]

---

1 It is interesting to note with respect to Freud's concept of analytic "neutrality" that Lynn and Valliant (1998), who studied his theory of technique against the communications he actually made to his patients, recognized a "substantial disparity between Freud's recommendations and his actual methods."

© 2006 CMPS/*Modern Psychoanalysis*, Vol. 31, No. 2

In fact, this patient could often sense what I was feeling, and what could be construed as his transference projections were often uncannily close to my emotional reality. The boundaries between self and other became at times so obscured for me that the term "neutrality" could not begin to define an analytic posture best suited for his treatment.

I have conceptualized the treatment in phases. These phases are not meant to be prescriptive of treatment in general. They describe, instead, changes in the material presented by this particular patient, which may have resulted from the resolution of transference and countertransference resistances. In reality, the phases were fairly indistinct; vestiges of each phase remained in practically all subsequent phases.

Fragmentation and Terror: Treatment Phase One

THE SEVEN RINGS OF HELL

Lying on the couch in my office during his first few sessions, Mr. M seemed agitated. He might spout a few words: "Your hair . . ." he'd whisper. "Your thigh . . ." He appeared to be in a state of agony or desire or both.

Mr. M did not exhibit the characteristics of a classic psychoanalytic patient; he did not seem neurotic, obsessional, hysterical, depressed, or anxious. He had suffered from an eating disorder in his early twenties. Although he had been diagnosed with schizophrenia during a brief stay at a hospital where his parents had taken him after he had tried to break the windshield of their car with an ax, he did not consider himself schizophrenic. Before beginning treatment with me, in fact, he had already been in a brief modern analysis.

Despite his interest in psychoanalysis, Mr. M did not feel he exhibited any "curable" symptoms. He felt hopeless. As the sessions progressed, he often talked about his wish to die. "There's no point," he'd say. "I should just die."

In his early twenties, after a series of adventures joining religious groups, meeting a variety of people, and working at fast-food joints across the country, Mr. M had returned to live in his original home. At the time he began treatment with me, he had been living with his parents for approximately eight years.

His life, when he started treatment, was fairly circumscribed. He had started juggling a few years earlier, which occupied much of his attention. He did not seem interested in doing much more than coming to his sessions, visiting his sister in another state, and working out daily at his neighborhood gym. Despite his great mental acuity, he did not find it possible to read or write. This was a source of disappointment to him and added to his hopelessness.

Mr. M could describe his daily life and experiences fairly lucidly. However, it was very difficult for him to talk about upsetting events. Often, he was upset by his parents and sister as well as by people he encountered in his daily outings. Whenever he felt upset, he would interrupt his thoughts by saying, "My sister . . . nooo. I can't talk about that." If I asked him why he couldn't talk about something, he'd say, "It's hopeless," and turn his head to the wall.

Physical sensations were very prevalent for Mr. M when treatment started. He talked a lot about his body: his arm ached; his hands were too sweaty; he had an upset stomach. These bodily sensations disturbed him and the juggling often brought them on. The juggling both fascinated and tormented him.

Mr. M had also had some sex therapy, which he had found helpful because he had felt thwarted in his sexual development in his early twenties. He had been helped and encouraged to touch the sex therapist. She was apparently no longer available, and he could not find any other office that provided that form of treatment.

In two ways he expressed disappointment that I could not provide sex therapy. The first was to say, "We should just have sex. That is the only thing that would help." The second was to interrupt his sentences with sad rhapsodies: "Yesterday I . . . your thigh . . . your hair . . . " His intense longings and hopelessness were both embodied in these communications.

During the first few months of treatment, I would emerge from sessions with Mr. M feeling surreal and fragmented. It was a struggle to find language to describe my emotional experience with him. The analytic office felt at once enclosed and intense to me. There was no sense of time or space, as if the sessions could go on forever. Mr. M's extreme sensitivity to sensory impressions did not apply only to me. If Mr. M was talking and the overhead heating fan suddenly went on, its whooshing sounds were capable of completely silencing him because of frustration over the interruption.

I struggled to defend against the degree of fragmentation and tension in the initial months of treatment by working with Mr. M to bring me a check each week. He said, "Talk to my father." His passivity paralleled his hopelessness. He would say, "I can't bring you anything. I can't talk to my father. I can just come here. That's all I can do."

It seemed important to me to keep Mr. M's parents out of the treatment and to establish a therapeutic relationship and contract that would include only him and me. Fortunately, my insistence on his obtaining and bringing me the check did lead to his cooperation. In fact, he began to drive himself to the sessions instead of having his father drive him.

Perhaps Mr. M experienced my wish to keep his parents out of the contract as an expression of my interest in being "in synch" with him. In fact, shortly after he began bringing me the checks, he bought a watch, which he would wear only for his sessions. He insisted that we synchronize our watches to the minute, if not the second, at the start of each session.

On several occasions, Mr. M came early for his sessions to adjust the clocks in the other treatment offices to further ensure that we would be in synch even if we should have to switch rooms. I tried to explore the meaning of his actions in the hope of influencing his patterns of discharge in order to channel expression from action to verbalization (Spotnitz, 1976). Mr. M's response to my questions and explorations, however, was to shut down and become sullen. He would turn his head to the wall and not talk. My efforts to get him to put his actions into words were experienced by Mr. M, I believe, as rejecting and confusing.

Also during this period, Mr. M went into action by turning on the overhead fan in my office. As it began to swirl violently above me, I became anxious that it was going to fly off the ceiling and behead me. When I looked at him, he seemed to be gazing at the fan, smiling. I sprang up from my chair, turned the fan off, and commanded him not to alter it again.

Mr. M picked up on my terror and began to talk in earnest about not returning to treatment after this incident. It is as yet unclear to me from whose mind the violent fantasy originated: whether I was in touch with murderous impulses in him or generating my own; whether he felt terrified by his own impulses or mine. The difficulty knowing where I began and where the patient ended was very characteristic of this case.

THE PUZZLE

The intensity in the room, in combination with all the acting out, his difficulty talking, and the hopelessness about not having sex therapy, was frustrating for me. Treatment was becoming laborious. I was unsure as to whether I could manage the case. After each session Mr. M would say, "Should I come back? I don't know. . . ."

In the midst of my hopelessness, I asked Mr. M what he enjoyed doing. He said, "My father and I do puzzles. We could do a puzzle." Mr. M and I embarked on a discussion about doing a jigsaw puzzle in the session. We talked about how the puzzle was to be started, where we would keep it, and how we would work on it. After a few weeks, it became apparent that Mr. M was not just *talking* about doing a puzzle—he was expecting that we really would.

I felt very conflicted about actually doing the puzzle, or going into any kind of action, especially in light of the emerging eroticized transference. Trying to adhere to the standards of modern analytic techniques, I was working to understand contact functioning and to design effective object-oriented questions (Spotnitz, 1969). Furthermore, the patient's struggle to get money from his father and his switching clocks around and turning fans on all aroused anxiety in me. A part of me wanted to reject him to free myself of these tensions.

During this time, I presented this case at a psychoanalytic colloquium led by Dr. Meadow, who suggested that I relax my parameters around technique. She explained that going into action with the puzzle would not be analogous to going into action sexually. Mr. M was not looking *primarily* for interaction and sexual gratification. Rather, he was interested in finding a means of decreasing the tension in the room. Dr. Meadow directed me to read Ferenczi and to try my hand at the "active technique" (Ferenczi, 1950; Freud, 1924).

It is possible that Ferenczi might have given Mr. M an injunction to bring in the puzzle. However, Meadow's recommendation to use an active technique did not have the effect of forcing repressed material as Ferenczi might have hoped. It did succeed, however, in overcoming a corrosive impasse in the treatment.

The puzzle—all 2,000 pieces of it—was extraordinary. It was round, with an image of a bird of paradise in brilliant colors. It felt at once meaningful and daunting, like a giant, dharmic wheel of life. The puzzle brought to the sessions the first semblances of peace and cohesion for me, despite the fact that I still felt somewhat inhibited and reserved. Still, it distracted me and Mr. M from language. In doing the puzzle, I let Mr. M know that I could tolerate him.

As I sat in my chair, I would watch Mr. M on the floor, his gangly limbs usually folded in, working diligently. The puzzle held the promise of integration and of paradise. If I saw a piece that could fit, I would point it out to him, and he would insert it. We worked together peacefully this way for many weeks. Toward the latter part of this period, he would sometimes tire of the puzzle and take the couch, where he would remain in silence or sometimes talk about the events of his week. Once or twice he dozed. We never finished the puzzle. During this period I had a dream.

Encapsulation: Treatment Phase Two

THE DREAM

My dream occurred on a morning before I was to meet with Mr. M Unlike any other dream I have had before or since, this one featured a large, colorless, undulating blob (Figure 1).

At the time, I likened the image in my dream to that of an amoeba. I had once studied amoebas and paramecia under a microscope. It seemed to me that they moved as if pushed from within causing them to undulate and roll. In the dream, too, it was as if something inside the amoeba was trying to emerge. Years later, pregnant with my first

Figure 1   The Amoeba

child in the final days of gestation, her tiny fetal hands and feet pressing against my abdomen, I realized that perhaps I had dreamt of my patient in intrauterine life. Or maybe, I was dreaming about my own containment.

Whether I was dreaming about him or about myself, the dream provided me with an emotional model for how I needed to understand the treatment. As I awoke from the dream, I felt rested and at peace, with no tension about seeing him later that day. I looked forward to seeing him.

As Mr. M lay on the couch that day, armed as I was with my newly found understanding, the words I uttered and his words and how he spoke them no longer mattered. Our voices became a series of undulations—rhythmic, contrapuntal utterances—mere cadences of sound. I experienced him as my amoeba, pushing gently against the walls of his interior. I felt that he and I were to roll comfortably within these walls, and this understanding, at the sensory level, centered me.

Mr. M's unfinished sentences, eroticized language, hopelessness, and torment no longer disoriented me. I entered instead a world of sensation where there were no complete thoughts, where there was neither eroticism nor violence. There was only a physical sensation of the other, muffled and indiscernible, yet palpable and strong. I had finally found a psychic place that could contain Mr. M. It was a place where I could finally tolerate being with him in a pre-object state, regressed, perhaps, to a level of intrauterine experience (Meadow, 1991).

JUGGLING

Several years prior to his analysis Mr. M had started learning how to juggle. In the first few years of treatment, his discussion of the juggling centered largely on bodily sensations. "My palms sweat so much. I don't know what to do about it." Sometimes, the juggling created aches and pains that tormented him physically. It was as though he were being prodded and pushed in directions he was uncomfortable with physically.

Throughout the analysis, the juggling was presented largely as a frustrating force to contend with. Over the next 15 years, juggling never brought him any sense of achievement. As soon as he mastered a technique, he set himself a new challenge: first three balls, then four balls, five pins, juggling on a unicycle, balancing balls on his nose, bouncing as well as throwing balls. In this way, the juggling never provided a real sense of achievement or progress but acted instead as a continuous source of frustration, torment, and rage.

The juggling served a dual purpose. First, it provided some discharge for psychomotor agitation; it seemed an effective drain for much of his tension. Secondly, the juggling *aroused* tension. The endeavor epitomized a struggle for containment. Balls had to be juggled in an arc or closed pattern. If they broke the pattern, he felt tormented and frustrated. At times, his rage would be so great that he would bang his head against a wall or floor. More often, however, he ranted and raved in frustration.

The intense struggle to keep the balls together in a closed pattern and control their movement is in keeping with my dream about an amoeba pushing against boundaries of interior space. New levels of achievement with juggling are symbolic attempts to push against the boundaries of his interior space. He must not break the closed pattern of the pins or allow them to collapse into chaos. They epitomize the life drive *and* the death drive: at once the will to progress and the force to restrict satisfaction and growth.

The rage and frustration involved in keeping the "juggling" energies contained in a controlled, enclosed form epitomize Mr. M's internal struggle to keep within the boundaries of his internal space. And yet, in trying to physically *expand* the boundaries of a closed form, Mr. M reveals his unconscious wish to expand the boundaries of his interior space. Juggling also illuminates the role of outside forces in influencing the dynamic: the work is totally up to him.[2]

Symbiosis: Treatment Phase Three

By his second year of treatment, Mr. M had become very absorbed in daytime talk shows. He spent almost all of his sessions providing fascinating philosophical ideas and scathing commentary about current events.

I think of this as a phase of symbiosis because Mr. M discovered that we shared a very enjoyable similarity in our thinking about repressed

---

2 It is interesting to note Tustin's (1990) idea that bodily separateness is the heartbreak at the center of all human existence. Juggling can also be seen as a means of using the body to create a physical experience of integration.

sexual and aggressive impulses, about people, and about the world. In fact, Mr. M did not even want to talk about any subject if I had not heard about it on TV or read about it in the paper. The requirement that he and I watch or read the same material in order for him to provide his commentary persisted for the next 12 years.

I had mixed feelings about Mr. M's requirement. On the one hand, I could understand why it might have been too frustrating for him to explain something to me that I had not also experienced. On the other hand, I was very interested in all of Mr. M's thoughts and ideas while frustrated by his refusal to share his experiences with me unless I had experienced them too.

If I told him that I had not had a chance to see or hear something, I believe he became sullen. At times I tried to work on this resistance. If he refused to talk about something he thought I hadn't also seen or read, I might ask, "What would happen if you talked about it?" Mr. M would become agitated by these explorations, however. "I can't. That's all." Perhaps my having seen or watched the same things as he during our absence from each other meant that we not only shared the same ideas, but also that we would have, since our last session, been doing the same things at the same time. By doing so, we were creating a transitional presence for each other, sustainable throughout the week via the newspaper or TV.

To support his need for a sustainable presence, I decided to assert that I *had* seen or heard about various events even if I hadn't. Analytic transparency, in this case, was achieved by removing any barriers created by reality that might serve as impediments to further communication. To remove those barriers required that I refrain from exploring or interpreting his resistance and thereby avoid becoming a visible dystonic presence.

Mr. M's views about the daytime television talk shows revealed to me that he had a very fine mind. He was able to analyze the unconscious motives and impulses of the hosts and of their guests. He scorned their inability to recognize and take responsibility for their own exhibitionist, erotic, or aggressive motives, and he talked lucidly about the dynamics at great length. "Look at the way she wore her pants! She's not there to talk about whether her boyfriend cheated on her or not! She's there because she's trying to show off her body to everyone! Don't they know they just want to have intercourse and kill each other?"

A powerful narcissistic transference developed as Mr. M discovered just how much I shared his views and how completely likeminded we were about the lack of understanding of sexual and aggressive forces among the talk-show hosts, their guests and, ultimately, people in general.

During this phase, Mr. M began to delve into myriad topics, and he began to read about them. He even read Einstein's theory of relativity, complaining that he couldn't understand it as well as he would have liked. For the next seven years, his sessions continued to be taken up with psychoanalytic and social commentary on news events and daytime TV. Occasionally, however, he would offer a short anecdote about how much his father, mother, or sister frustrated him. At first, he could barely describe an unpleasant interchange. A sentence or two was all he could manage. Sometimes, even before uttering a word, he would say, "Oh, no . . . can't talk about that."

Sometimes, in talking about his family, he descended into bitterness and hopelessness. "What's the use? You weren't there. It would have been different if you could have been there when I was a child. Now, it's too late."

TELEPATHY

In his eighth year, Mr. M finally put in words, with sadness, what his hopelessness and inarticulateness had perhaps belied: "I wish you could just enter my mind and read my thoughts so I wouldn't have to describe things to you."

I was surprised to hear that Mr. M wished for telepathy because I often thought that I *could* tell what he was thinking and feeling. Likewise, Mr. M had an uncanny ability to know whether I was listening to him or not. If my mind wandered, for example, he would say, "I'm boring you," even though I do not believe I was talking to him any more or less than usual. In fact, by this point in the treatment, Mr. M's attunement to my mind sometimes bordered on the uncanny.

I used my perceptions by responding to Mr. M's lament in a somewhat hurt tone. "You think I *can't* read your mind?" "That's true," he confirmed, "You can. We have a kind of telepathy. Then why do you always want me to say things?" I answered him by asserting matter-of-factly, "Because it's good practice to put things into words."

This emotional communication marked a change in Mr. M's experience in talking to me. He could consider talking as an additional method for our telepathy, frosting on our cake of confluence. Language no longer served as a painful reminder of our separateness; it was an exercise we could enjoy together, like doing the puzzle.

PSYCHOANALYSIS

It is perhaps not surprising, given the degree of symbiosis in this case, that Mr. M should have become interested in two of my own great passions: psychoanalysis and music.

In his fifth year of treatment he began to read Freud. At first, he felt very daunted and ignorant. "I don't know if I can understand it. I don't get all of it," he said. I suggested he simply run his hands along the *Standard Edition* at first. Mr. M, however, did much better than that: he began to devour Freud.

This period marked the height of what I have conceptualized as Mr. M's symbiotic phase. Mr. M loved Freud. I experienced his newfound interest as a further solidification of his attachment to me. During this phase, he and I enjoyed many, many hours of discussing psychoanalysis and the world. He was intolerant of Freud critics and refused to read most other psychoanalysts. It often felt as though only he and I, through Freud, could understand the erotic and murderous impulses of the people around us. We bemoaned the countless daily illustrations of the world's ignorance and lack of enlightenment.

Psychoanalysis also provided him with new conceptual tools with which to understand his family and himself. Mr. M soon extended his commentary to include discussions about his family's frustrated impulses. He began to analyze his mother's castrating behaviors, his sister's repressed desires, and his father's passive aggression.

Mr. M also found new language to understand himself. "I'm not neurotic, you know. I don't have any hysterical symptoms. That's why you can't cure me. There's nothing wrong with me, you see. I'm just hopeless, that's all. We just have to live with it; there's nothing that can be done for me. Now we know."

His juggling also came under the scrutiny of his recently acquired understanding of Freud. "The unicycle is a regression to homoerotic tendencies. You don't walk, like an infant, but the emphasis on the buttocks is what makes it homoerotic."

Mr. M even joined a juggling club in his seventh year of treatment and studied the jugglers. "Jugglers in general are just engaging in autoerotic behaviors as well as exhibitionist tendencies. They are sublimating their real erotic desires for intercourse," he explained.

Emergence of Negativity: Treatment Phase Four

While I was fascinated with Mr. M's interpretations and commentary, I continued to be frustrated by his difficulty in talking about painful feelings and memories. I wanted him to let me in. Perhaps the separateness I felt when he could not talk frustrated me as well. Whether my countertransference feelings were induced or subjective, they led me to push him into talking about things he did *not* want to talk about.

One of Mr. M's chief complaints was: "I'll never progress." Out of frustration, I would ask, "Well, how would you *like* to progress? What's wrong with how you are now?" He could not answer this question. Trying to explore the communication or interpret his resistance only led to impasse.

Mr. M's expressions of extreme hopelessness and his inability to talk about his feelings were attempts to keep himself contained psychologically, to keep the balls aloft, so to speak, in a closed, manageable form. I was trying too hard to push against the boundaries of his interior space, and that pressure made him uncomfortable. He needed a transparent presence, one that could permeate the boundaries or sensations without imposing any of her own impulses, thoughts, feelings, or desires. When I could not achieve this state, Mr. M's discomfort became too great, and he would discontinue treatment.

After a few months' respite, I would once more be able to conceptualize the case in terms of the undulating amoeba. This helped me manage my frustration and respect his boundaries. Once I regained my motivation to work with him, I would invite Mr. M to return to treatment, which he would willingly do. This repeated itself every three or four years.

EROTICIZATION

One of the clues that the treatment was pushing too hard against the boundaries of Mr. M's internal space was the repeated emergence of the eroticized transference. For example, in his sixth year of treatment, the eroticizations often lost their quality of plaintive cries and seemed to express not only longing, but anger. "We should just have sex," Mr. M would assert if I was trying to explore or interpret a thought or behavior. "That's the only thing that would help anything."

When I lost my ability to be transparent, Mr. M felt pushed or prodded psychologically. At those times he conjured up sexual fantasies about me or expressed his desire to touch me, have sex with me, or be touched by me. Mr. M's flight into sexual fantasy enabled him to simultaneously discharge and extinguish aggressive feelings. The discharge of aggressive feelings was achieved by the indirect expression that the treatment was hopeless, that only having some form of sex would help him. The extinguishing of aggressive feelings was achieved by conjuring pleasure: "I could touch your hair, your leg . . . "

The eroticized communications decreased when I did not prod him to talk about things he didn't want to talk about or explore ideas he didn't want to explore. As long as I did not explore, interpret, or press Mr. M to talk or influence him to alter his psyche or behavior in any way, he could stay in regular treatment and talk progressively.

It was well into the second decade of treating Mr. M that I was finally able to consistently respect two of his major resistances. The first was not to press him to talk when he said, "No, not that." The second was not to explore any acting-out behaviors unless I felt he was a danger to himself, in which case I might ask him if he was trying to get himself hospitalized again.

PREGNANCY

During Mr. M's sixth year of treatment I became pregnant with my first child. This event passed, for the most part, almost without his notice except for his complaint that I might lose interest in him and then later a fantasy that a baby might bite my nipple off. In both scenarios I figured as a depriving breast. I reassured him that I had a lot of other people to take care of the baby and agreed with him that the baby might indeed bite me. These communications were designed to help him accept his fears and longings as well as his aggressive impulses. Part of being analytically transparent involved responding in a relaxed, accepting manner to the fantasies of neglect and sadism.

BORROWING FREUD

I rented my office in a building that also housed a psychoanalytic
library. Starting in his ninth year of treatment, before or after each session, Mr. M would surreptitiously remove a book, usually by Freud,
from the library and exhange it for another the following week.
Although Mr. M actually had a public library card, he complained that
it was too complicated for him to check out books there. "No, I can't
do that," he explained. "I would have to deal with repressed, controlling
people."

Mr. M seemed to be communicating that the books upstairs from my
office made it worth his while to come to sessions since the sessions
themselves were useless—he was, after all, not amenable to treatment.

In addition to symbolically communicating to me that the sessions
were not enough to travel into town for, taking the books also provided
him with a means of obtaining gratification and maintaining a transitional presence in me. By taking books home from the building where
we met each week, he was characteristically managing his own frustration and gratification levels.

I soon became afraid that the librarian (to whom I was known) would
find out about Mr. M and that I would get in trouble for colluding with
my patient. I went so far as to explore with her whether the patient
could receive a special dispensation. He couldn't. I decided to leave
him to his own devices, which was very uncomfortable for me. I was
afraid we would be "found out."

I seriously questioned my feeling that I could not explore Mr. M's
acting-out behavior with him. Was it because of my own fears of managing his aggression? Was I afraid he would leave my worthless treatment if I did not subsidize it with the books, and if I should stand up
for myself? I felt like both a coward and a renegade.

Despite these nagging doubts about my treatment plan, however, setting up prohibitions, interpreting, or embarking on a program of exploration was simply not in keeping with the concept of the amoeba, which
had been most effective for me in directing the treatment. Intuitively, I
decided against introducing "reality" into the sessions. I opted instead
for the analytic transparency that might even entail my participating in
conceptualizing how he might best escape with a book under his arm,
unnoticed.

Both the patient and I felt at least good and at times euphoric. The
required oceanic state means that the analyst will not experience reality; it is a state in which ego functions have no immediate role and judg-

ment and perceptual functions are temporarily suspended. Meadow (1991), writing about this case, notes:

> A prohibition, however, soon arrived. Mr. M got "caught" by the librarian, who, being familiar enough with psychoanalysis, suggested he "discuss with his analyst" how he should be borrowing books. Mr. M showed up at his session in a state of extreme agitation, anxious, and enraged. He was not sure he could stay in the room, and he could not take the couch. (p. 101)

I affected a light-hearted, amused response as a way to buffer his extreme agitation, and he tentatively agreed to stay. He announced he was going to have to leave therapy, though. The librarian's control over the books was just another symptom of a repressed society trying to repress him and sublimate its own sexuality. He couldn't go on this way.

In this moment, a great anxiety surged through me, along with an impulse to control the anxiety by finally having a talk with Mr. M about not withdrawing the books and once and for all putting a halt to his acting-out behavior. I also realized, however, that the librarian's mere suggestion that he discuss the borrowing was producing tremendous agitation. I sensed that the borrowing provided Mr. M with a means of both expanding and containing his energies. He could grow intellectually while gratifying himself so as not to be too frustrated by his sessions. On several different levels, it provided him with an effective means of juggling his energies. In the general scheme of his restricted life, taking the books out was positive.

I therefore opted to remain transparent with Mr. M by joining him. I agreed with him that the librarian made it very difficult for people to read and that she was a dictator. I expressed no interest in curtailing his behavior or addressing the resistance. I even suggested we meet on a different day when that librarian might not be there so he could continue to withdraw books.

Supporting Mr. M's unorthodox way of expanding the boundaries of his psyche (instead of encouraging him to do it in a way that might have felt more acceptable to me or the librarian) enabled Mr. M to continue coming to his sessions and to continue reading Freud. He was not ready for me to explore the resistance. It was only many years later, as will be described in the seventh phase of treatment, that the resistance could finally be resolved.

Music

In tandem with Mr. M's increasing ability to express and enact negative feelings about his family and about me came an intense passion for classical music in his ninth year of treatment. Not surprisingly, classical music was one of my own great passions.

This expansion into new, pleasurable levels of sensory experience typified his intense symbiosis with me. It also marked a change, however, from his interest in reading classical psychoanalysis and Freud. This new interest was purely libidinal. While his love of Freud was also libidinal, it had an aggressive component in that it provided him with language to describe the failure in the world to understand unconscious process. With music, however, he was pushing against the boundaries of his inner space into new areas of pure pleasure.

The interest also affected his external boundaries. He visited record stores, talked to family members about music and about their collections, and experimented with listening to different kinds of music. While he was still firmly grounded in his unhappiness, he could experience pleasure, too. He never talked any more about wishing he could just die.

His newfound interest in music correlated with a reduced need to "juggle" negative energies, which were increasingly verbalized. Perhaps his psychic energy was freer to seek new libidinal interests. Mr. M brought in many CDs for me so we could listen to the same music. One CD was of an esoteric new classical music ensemble. I was somewhat intimidated by his fine, sophisticated ear.

Coinciding with my admiration for Mr. M was his first positive communication to me in 13 years: "I guess this is a good place for me to be. I feel like I'm smart here. I may never get better, we know that, but at least I can feel a little better." Indeed, Mr. M had new ideas for what he wanted to listen to and read; he could appreciate his superior cognitive abilities and the challenges of conforming to an inadequate world. He stopped talking about whether he should remain in treatment and accepted that, despite the fact that he could never be "cured," being together was enough.

Loneliness: Treatment Phase Five

Mr. M's budding awareness of human behavior as understood by Freud and psychoanalysis also led to an increased awareness of loneliness.[3]

---

3 This phase, "loneliness," occurred almost in tandem with the phase described after this one, which I call "individuation."

THE MOVE

Although Mr. M's loneliness was somewhat abated by an increasingly richer relationship with his sister and by trips to juggling clubs and record stores, the problem became quite exacerbated when his parents, in the eleventh year of treatment, decided to sell their house. This created a tremendous upheaval and rage in Mr. M's life. He was tortured by visits from real estate agents and by the prospect of losing his home and having to move.

Nonetheless, Mr. M was able to talk in full sentences and without hesitation about the tremendous upheaval of losing the home in which he had spent his entire life. He posted signs on the doors for realtors to see: "I don't want this sale" and so on. Although he knew his efforts were hopeless, I admired his direct expression and saw it as psychologically constructive. It was certainly a marked change from how he used to manage unbearable tensions, by lying immobile on the floor for long periods of time.

Despite numerous attempts to dissuade his parents from selling the house, it became clear that he was going to have to separate from his family home and make a new life. This reality aroused a great deal of anxiety and depression. Forced to expand his physical boundaries, he despaired about his ability to acclimate to a new space. The move would place him more than an hour and a half from my office. The potential loss of the house greatly exacerbated his loneliness.

After well over a year of discussion about the move, Mr. M was able to negotiate with his parents enough benefits to soften the reality of the move. For one thing, he was going to participate in the selection of a new house. The move was also going to ostensibly provide him with more financial freedom. He decided to buy himself a new car, and unlike the broken-down jalopies he had always driven, it was new and very sharp. His monthly income increased. The move forced him to negotiate compensatory arrangements that ultimately benefited him and perhaps opened his mind to the possibility that he could manage change effectively despite the difficulties.

SMALL CREATURES

The new house was bordered by a large wooded area. Mr. M had nurtured a few cats in his old neighborhood, but in this more secluded and rural location, he found much solace in tracking and identifying a variety of small animals.

Mr. M's identification with the small animals became evident to me when he started taking pictures and sending them to me through the internet. During this period, he wrote emails to me, sometimes daily or several times a day if something agitated him. He mostly sent me digital photographs in which he depicted animals as solitary, lost creatures: a lone fox; an oversized fly unlike any other, out of place.

Mr. M wanted to feed these animals. He was afraid that they would starve. At one point, to avoid feeding them a potentially harmful substance, he diligently tracked and dissected their feces to better understand what they were ingesting. His mother was upset by the bags of feces he left lying around, but by understanding what the animals ate and protecting them from eating food that might hurt them, he was actively insuring that his own, ambiguous relationship to eating would not be extended to his new friends.

Klein (1946) writes about persecutory fears "arising from the infant's oral sadistic impulses to relieve the mother's body of its good contents, and the anal-sadistic impulses to put his excrements into her (including the desire to enter her body in order to control her from within)" (p. 99). I regarded Mr. M's active interest in dissecting and analyzing what the animals ingested as a new, active means of addressing and controlling his own struggles with absorption.

The scientific means he used to correct and avoid potential poisoning of the animals was in sharp contrast to his more characteristic way of dealing with his anger passively. I admired the systematic way he executed his investigation.

Once, Mr. M discovered a small pond with thousands of beautiful tadpoles. Later that week, they were all devastated by a single, hot day. I sometimes felt his own days were like that; he might be able to enjoy himself somewhat on one day and then feel devastated on the next.

The photos he sent me of little frogs were completely enchanting. They were beautiful little brilliantly colored creatures with tiny webbed feet. Mr. M arranged a montage of small frogs in a new photo design. I felt the frogs depicted a vibrancy that was increasingly mirroring his inner life. While the montage depicted a pattern that was still closed, controlled, and contained, the frogs also felt celebratory and alive. (See Figure 2.)

Mr. M's focus on animals also expressed an emerging sense of his own loneliness and interest in forming new attachments. The animals were often depicted as lost in a depriving world. While all the photos were very beautiful, many of them communicated a feeling of being out of place in the world. (See Figure 3.)

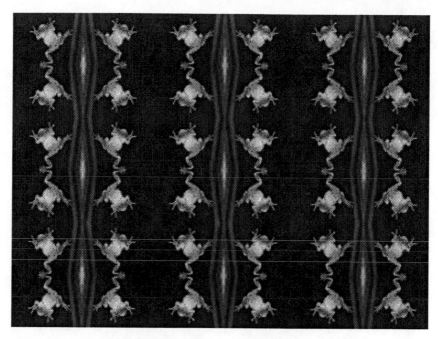

Figure 2   Vibrant frogs in a controlled pattern.

Figure 3   Frog struggling in its surrounding.

Mr. M also began to talk more about feeling isolated. I suggested he take a class or mix with people. This idea seemed to depress him: "I can't do that."

I was prepared to abandon any ambitious plans for Mr. M in favor of allowing him to push against his own internal boundaries. He surprised me, however, by being able to talk about his resistance. "You're trying to get rid of me," he said. "You don't want me near you."

To correct his erroneous interpretation, I said, "Well, why don't you take a class with me?" He liked this idea because it meant that expanding the boundaries of his external and interior spaces did not have to preclude being with me; from within the context of our relationship, he was willing and able to venture onto new ground.

In fact, I marveled at the enthusiasm and energy Mr. M found in the enrollment process for the class. His passivity, apathy, and hopelessness had given way dramatically to real organization and ambition. He set up appointments with registrars and the dean of admissions and made special trips to submit checks and materials. He got himself admitted to a continuing education class of which I was a member. The boundaries of his internal and exterior life were expanding to new heights not only of experience but also, seemingly, of excitement and emotional involvement.

Individuation: Treatment Phase Six

THE CLASS

The class Mr. M and I attended was on psychoanalysis. Readings about schizophrenia, advancements in psychoanalysis since Freud, and theoretical papers about aggression and infant development predominated. Mr. M was shocked and enraged to read about the emphasis on early life and on aggression in the development of pathology.

Despite his distaste for the material, he began to conceptualize his illness as one of sexual inhibition. The readings aroused memories of his twenties, during which time he had felt unable to date women. The frustration of libidinal impulses was of more interest and consequence to Mr. M than any discussion of early trauma, innate disposition, or drive theory. "I have no problem with aggression," he said. "I can be angry. My problem is that I was inhibited in the expression of my sexuality. In my twenties, when my problems started, they were sexual."

The revolving faculty, meanwhile, recognized Mr. M as a Freud scholar and expressed their respect accordingly. Mr. M was not only able, ultimately, to refine and articulate his position, but also to produce an erudite term paper.

Some weeks after the class had ended, Mr. M was describing thoughts and feelings in an animated session. He had read an article anthropomorphizing a large shark on a website. "Did you read it?" he asked. Before I could answer, Mr. M said, with some impatience in light of his anxiousness to describe his thoughts, "Well, I don't care if you did or not. I'm going to talk to you about it anyway." This was the first time that Mr. M's need to establish our synchronicity took second place to his desire to communicate something new to me. It was quite evident now that Mr. M felt freer to push against the boundaries of his inner space and of our symbiosis. This moment, for me, was much like seeing a child constricted for years by leg braces set free to run joyfully. His energy and vibrancy were palpable.

Later that month, I felt Mr. M was in a good place with himself and, therefore, with me. He had become a legitimate student, with rights to the library. It was only then that I finally said to him, in as soft a voice as I could muster, "You know, you have to stop taking the books." He replied in a quiet voice, "I know," and he stopped.

ADVENTURES

In tandem with taking the class with me, Mr. M decided to seek additional therapy since he felt more and more strongly that the locus of his problems might be oedipal in nature and therefore might benefit from sex therapy. Since the onset of his unhappiness had really manifested in his twenties, when he felt he should have become sexually active, he hoped that becoming sexually active now could somehow reverse the damage. I encouraged and supported both his hypothesis and expansion into new realms of experience.

The sex therapy aimed to teach him how to make meaningful emotional contact with a woman. While Mr. M found it illuminating, it was also disappointing since it did not satisfy his immediate sexual aims.

Shortly after discontinuing the therapy, however, Mr. M began an internet relationship with a young woman in Europe with whom he corresponded regularly via videoconferencing that was not sexual in nature. He emailed me a picture of her. Not surprisingly, she looked very much like me and had my middle name.

Mr. M decided not to take another class with me. Instead, he decided to explore New York City and take up golfing at a new weekend house he was going to with his sister. He chose to juggle regularly in Central Park, only two blocks, uncannily, from where I grew up. Despite the vicinity of his new juggling haunt to my native home, the activity itself was further evidence of the expansion of his physical as well as his psychic boundaries.

Another expansion of the boundaries of his psychic space occurred in his constricting relationship to unhappiness. His attitude toward his hopelessness shifted. "You know," he explained, "It's not about 'progress.' It's just about . . . doing what you can." This move away from a concept of "progress" to a decision to continue having "adventures" marked a shift in his consciousness; he no longer needed hopelessness to contain his impulses. He was learning to feel more comfortable with a variety of aggressive and libidinal impulses and with a general excitement about his feelings and experiences.

The expansion of Mr. M's internal boundaries, with an ensuing ability and interest in exploring the world, coincided predictably with a decrease in his compulsive need to juggle. "I don't want to create too much stress on myself with juggling," he explained. "I have these other things that tax me. I don't want to tax myself too much." By managing the dynamics of his tension states with a mixture of new experiences in the world and by talking, his compulsion to juggle patterns in closed, but increasingly complex, shapes seemed to decrease. He was extending his ability to juggle boundaries onto the real world.

Here is a recent email communication from Mr. M:

Subject: weather or not

I have a tentative plan to submit for your approval.. perhaps on next Wed. I will go to practice juggling near where you are having the conference.. there might be some public park there that would suit. I'll try to do it in the morning, while the programs are in session. This way, I would maintain some connection, without it being too close. I hope the weather is good next week. Do you like this frog?

Figure 4 depicts a frog, almost indiscernible from his monochrome surrounding, emerging tentatively through a barrier that looks at once like water, slimy and crystalline. The barrier is itself beautifully transparent. It depicts, with sublime perfection, Mr. M's own incredible achievement: pushing through barriers of his own interior space.

Figure 4   Emerging frog

Discussion

Analytic transparency, in which the analyst can allow herself to be known to the patient in any aspect of emotional reality or projection, is achieved via an amalgam of modern analytic concepts and techniques. On the level of technique, it involves following the contact and joining the patient. Theoretically, it involves understanding drive theory as a means of deciphering and working with resistance. And finally, it requires resolving countertransference resistances to being fully available to the patient in an emotionally therapeutic way. I will discuss below the specifics of how these concepts and techniques worked in this case.

THE CONTACT FUNCTION

I had worked analytically with psychosis in the locked chronic wards of Metropolitan State Mental Hospital, where I had first learned to identify, tolerate, and stay with the psychotic experience. In the underground, unsupervised inner sanctum of the hospital, where I was sometimes taken by one of the patients, I would sit with them as they smoked, ate, and rocked. I had come to enjoy a certain restfulness in learning how to follow the patient's "contact" (Spotnitz, 1969) and had grown accustomed to tolerating a low-grade terror, allowing myself simply to observe.

One of the major contributions of modern psychoanalysis to the theory of technique has been following the patient's contact. The image in my mind was of a circle within a circle, the small inner circle representing the ego, which I was to stay away from psychologically at all times by asking neutral, object-oriented questions (Spotnitz, 1969).

Somehow, I did not experience Mr. M as I had the chronic patients in the mental hospital, who were content to let me sit there and for whom I did not, at least initially, seem to exist. With Mr. M everything felt eroticized and raw—his bodily sensations, the room, the weather, my voice. Silence felt too frustrating, and yet when I asked a question, it felt dystonic. I felt my interventions created too much space between us, and yet the silence was oppressive.

At the initial stages of treatment with Mr. M, just thinking of being object-oriented with him did anchor me; I was at least tethered to a sense of purpose or direction. Ultimately, however, it did not serve to help me feel at ease. It translated, somehow, into a form of analytic neutrality that made me feel, and also probably appear, removed or distant.

After my dream of the amoeba, however, I realized that following the contact required more than waiting for a verbal or nonverbal cue to ask a neutral question. It also required finding an emotional space that could adequately match the patient's. To do so, the feeling tones in the room had to be discerned.

The theoretical orientation that feeds sound clinical method and scientific investigation has to be fueled by a creative capacity to use feelings and intuition to gauge the feeling tones.

DRIVE THEORY AND ACTING-OUT BEHAVIORS

Gauging Mr. M's specific, seemingly intractable resistances in terms of how he managed his tension rather than as character defenses was very important in achieving analytic transparency. Traditionally, it is via resistance that we explore and understand how defenses are constructed. For most patients the rules of treatment—to come on time, pay on time, and lie on the couch and talk—are fraught with resistance.

Mr. M's varied and enduring acting-out resistances, such as doing the puzzle in the session, setting clocks, taking books from the library, bringing the analyst materials, and emailing in between sessions, were not, however, amenable to interpretation or any form of psychological exploration. Exploration inevitably led to impasse. The behaviors had to be studied at length, sometimes for years, before they could be addressed.

Meadow (2003) writes about behaviors that may be primitive in nature: "Spotnitz (1969, 1985) observed that these behaviors were more than resistances. They were also nonverbal messages. He refers to them as survival devices that should be respected as such" (p. 70). Understanding Mr. M's acting out as a mode of expression made it possible to understand how he constructed himself. These types of resistances, survival devices that precede feeling, thought, and language, can be successfully mitigated by drive theory. Meadow (1996) writes: "It helps if we view these solutions as organized mental activity in which the flow of energy can be understood as a method for mastering tension" (p. 201). Interpretation and exploration, with this understanding, no longer have to serve as primary clinical interventions.

Doing the puzzle, in fact, served as a therapeutic means for the patient and me to achieve a comfortable way of staying in the room together. Meadow (1987) writes: "One can learn a lot of techniques and never go beyond rote performances. Eclectic training is best, since it provides tools to be used when needed, while not freezing the therapist into an idea" (p. 149). Allowing Mr. M to do the puzzle with me helped him understand that I was primarily interested in his psychological comfort. At various points in the treatment, if Mr. M felt particularly frustrated, I would ask him, "Should we do the puzzle again?" This intervention alone often served to reduce tension to tolerable levels and restore progressive communication.

Over the course of time, helping the patient put into words what his behaviors communicated had, paradoxically, to happen without words. Opening the door from my psyche to his, with a deep understanding and appreciation for what his behavior communicated and without expressing any wish to alter his patterns of nonverbal communication, may ultimately have made it possible for this patient to resolve his resistances to talking spontaneously, without undue influence from the analyst.

RESISTANCES TO VERBALIZATION

Mr. M's resistances to verbalization included his inability to articulate full sentences, particularly when under the sway of difficult feelings. His retreat into hopelessness was another way of avoiding talking. Neither of these resistances was amenable to exploration or interpretation.

Understanding the resistances by means of gauging his tension levels again made it possible to achieve analytic transparency. I came to understand that if and when Mr. M did talk, however haltingly, about a real feeling and thereby push against the boundaries of his interior space, it could sometimes lead to his feeling bruised, battered, or agitated. This became excruciatingly clear when he began to interact more with family and friends: his extreme sensitivity and the arousal of tremendous amounts of rage could be very intense. Exploration, therefore, did not foster progressive communication because he experienced it as being overly prodded and aggravated or even battered.

Likewise, Mr. M's intense hopelessness and insistence that he could not "progress" was not with a view to any particular ideal or goal he refused to consider. Rather, the hopelessness served as a major facilitator for the containment for his newfound excitation given the gradual expansion of his energies. The resistance helped to decrease any potential anxiety about expanding the boundaries of his inner space. It soothed him to believe "I'm hopeless." In reality, Mr. M was progressing quite a lot.

JOINING THE PATIENT

What seemed to help Mr. M with the resistances outlined above, therefore, was not to explore or interpret. Instead, it seemed helpful for me to make emotional communications that indicated to him that I was psychologically in tune with him.

On the most basic level, these communications involved enjoying our mutual love of psychoanalysis and music. Our becoming psychological twins provided Mr. M with a much-needed symbiosis. Joining this patient psychologically also involved making light remarks when he expressed difficult feelings. These remarks would soothe and serve as a buffer for him. Emotional communications worked best that neither encouraged more talk nor put an end to it, but rather normalized his emotional experiences.

These types of remarks might include: "It's hard to be with family." or "People just don't get it, do they?" Sometimes I would say, "Now *that* is hard to talk about." After his first five-minute description of a very difficult interchange he had with his sister in his eleventh year of treatment, I said, with real feeling, "I can't believe how long you were able to talk about that."

These types of soothing emotional communications, designed to address a patient's terror in light of emerging feelings and sensations, often lead to progressive communication (Meadow, 1996). Accepting the patient's communications without exploration or interpretation and, when required, with a soothing communication or agreeable confirmation of a particular view, may create the psychic bridges necessary for new patterns to emerge. Ultimately, over time, dangerous sensations can be understood and experienced in new ways.

Under these conditions, the analyst serves best as a strengthening, reassuring, and supporting presence. Emotional communications directed at working with tension levels create ego strength and increase verbalizations. In a sense, the patient is being helped to create a new stimulus barrier; a form of psychological myelination takes place that can endure a more intense emotional stimulation as the patient slowly learns to accept his own impulses. This was particularly true during phases of his treatment when his reactions to certain stimuli were strictly on the level of impulse, even before the advent of discernible feeling, thought, and language.

COUNTERTRANSFERENCE CONSIDERATIONS

To work transparently with this patient, I had to communicate a complete openness and receptivity. This openness required my becoming free of a number of defenses. At several distinct junctures in the treatment, my own unanalyzed defenses interfered with the openness and receptivity he required.

For example, I initially had great difficulty accepting Mr. M's hopelessness. Early on, I tried to mirror his hopelessness. "*I'm* hopeless," I might say. Mirroring, which is designed to safely reverse self-attack or help project it (Margolis, 1994), did not work with Mr. M. In fact, the mirroring, while providing me with some aggressive discharge for my own frustrations, confused him. Trying to influence Mr. M's patterns of discharge interfered with my ability to work with him transparently.

In addition to my difficulty with his extreme hopelessness, was the difficulty I had with his inability to talk fluidly about his challenging feelings. McAloon (1987), in discussing a patient's resistance to using the couch, describes her countertransference need to "feel like an analyst" as a resistance. I experienced a similar resistance with Mr. M, wanting him to talk more about his negative feelings to gratify my own interest in feeling like an analyst. Helping Mr. M talk about his feelings meant that I, at least, was not hopeless. I would fight against my own hopelessness by pushing against his boundaries.[4] It was only after I was finally able to acknowledge and access my own deep-seated feelings of hopelessness that I could finally understand how psychically disorganizing it could be to actually relinquish them. Only then could I understand how the hopeless feeling helped reduce the terror that could be evoked in light of new experiences that aroused impulses.

My defense against accepting and understanding his hopelessness also led me to erroneously interpret his passivity as stubbornness and even defiance, which were my own characterological defenses. My interpreting the intransigence of his hopelessness as defiance made it particularly difficult for me to work transparently with Mr. M. In the first place, I did not feel it was "right" for him to defy me. I felt that he was behaving aggressively toward me, and that I should not tolerate it. At times, I even had the idea he was walking all over me.

Among other ineffective exploratory interventions, my erroneous hypotheses about him led me to question Mr. M by asking "Should I feel tortured by you?" The intervention shocked and upset him. He felt not only confused and hurt by it, but also more hopeless. He left treatment for several months. I could not adopt this position with Mr. M and was helped to abandon it with a renewal of my conceptualization of the treatment as like an amoeba.

In addition to tolerating my projection that Mr. M was defiant and stubborn, I also had to tolerate other ways that I experienced his aggression. My defense against feeling hated or devalued by him proved to be another major obstacle to the treatment.

I had, for example, to accept for many years that the treatment alone was not always worth Mr. M's visit to my office. I had to accept feeling that his intellectual and musical prowess were superior to mine, knowing that if I were to compete with his ideas or in any way vie for intellectual superiority, it would prove destructive.

---

4 My frustration and hopelessness may also have been induced. Certainly, the experience of being with me was often frustrating for Mr. M. It is important to note that the difficulty distinguishing between self and other can obscure the dynamics of subjective vs. objective countertransference reactions.

Ironically, working on my own hopelessness, aggression, and even insecurity made it more possible for me to tolerate feeling both worthless *and* inadequate enough to prevent myself from fruitlessly fighting to address his behaviors. It was only when I could stop defending against those feelings, and therefore against him, that I could become truly transparent. Meadow (1989) notes, "The patient has successfully created the image of a friendly presence in his mind and it brings with it a sense of well-being. I've found it is difficult for the patient to maintain this state if the analyst is too full of herself or makes intrusive statements" (p. 151). As long as I acted on my projections, rejected him, or competed with his intellectual and aesthetic prowess, treatment was strained.

It is important to note here that Mr. M was extremely helpful in forgiving me my trespasses. For example, I believe, in retrospect, that the struggle to achieve the goal of having him bring me a check each week was largely a resistance on my part. It helped me to defend against the passivity, torment, fragmentation, and hopelessness that dominated the sessions and made it possible for me to continue to treat him. Mr. M cooperated with my wishes because, I believe, patients are sometimes willing to tolerate the therapist's need to feel at ease.

When my resistances had been worked through such that new levels of analytic transparency could be attained, I felt the treatment really soared. When I could truly accept feeling hopeless, worthless, and inadequate, I could appreciate, embrace, and support the marvelous ways Mr. M was learning to find expression for his aggressive and libidinal impulses. Both deep emotional experience and rigorous scientific investigation and methodology were inexorably bound to the momentum in the case.

Final Note

Mr. M's journey from passivity to being an active agent in changing his life will, I am quite sure, continue. "I can't be passive any more," he said to me recently, somewhat anxiously. His goals—to continue to expand his mind, have new adventures, and repair the sexual inhibition that has dominated his life—will, I have no doubt, be reached. For a patient like Mr. M, whose stunning intellect and fascination with the world is insuppressible, I imagine an ever increasing capacity for adventure.

Despite the many resistances both he and I presented over the course of approximately 17 years of work, a powerful bond, facilitated by a dream, enabled us both to tolerate the challenges and discomforts of working together enough to move us both along to new levels of experience and achievement.

Mr. M no longer spends entire sessions mesmerizing me with his diatribes against humanity. Nor does he often frustrate me with an inability to articulate a painful sensation or thought. He is thoughtful, feelingful, vulnerable, clear-headed, and engaged. His struggles are very, very difficult, and he has a long road ahead of him, but he is no longer passive. He is an active participant in the adventures that fascinate him and torment him, and which he brings to his sessions with increasing facility.

I trust that Mr. M will continue experiencing new levels of engagement with the world and that, together, the journey will continue to expand the boundaries of both of our interior space. I look forward to subsequent phases of treatment and to a lifetime of getting to know each other more.

REFERENCES

Ferenczi, S. (1950), *Further Contributions to the Theory and Technique of Psycho-analysis.* 2nd ed. New York: Brunner/Mazel, Inc.

Freud, S. & S. Ferenczi (1924), *The Correspondence of Sigmund Freud and Sándor Ferenczi.* Vol. 2, 1914–1919. Cambridge, MA: Belknap Press/ Harvard University Press, 1996.

Klein, M. (1946), Notes on some schizoid mechanisms. *International Journal of Psychoanalysis*, 27:99–110.

Margolis, B. D. (1994), Joining, mirroring, psychological reflection: terminology, definitions, theoretical considerations. *Modern Psychoanalysis,* 19:211–226.

McAloon, R. (1987), The need to feel like an analyst: a study of countertransference in the case of a patient who refused to use the couch. *Modern Psychoanalysis*, 12:65–87.

Meadow, P. W. (1987), The myth of the impersonal analyst. *Modern Psychoanalysis,* 12:131–150.

Meadow, P. W. (1989), How we aim to be with patients. *Modern Psychoanalysis*, 14:37–154.

Meadow, P. W. (1991), Resonating with the psychotic patient. *Modern Psychoanalysis*, 16:87–103.

Meadow, P. W. (1996), The preoedipal transference. *Modern Psychoanalysis*, 18:191–200.

Meadow, P. W. (2003), *The New Psychoanalysis*. New York: Rowman & Littlefield.

Meadow, P. W. (1981), Drive theory in diagnosis and treatment. *Modern Psychoanalysis,* 6:141–170.

Spotnitz, H. (1969), *Modern Psychoanalysis of the Schizophrenic Patient*. New York: Grune & Stratton.

Spotnitz, H. (1976), *Psychotherapy of Preoedipal Conditions*. New York: Jason Aronson.

Spotnitz, H. (1985), *Modern Psychoanalysis of the Schizophrenic Patient*. 2nd ed. New York: Human Sciences Press.

Tustin, F. (1990), *Autistic Encapsulation in Neurotic Patients*. Lanham, MD: Jason Aronson Inc.

Vaillant, G. & D. Lynn (1998), Anonymity, neutrality, and confidentiality in the actual methods of Sigmund Freud: a review of 43 cases, 1907–1939. *American Journal of Psychiatry*, 155:163–171.

18 LaSalle Road
Westwood, MA 02090
cluiz@post.harvard.edu

Modern Psychoanalysis
Vol. XXXI, No. 2, 2006

Hysteria as a Concept: A Survey of Its History in the Psychoanalytic Literature

STEPHEN R. GUTTMAN

The author traces the concept of hysteria in the psychoanalytic literature from early Freud to the present, revealing its multifaceted and elusive character. For example, depending on the theoretical viewpoint from which hysteria is viewed, it can be seen as either a preoedipal or an oedipal phenomenon—or both. Implications for treatment based on these varying viewpoints are discussed.

The origins of psychoanalysis can be located in Breuer and Freud's innovative approach, in the late 1880s, to curing hysteria—already then an ancient diagnostic entity. The term, obviously derived from the Greek word *hystera*, "uterus," reflects the prevailing views on the nature of the disease (and on human nature) at the time of its coinage— it was identified with symptoms seen as typical of women. But this association of hysteria with the female generative system was an expression of an even more ancient awareness of the malign effect of disordered sexual activity upon emotional stability, not only in women. Indeed these concepts are found in humanity's earliest surviving speculations about health and disease (long predating the term "hysteria"), and they indicate the prominent role that sexual life played in our general sense of well-being even in remote antiquity. They are documented in the first recorded medical literature of ancient Egypt, two thousand years before the Common Era (Veith, 1965, pp. 1–2.).

© 2006 CMPS/*Modern Psychoanalysis*, Vol. 31, No. 2

Since the early work of Breuer and Freud, as different schools of psychoanalysis emerged and interacted with one another, psychoanalysts have regarded hysteria in myriad ways. As they applied psychoanalytic understanding to a widening array of mental phenomena, they continually returned to hysteria, assessing it anew from a variety of evolving theoretical viewpoints.[1] Because of this complex history, the terms *hysteria*, *hysteric*, and *hysterical* can generate confusion when used in present-day case presentations and theoretical discussions.

I decided to look at the psychoanalytic literature on hysteria dating back to the 1880s to determine what differences could be found in the way it has been conceptualized and to determine what implications for current treatment might ensue from those differences with particular attention to the following:

- the definition of hysteria, including what symptoms are considered indispensable to the diagnosis of hysteria and what psychic dynamics and psychic structure, if any, are peculiar to hysteria
- the etiology of hysteria, including what factors are considered pathogenic, when those factors impact a particular person in the developmental sequence, and the relative influence of the drives and innate fantasy vs. that of traumatic experience
- the treatment approach specifically recommended for hysteria

Early Freud

Although Freud adjusted and adapted his understanding of hysteria throughout his career, Freud's work is undoubtedly the best place to begin a psychoanalytic investigation of hysteria. Even in his earliest writing on the subject, Freud noted how the diversity and complexity of the topic seemed to generate confusion. In his 1888 contribution to Villaret's encyclopedia, he wrote: "German, as well as English, authorities are still in the habit today of allotting the descriptions 'hysteria' and 'hysterical' capriciously, and of throwing hysteria into a heap along with general nervousness, neurasthenia, many psychotic states and many neuroses which have not yet been picked out from the chaos of nervous diseases" (Freud, 1888, pp. 41–42). Acknowledging that the term "hysterical" had a multifaceted meaning even among the general public, he commented, "What is popularly described as a hysterical

---

1 "Hysteria constantly follows in the footsteps of psychoanalytic theory and changes with it" (Halberstadt-Freud, 1996, p. 987).

TMT. worldview self-esteem

temperament—instability of will, changes of mood, increase of excitability with a diminution of all altruistic feelings—may be present in hysteria, but is not absolutely necessary for its diagnosis" (p. 49). Freud took nearly 10 pages of the encyclopedia entry to discuss the symptoms of hysteria, describing them as an "extremely rich series of symptoms" that he conceptualized into seven categories: convulsive attacks; hysterogenic zones, or "supersensitive areas of the body"; disturbances of sensibility (to touch and feeling), i.e., anesthesias; disturbances of sensory activity (such as sight); paralyses; muscular contractures, or spasms; and general characteristics (pp. 42–51).

Except for the last category, all the symptoms Freud discusses are of a physiological nature. He calls these physical symptoms stigmata as they are clearly apparent in the body of the patient. However, in discussing the seventh category, general characteristics, Freud (1888) notes that "hysterical manifestations have, by preference, the characteristic of being *excessive*"[2] and that "hysterical symptoms shift in a manner which from the outset excludes any suspicion of a material lesion" laying the groundwork for his contention that the causes of the disorder are psychical rather than physical (p. 48). He still claims, as did his teacher Charcot, that heredity is of paramount importance in the etiology of hysteria and that the "incidental" or "accidental" causes merely trigger the hysterical outbreaks.[3] Among these "accidental" causes Freud includes "mollycoddling, premature awakening of mental activity, frequent and violent excitements . . . trauma, intoxication, grief, emotion, exhausting illness—anything, in short, which is able to exercise a powerful effect of a detrimental kind" (p. 50). He has not yet restricted this roster of triggers to the sexual sphere, even arguing that the influence of sexual abnormalities was as a rule overestimated.[4] Freud's idea is that real events or environmental influences stimulated an excess of energy in the mind that had to be discharged, and that if these influences impinged upon a person who possessed a genetic disposition towards hysteria, this excess stimulation could be discharged

2 "A hysterical pain is described by patients as extremely painful, an anesthesia and a paralysis may easily become absolute, a hysterical contracture brings about the greatest retraction of a muscle of which it is capable. . . . *It is especially characteristic of hysteria for a disorder to be at the same time most highly developed and most sharply limited*" (Freud, 1888, p. 48).

3 "Compared with the factor of heredity all other factors take a second place and play the part of incidental causes, the importance of which is as a rule overrated in practice" (Freud, 1888, p. 50).

4 "As regards what is often asserted to be the preponderant influence of abnormalities in the sexual sphere upon the development of hysteria, it must be said that its importance is as a rule overestimated." A few lines later Freud added the following qualification: "It must, however, be admitted that conditions related *functionally* to sexual life play a great part in the aetiology of hysteria (as of all neuroses), and they do so on account of the high psychical significance of this function especially in the female sex" (Freud, 1888, pp. 50–51).

in a wide variety of unconsciously selected hysterical symptoms.[5] He does not at this point suggest the reason certain ideas were selected to become associated with the excess stimulation other than to point out that a physical trauma to a specific body part, such as a contusion to the hand, could lead to hysterical symptoms in that part, such as contractures in that hand (p. 51).

In discussing the recommended course of treatment for the disease in the encyclopedia, Freud (1888) mentions a variety of techniques, including bed rest, hydrotherapy, gymnastics, and massage, before citing "a method first practiced by Josef Breuer in Vienna" that "produces successful cures which cannot otherwise be achieved." This method recommended that the physician "lead the patient under hypnosis back to the psychical prehistory of the ailment and compel him to acknowledge the psychical occasion on which the disorder in question originated" (p. 56). This statement reflects Freud's then current thinking that the physician, in the position of power and knowledge, could forcefully influence the patient (under hypnosis) to consciously assimilate an actual event or series of events (and concomitant emotional reactions) that had occurred in the past but had been relegated to an unconscious state. Freud claims that this is "the method most appropriate to hysteria because it precisely imitates the mechanism of the origin and passing of these hysterical disorders," and that this method would become the treatment of choice "when the understanding of suggestion has penetrated more deeply into medical circles" (pp. 56–57). The "mechanism of the origin" is left unspecified, however.

Freud and Breuer

Through his work with Breuer in the 1890s, Freud's ideas about hysteria begin to deepen and expand. It is during this period that he comes to the famous conclusion: "*hysterical patients suffer mainly from reminiscences*" (Freud & Breuer, 1893a, p. 7), reflecting his idea that actual experience in the past lay at the root of hysteria. He comes to believe that psychic trauma had occurred in the life of a young child—caused

---

5 "The psychical changes which must be postulated as being the foundation of the hysterical status take place wholly in the sphere of unconscious, automatic, cerebral activity. It may, perhaps, further be emphasized that in hysteria the influence of psychical processes on the physical processes in the organism (as in all neuroses) is increased, and that hysterical patients work with a surplus of excitation in the nervous system—a surplus which manifests itself, now as an inhibitor, now as an irritant, and is displaced within the nervous system with great freedom" (Freud, 1888, pp. 49–50).

by either a single event or a series of events—that was being expressed in the hysterical symptom, and that the trauma had been sexual in nature.[6] Although some contemporary authors have argued that Freud did not intend to restrict his notion of trauma even in this early period to *actual* events and that he always allowed for the possibility that the trauma was inherent in the child, e.g., with the eruption of an unacceptable or forbidden wish,[7] Freud (1896b) is very explicit on this point in "The Aetiology of Hysteria": "The sexual experiences in childhood consisting of stimulation of the genitals, coitus-like activities, etc. are therefore in the final analysis to be recognized as the traumata from which proceed hysterical reactions" (p. 190).[8]

Freud's (1895) writing from this period is much more detailed regarding the mechanism of origin—the mental operations—that generate hysterical symptoms. He explains that an "excessively intense idea" intrudes into the consciousness of a hysteric, and that this idea has a compulsive aspect beyond the patient's control.[9] This idea generates a hysterical symptom—Freud gives the example of hysterical weeping—that strikes even the patient as outlandish and inappropriate with respect to the "excessively intense idea."[10] Freud explains that the

6 "I put forward the proposition, therefore, that at the bottom of every case of hysteria will be found one or more experiences of premature sexual experience, belonging to the first years of childhood, experiences which may be reproduced by analytic work though whole decades have intervened. I believe this to be a momentous revelation" (Freud, 1896b, p. 187). Alternate translation from the *Standard Edition*: "I therefore put forward the proposition that at the bottom of every case of hysteria there are one or more experiences of *premature sexual experience*, occurrences which belong to the earliest years of childhood but which can be reproduced through the work of psychoanalysis in spite of the intervening decades. I believe this to be an important finding" (Freud, 1896a, p. 203).

7 "Psychic trauma calls for more detailed elucidation because the concept has given rise to misunderstandings about the role of the internal and external worlds. Even before 1895, Freud had noted that an idea was always involved, whether or not linked to a trauma that had been actually experienced. The decisive element was not the objective event but the significance assigned to it by the individual. A forbidden wish could also act as a trauma" (Halberstadt-Freud, 1996, p. 985).

8 Alternate translation in the *Standard Edition*: "Sexual experiences in childhood consisting in stimulation of the genitals, coitus-like acts, and so on, must therefore be recognized, in the last analysis, as being the traumas which lead to a hysterical reaction to events at puberty and to the development of hysterical symptoms" (Freud, 1896a, pp. 206–207).

9 "Hysterical patients are subject to a *compulsion* which is exercised by *excessively intense ideas*" (Freud, 1895, p. 347).

10 "Hysterical and excessively intense ideas strike us . . . by their oddity; they are ideas which in other people have no consequences and of whose importance we can make nothing. They appear to us as intruders and usurpers, and accordingly as ridiculous. Thus, *hysterical compulsion* is (1) *unintelligible*, (2) *incapable of being resolved by the activity of thought*, (3) *incongruous* in its structure" (Freud, 1895, p. 347). "*The reaction of the hysteric is only apparently exaggerated; it is bound to appear exaggerated to us because we only know a small part of the motives from which it arises*" (Freud, 1896a, p. 217).

real cause for the weeping has been repressed (i.e., unconsciously repudiated from the patient's conscious mind), and that any idea associated with the real cause has been replaced by a substitute idea.[11] This substitute, the "excessively intense idea," was related to the original by an actual occurrence at some point in the patient's past. He refers to the substitute as an "incidental circumstance" that becomes "a symbol" for the original idea and says that if the original idea were to become conscious, its effects would be justifiable and intelligible and could be combatted (p. 349). The "excessively intense" substitute, however, remains unintelligible and beyond the patient's control because the circumstances of its origin remain unconscious. This process of substitution of one idea for another, which Freud refers to as "symbol formation," goes beyond the defense ordinarily employed to keep unpleasant ideas out of consciousness.[11] Even in obsessional neurosis, he points out, this "displacement" does not occur (p. 352).

It is in this period of collaboration with Breuer that Freud first discusses *splitting*, the creation of a quasi-independent nucleus of "second consciousness,"[12] for a time acquiescing in Breuer's use of the term "hypnoid state" for this dissociated sector of the psyche.[13] He writes that traumatic memories become shut off from consciousness because the affects attached to them are not sufficiently discharged immediately following the trauma.[14] With the discovery that the early traumatic memories had not been destroyed or completely eradicated from consciousness (since

---

11 "The *hysteric*, who weeps at *A*, is quite unaware that he is doing so on account of the association *A–B*, and *B* itself plays no part at all in his psychical life. The symbol has in this case taken the place of the *thing* entirely. . . . Whenever anything is evoked, from outside or by association, which would in fact cathect *B*, *A* enters consciousness instead of it" (Freud, 1895, p. 349).

12 "When this process occurs for the first time there comes into being a nucleus and centre of crystallization for the formation of a psychical group divorced from the ego—a group around which everything which would imply an acceptance of the incompatible idea subsequently collects. The splitting of consciousness in these cases of acquired hysteria is accordingly a deliberate and intentional one. At least it is often introduced by an act of volition; for the actual outcome is something different from what the subject intended. What he wanted was to do away with an idea, as though it had never appeared, but all he succeeds in doing is to isolate it psychically" (Freud & Breuer, 1893a, p. 123).

13 "The basis and *sine quâ non* of hysteria is the occurrence of peculiar dreamlike states of consciousness with a restricted capacity for association, for which [Breuer] proposes the name 'hypnoid states'. In that case, the splitting of consciousness is secondary and acquired; it comes about because the ideas which emerge in hypnoid states are cut off from associative communication with the rest of the content of consciousness" (Freud, 1894, p. 46).

14 "The injured person's reaction to the trauma only exercises a completely 'cathartic' effect if it is an *adequate* reaction—as, for instance, revenge" (Freud & Breuer, 1893a, p. 8).

they could be recovered under hypnosis),[15] he views their splitting-off as a basic attribute of hysteria.[16] But Freud maintains that splitting-off is not the end of the process since the excitation attached to the walled-off affect still needs an avenue of discharge:[17] "In hysteria," he (1894) writes, "the incompatible idea is rendered innocuous by its *sum of excitation* being *transformed into something somatic*. For this I should like to propose the name of *conversion*" (p. 50). It is this concept of conversion that Freud uses to explain the wide variety of physical symptoms—the stigmata—that he encounters in his hysterical patients. He suggests that to a greater or lesser extent symptoms are related to the body parts that were flooded with nervous excitation during the original trauma, and that subsequent traumata of a similar nature can reawaken memories of the original trauma, triggering conversion anew.[18]

In his clinical work with hysterics, Freud discovers that not only can memories be recovered to consciousness, but that talking about them in an emotional way leads to the disappearance of the symptoms.[19] He

15 "The operation of Breuer's cathartic method lies in leading back the excitation . . . from the somatic to the psychical sphere deliberately, and in then forcibly bringing about a settlement of the contradiction by means of thought-activity and to discharge of the excitation by talking . . . hypnosis regularly widens the restricted consciousness of a hysteric and allows access to the psychical group that has been split off" (Freud, 1894, p. 50).

16 "*Splitting of consciousness . . . is present to a rudimentary degree in every hysteria, and that a tendency to such a dissociation, and with it the emergence of abnormal states of consciousness (which we will bring together under the term 'hypnoid') is the basic phenomenon of this neurosis.* . . . These hypnoid states share . . . one common feature: the ideas which emerge in them are very intense but are cut off from associative communication with the rest of the content of consciousness" (Freud & Breuer, 1893a, p. 12).

17 "Both the memory-trace and the affect which is attached to the idea are there once and for all and cannot be eradicated. . . . *But the sum of excitation which has been detached from it must be put to another use*" (Freud, 1894, pp. 48–49).

18 "The conversion may be either total or partial. It proceeds along the line of the motor or sensory innervation which is related—either intimately or more loosely—to the traumatic experience. . . . Consequently the memory-trace of the repressed idea has, after all, not been dissolved; from now on, it forms the nucleus of a second psychical group. . . . When once such a nucleus for a hysterical splitting-off has been formed at a traumatic moment, it will be increased . . . whenever the arrival of a fresh impression of the same sort succeeds in breaking through the barrier erected by the will, . . . re-establishing for a time the associative link between the two psychical groups, until a further conversion sets up a defense. . . . The excitation which is forced . . . into somatic innervation now and then finds its way back to the idea from which it has been detached, and it then compels the subject either to work over the idea associatively or to get rid of it in hysterical attacks . . ." (Freud, 1894, pp. 49–50).

19 "For we found, to our great surprise at first, that *each individual hysterical symptom immediately and permanently disappeared when we had succeeded in bringing clearly to light the memory of the event by which is was provoked and in arousing its accompanying affect, and when the patient had described an event in the greatest possible detail and had put the affect into words. Recollection without affect almost invariably produces no result*" (Freud & Breuer, 1893a, p. 6).

concludes that the best way to address hysteria in treatment is by use of this cathartic method—that is, by facilitating the abreaction of the pent-up affect attached to the original trauma.[20] Freud at first tries to use hypnosis as the means of facilitating the cathartic abreaction, but he discovers that he is not personally suited for it, and he has difficulty inducing somnambulism in many of his patients (Freud, 1893c, pp. 107ff).[21] He begins asking his patients only for "concentration," directing them to lie down and shut their eyes; occasionally, he applies pressure to patients' foreheads with his hands and commands them to communicate whatever comes into their minds at the moment he releases the pressure. He finds that this approach, though more laborious, yields the precise result he is seeking: a point of entry into the forgotten, enabling the patient to recall more and more of the circumstances surrounding the appearance of symptoms. Freud concludes that the forgetting is only apparent and that everything is retained in the unconscious.[22] Within a few years—by 1904 at the latest and probably by 1900 according to the editors of the *Standard Edition*—Freud abandons this pressure technique, explicitly saying that he avoids touching his patients in any way and that he does not recommend having the patient keep his eyes shut during analysis.[23]

Freud (1895) says clinical experience has shown that two preconditions are necessary for the formation of the "pathological defense" of hysterical repression. First, the original idea/memory must "evoke a distressing affect (unpleasure)," and second, the idea must be "from sexual life" (p. 350). That sexual life is *always* implicated is known, Freud says, from clinical experience,[24] but he goes on to explain this fact by referring to the delayed sexual development of children (and by assuming that children do not fully experience or understand sexual feelings until puberty). He gives the example of Emma, a young woman who had a "compulsion of not being able to go into shops alone. As a reason for this, [she produced in treatment] a memory

20 "By providing an opportunity for the pent-up affect to discharge itself in words the therapy deprives of its affective power the idea which was not originally abreacted; by conducting it into normal consciousness (in light hypnosis) it brings it to into associative readjustment" (Freud & Breuer, 1893b, p. 49). Also in the *Standard Edition*, 1893a, p. 17.

21 The editors of the *Standard Edition* (1893a, p. 111) place Freud's use of hypnosis approximately between the years 1887 and 1896.

22 "The conclusion I drew from all these observations was that experiences that have played an important pathogenic part, and all their subsidiary concomitants, are accurately retained in the patient's memory even when they seem to be forgotten" (Freud, 1893c, p. 112).

23 *Standard Edition*. London: Hogarth Press, 2:110; 7:250; 7:260.

24 "We know from clinical evidence that all this only occurs in the sexual sphere" (Freud, 1895, p. 353).

from the time when she was 12 years old (shortly after puberty)" (p. 353). In her memory, she ran from a shop in fright upon witnessing two shop assistants laughing together and surmising that they were laughing at her clothes; she also recalled that she had been attracted to one of the shop assistants. Freud traces this reaction to a forgotten memory Emma produced of two earlier incidents that had occurred when she was eight years old—before puberty. She had gone into a shop alone, and the shopkeeper, with a grin on his face, had groped her genitals through her clothing. A while later, she had again gone into the shop alone, and the same thing happened, after which she never went into the shop again. In the treatment, "she . . . reproached herself for having gone there the second time as though she had wanted in that way to provoke the assault" (p. 354). Freud concludes that the only possible explanation for this scenario was that the sexual feelings aroused in Emma at age eight took on new meaning after puberty—an unacceptable meaning—that was driven from her consciousness through the mechanism of her ego directing her attention to the substitute ideas ("symbols") of *shops* and *clothes* and away from feelings of sexual arousal.[25]

In short, Freud sees the eruption of sexual impulses at the onset of puberty as setting the stage for a triggering incident to re-awaken traumatic sexual memories from earlier childhood.[26] (In this way, Freud also explains the fact that hysterical symptoms rarely emerge until adolescence.[27]) He calls this concept *Nachträglichkeit* (translated in the *Standard Edition* as *deferred action*), holding that "the subject revises past events at a later date, and that it is this revision which invests them with significance . . . or pathogenic force" (Laplanche & Pontalis,

---

25 "Here we have the case of a memory arousing an affect which it did not arouse as an experience, because in the meantime the change [brought about] in puberty had made possible a different understanding of what was remembered" (Freud, 1895, p. 356).

26 "Now this case is typical of repression in hysteria. We invariably find the memory is repressed which has only become a trauma by deferred action. . . . Every adolescent individual has memory-traces which can only be understood with the emergence of sexual feelings of his own; and accordingly every adolescent must carry the germ of hysteria within him. There must obviously be concurrent factors as well, if this universal determining effect is to be limited to the small number of individuals who actually become hysterics. Now analysis indicates that what is disturbing in the sexual trauma is evidently the release of affect; and experience teaches us to recognize hysterics as individuals of whom one can assume in part that they have become *prematurely* sexually excitable owing to mechanical and emotional stimulation (masturbation), and of whom one can assume in part that a premature sexual release is present in their innate disposition. But premature *beginning* of sexual release or prematurely *intensified* sexual release are clearly equivalent" (Freud, 1895, pp. 356–357).

27 "In boys and girls of intense hysterical disposition, the period before and after puberty brings about a first outbreak of the neurosis. . . . As is well known, an early age, from 15 onwards, is the period at which the hysterical neurosis most usually shows itself actively in females" (Freud, 1888, p. 52).

1973, p. 112). Now events whose significance had not been grasped in the past were seen in a new light based on fresh personal experience, unleashing unacceptable or frightening memories, fantasies, and emotions.[28] Freud's idea is that the repudiation by the ego of these memories, fantasies, and emotions is due to their connection with forbidden impulses, requiring that the subject employ some means of defense in order to keep them out of consciousness.[29]

After the "Seduction Theory"

The preceding rendition of the etiology of hysteria later acquired the label "seduction theory" or "trauma theory," reflecting the importance Freud assigns to actual traumatic experience of a sexual nature in his then current understanding. However, in the late 1890s, he begins to have doubts about the seduction theory. As he explains in a letter to his friend Wilhelm Fliess, his reasons for moving away from the trauma theory stem in part from his frustration in losing patients and having difficulty in bringing analyses to satisfactory conclusions,[30] but he also confides that he has come to believe that the prevalence of hysteria is too great to be accounted for by what he believes is the relatively rarer phenomenon of actual child abuse.[31] Freud begins to shift his emphasis

28 Freud's analysis of the Wolf Man relied extensively on the concept of *Nachträglichkeit* as well, although in this case the original trauma was seen as the Wolf Man's glimpsing the "primal scene" at age one and a half and the onset of neurosis at age four or so to be caused by "his development, his sexual excitations and his sexual researches" (Freud, 1914a, pp. 37–38).

29 "For these patients whom I analyzed had enjoyed good mental health up to the moment at which *an occurrence of incompatibility took place in their ideational life*—that is to say, until their ego was faced with an experience, an idea or a feeling which aroused such a distressing affect that the subject decided to forget about it because he had no confidence in his power to resolve the contradiction between that incompatible idea in his ego by means of thought-activity. In females incompatible ideas of this sort arise chiefly on the soil of sexual experience and sensation . . ." (Freud, 1894, p. 47).

30 "The continual disappointment in my efforts to bring a single analysis to conclusion, the running away of people who for a period of time had been most gripped [by analysis], the absence of complete success on which I had counted . . ." (Freud, 1897, p. 264). Also in *Standard Edition*. London: Hogarth Press, 1:259.

31 "And now I want to confide in you immediately the great secret that has been slowly dawning on me in the last few months. I no longer believe in my neurotica [theory of the neuroses] . . . Then the surprise that in all cases, the father, not excluding my own, had to be accused of being perverse—the realization of the unexpected frequency of hysteria, with precisely the same conditions prevailing in each, whereas surely widespread perversions against children are not very probable. The incidence of perversion would have to be immeasurably more frequent than the resulting hysteria because the illness, after all, occurs only where there has been an accumulation of events and there is a contributory factor that weakens the defense" (Freud, 1897, pp. 264–5). Also in *Standard Edition*. London: Hogarth Press, 1:259–260.

away from actual traumatic experiences as the key causal factor in hysteria to more universally experienced phenomena—such as masturbatory fantasies[32] and "the possibility . . . that sexual fantasy invariably seizes upon the theme of the parents" (1897, p. 265).[33]

Writing in 1908, for example, Freud explains how conscious fantasies used during masturbation in childhood become unconscious when the masturbatory act is later given up. Freud says these unconscious fantasies—if not successfully sublimated—retain their power and can become converted into hysterical symptoms. "In this way, unconscious fantasies are the immediate psychical precursors of a whole number of hysterical symptoms. Hysterical symptoms are nothing other than unconscious fantasies brought into view through 'conversion'."[34] In the same article, Freud (1908a) summarizes his understanding of hysteria in a series of formulas that refer both to fantasies and experiences:

> I will at this point . . . interpolate a series of formulas which attempt to give a progressively fuller description of the nature of hysterical symptoms. These formulas do not contradict one another, but some represent an increasingly complete and precise approach to the facts, while others represent the application of different points of view:
>
> (1) Hysterical symptoms are mnemic symbols of certain operative (traumatic) impressions and experiences.
> (2) Hysterical symptoms are substitutes, produced by 'conversion', for the associative return of these traumatic experiences.
> (3) Hysterical symptoms are—like other psychical structures—an expression of the fulfillment of a wish.

32 "Investigation of the childhood history of hysterical patients shows that the hysterical attack is designed to take the place of an autoerotic satisfaction previously practiced and since given up" (Freud, 1908b, p. 232).

"Longing is the main character trait of hysteria, just as actual anesthesia (even though only potential) is the main symptom. During this same period of longing, fantasies are formed and masturbation is (regularly?) practiced, which then yields to repression. If it does not yield, then no hysteria develops either; the discharge of sexual excitation for the most part removes the possibility of hysteria. It has become clear to me that various compulsive movements represent a substitute for the discontinued movements of masturbation" (Freud, 1897, pp. 274–275).

33 Also in *Standard Edition*. London: Hogarth Press, 1:260.

34 "[I]n so far as the symptoms are somatic ones, they are often enough taken from the circle of the same sexual sensations and motor innervations as those which had originally accompanied the [masturbatory] fantasy when it was still conscious. In this way the giving up of the habit of masturbation is in fact undone, and the purpose of the whole pathological process, which is a restoration of the original, primary sexual satisfaction, is achieved—though never completely, it is true, but always in a sort of approximation. Anyone who studies hysteria, therefore, soon finds his interest turned away from its symptoms to the fantasies from which they proceed" (Freud, 1908a, pp. 161–162).

(4) Hysterical symptoms are the realization of an unconscious fantasy which serves the fulfillment of a wish.

(5) Hysterical symptoms serve the purpose of sexual satisfaction and represent a portion of the subject's sexual life (a portion of which corresponds to one of the constituents of his sexual instinct).

(6) Hysterical symptoms correspond to a return of a mode of sexual satisfaction which was a real one in the infantile life and has since been repressed.

(7) Hysterical symptoms arise as a compromise between two opposite affective and instinctual impulses, of which one is attempting to bring to expression a component instinct or constituent of the sexual constitution, and the other is attempting to suppress it.

(8) Hysterical symptoms may take over the representation of various unconscious impulses which are not sexual, but they can never be without a sexual significance. (pp. 163–164)

Freud's gradual shift from understanding hysteria to be derived from actually experienced traumata to understanding hysteria to be derived from the universal phenomenon of sexual fantasy can be viewed in different ways.

On the one hand, the distinction between the repressed memory of a traumatic sexual experience and a repressed sexual fantasy of seduction may not be so great. In both cases, the objectionable content and its associated affect are relegated to the unconscious, and the sum of excitation attached to it presses for discharge. Dynamically, the picture is the same. Moreover, as Laplanche and Pontalis (1973) point out, Freud never completely abandons the seduction theory, and elements of it become reworked while his theories develop. For example, even to the end of his career Freud acknowledges the pathogenic influence of child abuse[35] although in these "actual" cases Freud stresses the involvement of fantasy. If, for example, a child is abused by an older child, he may later create a fantasy transposing the memory of this abuse onto one of his parents (Freud, 1916–1917, p. 191). Another example of the persistence of the seduction theory can be found as late 1933 in Freud's discussion of the child's preoedipal attachment to the mother in the "New Introductory Lectures," in which he addresses the possibility that the mother's physical ministrations generate sexual feelings in the child that could lead to fantasies of seduction.[36] Finally, Laplanche and Pontalis claim that in the

35 "Right up to the end of his life, Freud continued to assert the existence, prevalence and pathogenic force of scenes of seduction actually experienced by children" (Laplanche & Pontalis, 1973, p. 406).

36 "Here . . . the phantasy touches the ground of reality, for it was really the mother who by her activities over the child's bodily hygiene inevitably stimulated, and perhaps even roused for the first time, pleasurable sensations in her genitals" (Freud, 1932c, p. 120).

end "Freud [can] never resign himself to treating phantasy as the pure and simple outgrowth of the spontaneous sexual life of the child. He is forever searching, behind the phantasy, for whatever has founded it in its reality" (p. 406). As substantiation, they cite Freud's (1916–17) statement in the "Introductory Lectures" that "all the things that are told to us today in analysis as phantasy . . . were once real occurrences in the primaeval times of the human family" (p. 371).

On the other hand, the shift away from the seduction theory does constitute a major change since it frees Freud from being confined to attempting to elucidate the neuroses by tying them to the vagaries of the unique individual histories of his patients. From a theoretical point of view, this allows him to think in more general terms, and Freud acknowledges the impact of this freedom in later accounts, crediting it with his discoveries concerning childhood sexuality and the Oedipus complex.[37] From a technical point of view, this change allows Freud to begin to consider that working toward reconstruction of a patient's personal traumatic history and bringing it to consciousness may not be as important to therapeutic progress as is working toward a fuller understanding of what is transpiring between patient and analyst (i.e., the analysis of transference and resistance).[38] Freud's therapeutic technique during the post-seduction theory period is still primarily oriented toward the goal of making the unconscious conscious,[39] but by the time Freud (1916–17) publishes his "Introductory Lectures on Psycho-analysis," development and resolution of the "transference neurosis" have become his focus.[40] In

37 "If hysterical subjects trace back their symptoms to traumas that are fictitious, then the new fact which emerges is precisely that they create such scenes in phantasy, and this psychical reality requires to be taken into account alongside practical reality. This reflection was soon followed by the discovery that these phantasies were intended to cover up the auto-erotic activity of the first years of childhood, to embellish it and raise it to a higher plane. And now, from behind the phantasies, the whole range of a child's sexual life came to light" (Freud, 1914b, p. 17–18).

Freud was to acknowledge somewhat belatedly that with the seduction phantasies he "had in fact stumbled for the first time upon the Oedipus complex" (Freud, 1924, p. 34). "It was indeed only a short step from the seduction of the little girl by her father to the Oedipal love of the girl for her father" (Laplanche & Pontalis, 1973, p. 406).

38 "In Freud's early work, he attempted to reconstruct each patient's actual past; but by midpoint in his professional life, he was more concerned with resolving patients' resistances to knowing their past. His early trauma theory was replaced by a theory of fantasied experiences, and for contemporary analysts this brought recognition that fantasy may be more significant in the formation of mental structures than real events" (Meadow, 1989, pp. 57–58).

39 "The technique of psychoanalysis enables us in the first place to infer from the symptoms what those unconscious fantasies are and then to make them conscious to the patient" (Freud, 1908a, p. 162).

40 "When . . . the treatment has obtained mastery over the patient, what happens is that the whole of his illness's new production is concentrated upon a single point—his relation to the doctor. . . . When the transference has risen to this significance, work upon the patient's memories

the lecture XXVII, he recognizes that "the transference possesses . . . extraordinary, and for the treatment, positively central, importance in hysteria" (p. 445) and that the complete meaning of hysterical symptoms was not unraveled until transference was better understood.[41] "Transference is present in the patient from the beginning of the treatment and for a while is the most powerful motive in its advance," Freud writes, but "if it then changes into a resistance, we must turn our attention to it . . ." (p. 443). Freud's prescription for dealing with this emerging impediment to progress in the treatment is to analyze the resistance in a direct and interpretive way[42,43] although he straightfowardly admits that "the doctor's knowledge is not the same as the patient's and cannot produce the same effects" and that "if the doctor transfers his knowledge to the patient as a piece of information . . . it does not have the result of removing the symptoms . . ." (p. 281). Clearly, Freud's approach to treatment had evolved from the time when he was trying to get the patient to remember repressed traumatic experiences.

Late Freud

By the time Freud reaches the final stages of his career—after the publication of such seminal works as "Beyond the Pleasure Principle"

retreats far into the background. Thereafter it is not incorrect to say that we are no longer concerned with the patient's earlier illness but with a newly created and transformed neurosis which has taken the former's place. . . . All the patient's symptoms have abandoned their original meaning and have taken on a new sense which lies in relation to the transference; or only such symptoms have persisted as are capable of undergoing such a transformation. But the mastering of this new, artificial neurosis coincides with getting rid of the illness which was originally brought to the treatment—with the accomplishment of our therapeutic task" (Freud, 1916–1917, p. 444).

41 "It may be said that our conviction of the significance of symptoms as substitutive satisfactions of the libido only received its final confirmation *after the enlistment of the transference*" (Freud, 1916–1917, p. 445; italics added).

42 "We overcome the transference by *pointing out to the patient that his feelings do not arise from the present situation* and do not apply to the person of the doctor, but that they are repeating something that happened to him earlier. In this way *we oblige him to transform his repetition into a memory*. By that means *the transference*, which, whether affectionate or hostile, seemed in every case to constitute the greatest threat to treatment, *becomes its best tool* . . ." (Freud, 1916–1917, pp. 443–444; italics added).

43 "[W]hen the patient's free associations fail the obstacle can be removed every time by an assurance that he is now possessed by a thought which concerns the person of the physician or something relating to him. No sooner is this explanation given than the obstacle is removed—or at least the absence of thoughts has been transformed into a refusal to speak" (Freud, 1912, pp. 107–108).

(1920), "The Ego and the Id "(1923), and "Inhibitions, Symptoms and Anxiety" (1926)—he has introduced concepts that bear directly on his understanding of all the neuroses: concepts like the second topographical model, the death instinct, the Oedipus complex, castration anxiety, and the "sense of guilt." Writing in 1932, Freud (1931a) summarizes his understanding of the etiology of the neuroses by emphasizing internal conflict:

> It is a familiar fact that the aetiological preconditions of neurosis are not yet known with certainty. The precipitating causes of it are frustrations and internal conflicts: conflicts between the three major psychical agencies [id-ego-superego], conflicts arising within the libidinal economy in consequence of our bisexual disposition, and conflicts between the erotic and the aggressive instinctual components. (p. 220)[44]

When Freud says that conflict between the "three agencies" of the second typography or conflict "in the libido economy" is fundamental to the eruption of neurotic pathology, we have a clear indication that Freud considers the Oedipus complex (or at least arrival at the oedipal period) to be a "prerequisite" for all the neuroses, including hysteria.[45] This is because the constituent elements of these conflicts are those which develop as the child passes through the Oedipus situation. For example, the superego, the ego ideal, the conscience, and "the sense of guilt" all derive directly from the passage through Oedipus,[46] and they all figure prominently in Freud's reformulations of the dynamics of hysteria. Impulses that were originally described as objectionable to the patient's conscious mind and repressed into the unconscious are now described somewhat differently by Freud (1923) in the revised topographical model:

---

44 Alternate translation: "It is well known that all the etiological factors in neurosis are not yet clearly recognized. The precipitating causes of neurosis are frustrations and inner conflicts— conflicts between the three great psychic faculties [id-ego-superego], conflicts in the libido economy which result from the bisexual disposition, and [conflicts] between the erotic and the aggressive components of instinct" (Freud, 1932a, p. 6).

45 "In my opinion it is advisable in general, and quite especially where neurotics are concerned, to assume the existence of the complete Oedipus complex" (Freud, 1923, p. 33).

46 "The ego ideal is therefore the heir of the Oedipus complex, and thus it is also the expression of the most powerful impulses and most important libidinal vicissitudes of the id. By setting up this ego ideal, the ego has mastered the Oedipus complex and at the same time placed itself in subjection to the id. Where the ego is essentially the representative of the external world, of reality, the superego stands in contrast to it as a representative of the internal world, of the id. Conflicts between the ego and the ideal will . . . ultimately reflect the contrast between what is real and what is psychical, between the external world and the internal world" (Freud, 1923, p. 36).

The broad general outcome of the sexual phase dominated by the Oedipus complex may be taken to be the forming of a precipitate in the ego, consisting of . . . two identifications [a father-identification and a mother-identification] in some way united with each other. This modification of the ego retains its special position; it confronts the other contents of the ego as an ego ideal or super-ego. (p. 34)

The subject's superego, artifact of passage through the Oedipus complex, is now seen as determining what is acceptable to the subject's ego[47] and generating a sense of guilt when the ego does not rise to the standards of the ego ideal. What distinguishes hysteria from obsessional neurosis and melancholia, Freud (1923) adds, is that in hysteria this sense of guilt remains unconscious:

The hysterical ego fends off a distressing perception with which the criticisms of its superego threaten it in the same way in which it is in the habit of fending off an unendurable object-cathexis—by an act of repression. It is the ego, therefore, that is responsible for the sense of guilt remaining unconscious. We know that as a rule the ego carries out repressions in the service and at the behest of its superego; but this [hysteria] is a case in which it has turned the same weapon against its harsh taskmaster. . . . In hysteria the ego succeeds only in keeping at a distance the material to which the sense of guilt refers. (pp. 51–52)

In other words, in hysteria the ego uses the defense of repression to fend off criticisms of the superego as well as unacceptable impulses toward objects. It is only with this formulation involving the superego that the concept of aggression—the death instinct—starts to come into play in Freud's formulation of hysteria. While he does not discuss at length how a hysteric might react to the perception of unacceptable aggressive impulses arising within himself or herself[48] (as he does with

---

47 "The superego is, however, not simply a residue of the earliest object-choices of the id; it also represents an energetic reaction-formation against those choices. Its relation to the ego is not exhausted by the precept: 'you *ought to be* like this (like your father).' It also comprises the prohibition: 'you *may not be* like this (like your father)—that is, you may not do all that he does' . . ." (Freud, 1923, p. 34).

48 "It is remarkable that the more a man checks his aggressiveness towards the exterior the more severe—that is aggressive—he becomes in his ego ideal. . . . The more a man controls his aggressiveness, the more intense becomes his ideal's inclination to aggressiveness against his ego" (Freud, 1923, p. 54).

"The conflict due to ambivalence, for instance, is resolved in hysteria by this means. The subject's hatred of a person whom he loves is kept down by an exaggerated amount of tenderness for him and apprehensiveness about him" (Freud, 1926, p. 158).

the sexual impulses), Freud describes the Oedipus complex and its resolution—in his terms, an essential prerequisite for hysteria—with
abundant references to aggression: the boy feels rivalry and hostility
toward the father; the girl feels rivalry and hostility toward the mother;
the parents threaten castration if the boy masturbates; the girl perceives
her lack of a penis as cruel punishment. As the child introjects parental
imagoes and identifies with the parent of the same sex in order to avoid
the perceived threat of parental retaliation,[49] the aggression is deposited
into the superego, which deals cruelly with the ego.[50] In the case of hysteria, however, Freud argues that the cruelty of the superego is
repressed. The ego itself participates in the formation of hysterical
symptoms as it attempts to form a compromise between the "need for
punishment" (prompted by the superego) and the "need for satisfaction" (prompted by the id). The hysterical ego then adapts to the presence of the symptoms and, indeed, tends to bind them to itself, bringing about an alteration in the ego.[51] This is not, however, meant to imply
that these ego operations are willed or conscious. Freud is very clear
that they are not.[52] They, too, are repressed. In effect, Freud describes a
situation in which ego-sanctioned symptoms are unconscious but ego-

49 "Clearly the repression of the Oedipus complex was no easy task. The child's parents, and
especially his father, were perceived as the obstacle to a realization of his Oedipus wishes; so his
infantile ego fortified itself for carrying out the repression by erecting this same obstacle within
itself" (Freud, 1923, p. 34).

50 "Through its work of identification and sublimation *[the ego] gives the death instinct in the
id assistance in gaining control over the libido*, but in so doing it runs the risk of becoming the
object of the death instincts and of itself perishing. . . . But since the ego's work of sublimation
results in a defusion of the instincts and *a liberation of the aggressive instincts in the superego*, its
struggle against the libido exposes it to the danger of maltreatment and death" (Freud, 1923, p. 56;
italics added.)

51 "Hysterical symptoms which have been shown to be a compromise between the need for satisfaction and the need for punishment . . . participate in the ego from the very beginning, since
they fulfill a requirement of the superego, while on the other hand they represent positions occupied by the repressed. . . . The ego now proceeds to behave as though it recognized that the symptom had come to stay and that the only thing to do was accept the situation . . . and draw as much
advantage from it as possible. It makes an adaptation to the symptom—to this piece of the internal world which is alien to it—just as it normally does to the real external world. . . . The presence
of the symptom may entail a certain impairment of capacity, and this can be exploited to appease
some demand on the part of the superego or to refuse some claim from the external world. In this
way the symptom gradually comes to be the representative of important interests; it is found to be
useful in asserting the position of the self and becomes more and more closely merged with the
ego and more and more indispensable to it" (Freud, 1926, pp. 98–99).

52 "We have come upon *something in the ego itself which is also unconscious*, which behaves
exactly like the repressed—that is, which produces powerful effects without itself being conscious
and which requires special work before it can be made conscious" (Freud, 1923, p. 17; italics
added).

syntonic, and where they are bound by the ego to itself, resulting in an alteration of the ego.[53]

This type of repression requires a constant expenditure of mental energy, labeled an *anticathexis* by Freud. Although this is true in every case of repression, the anticathexis is particularly difficult to detect in hysteria because, Freud (1926) claims, "the hysterical anticathexis is mainly directed outwards, against dangerous perceptions. It takes the form of a special kind of vigilance which, by means of restrictions of the ego, causes situations to be avoided that would entail such perceptions, or, if they do occur, manages to withdraw the subject's attention from them" (p. 158). A similar strategy utilized by the ego in the service of minimizing the mental energy necessary to maintain an anticathexis is to give up certain functions that ordinarily belong to it. To cite an example of Freud's,

> [If] writing—which consists in allowing a fluid to flow out from a tube upon a piece of white paper—has acquired the symbolic meaning of coitus, or if walking has become a symbolic substitute for stamping upon the body of mother earth, then both writing and walking will be abstained from, because it is as though forbidden sexual behavior were thereby being indulged in. The ego renounces these functions proper to it in order not to have to undertake a fresh effort of repression—*in order to avoid a conflict with the id*. (p. 90)

Freud acknowledges that these scenarios—with the ego actively in conflict with the id impulses—present technical difficulties for the analyst.[54] But he also announces another even more powerful impediment to cure: the superego-induced "moral factor" or unconscious sense of guilt. "The most powerful of all obstacles to recovery, more powerful than the familiar ones of narcissistic inaccessibility, a negative attitude towards the physician and clinging to the gain from illness" is, Freud

---

53 "In hysteria, too, a certain amount of alteration of the ego through reaction-formation is unmistakable and in some circumstances becomes so marked that it forces itself on our attention as the principal symptom. . . . But the difference between reaction-formations in obsessional neurosis and in hysteria is that in the latter they do not have the universality of a character-trait but are confined to particular relationships. . . . *The reaction-formation of hysteria clings tenaciously to a particular object* and never spreads over into a general disposition of the ego" (Freud, 1926, pp. 157–158).

54 "From the point of view of analytic practice, the consequence of this discovery is that we land in endless obscurities and difficulties if we keep to our habitual forms of expression and try, for instance, to derive neuroses from a conflict between the conscious and the unconscious. We shall have to substitute for this antithesis another, taken from our insight into the structural conditions of the mind—the antithesis between the coherent ego and the repressed which is split off from it" (Freud, 1923, p. 17).

(1923) writes, what "may be called a 'moral' factor, a sense of guilt, which is finding its satisfaction in illness and refuses to give up the punishment of suffering. We shall be right in regarding this disheartening explanation as final" (p. 49). According to Freud, the only course of action open to the analyst in this situation is the laborious procedure of bringing the unconscious sense of guilt into consciousness.[55]

Although this synopsis may give the impression of completeness and certitude regarding the place of the Oedipus complex in the etiology of hysteria and the other neuroses, late in his career Freud also begins to explore the impact of the preoedipal period on these pathologies.[56] For one thing, he recognizes the daunting complexity of all the scenarios he has posited: "Insight into what takes place is made particularly difficult by the fact of its being so hard to distinguish the mental processes of this first [preoedipal] phase from later [oedipal] ones by which they are overlaid and are distorted in memory" (Freud, 1931b, p. 233).[57] But the primary impetus for Freud's investigation of the early mother-child relationship is the recognition that he must refine his formulation of the girl's passage through the Oedipus complex since, unlike the boy whose primary object, the mother, remains the object of his affection as he enters the oedipal period, the girl must eventually renounce her primary object in favor of a new one—the father.[58] In the 1931 paper "Female Sexuality,"

55 "The battle with the obstacle of an unconscious sense of guilt is not made easy for the analyst. Nothing can be done against it directly, and nothing indirectly but the slow procedure of unmasking its unconscious repressed roots, and thus gradually changing it into a conscious sense of guilt" (Freud, 1923, p. 50).

56 "[T]he Oedipus complex had a long prehistory and is in some respects a secondary formation (Freud, 1927a, p. 251).

57 "Everything in the sphere of this first attachment to the mother seemed to me so difficult to grasp in analysis—so grey with age and shadowy and almost impossible to revivify—that it was as if it had succumbed to an especially inexorable repression" (Freud, 1931b, p. 226). Alternate translation: "Everything connected with this first mother-attachment has in analysis seemed to me so elusive, lost in a past so dim and shadowy, so hard to resuscitate that it seemed as if it had undergone some specially inexorable repression" (Freud, 1932b, p. 281).

58 "During the phase of the normal Oedipus complex we find the child tenderly attached to the parent of the opposite sex, while its relation to the parent of its own sex is predominantly hostile. In the case of a boy there is no difficulty in explaining this. His first love-object was his mother. She remains so; and, with the strengthening of his erotic desires and his deeper insight into the relations between his father and mother, the former is bound to become his rival. With the small girl it is different. Her first object, too, was her mother. How does she find her way to her father? How, when and why does she detach herself from her mother? We have long understood that the development of female sexuality is complicated by the fact that the girl has the task of giving up what was originally her leading genital zone—the clitoris in favour of a new zone—the vagina. But it now seems to us that there is a second change of the same sort which is no less characteristic and important for the development of the female: the exchange of her original object—her mother—for her father" (Freud, 1931b, p. 225).

Freud (1931b) comes to a startling conclusion: "Since this [preoedipal] phase allows room for all the fixations and repressions from which we trace the origin of the neuroses, it would seem as though *we must retract the universality of the thesis that the Oedipus complex is the nucleus of the neuroses.*" But, perhaps as a means of attenuating this extreme conclusion, Freud then immediately suggests that the definition of the Oedipus complex be expanded "to include *all* the child's relations to *both parents*" (p. 226; italics added). Whether Freud meant by this that the triangular relationship child-mother-father exists from birth, or that the first phase of the Oedipus complex consists solely of the mother-child dyad remains a point of contention. (See André Green's comments, below.) At any rate, Freud now concludes that "the pre-oedipal phase in women is more important than we have hitherto supposed" (1932b, p. 282)[59] and that "this phase of attachment to the mother is especially intimately related to the aetiology of hysteria" (1931b, p. 227). He does not, however, explicitly rework his conception of the etiology of hysteria. Rather, he gives a more complete description of early childhood developments that factor into the etiologies he had outlined earlier in his career. For example, Freud describes two common fantasies originating in the preoedipal period of girls: the fantasy of being sexually seduced by the mother[60] and the fantasy of being devoured, murdered, or poisoned by her.[61] Both of these fantasies (which should equally apply to boys as well as to girls, it would seem) would in themselves constitute logical candidates for repression and possible conversion into hysterical symptoms in

59 *Standard Edition* translation: "Indeed, we had to reckon with the possibility that a number of women remain arrested in their original attachment to their mother and never achieve a true change-over towards men. This being so, the pre-Oedipus phase in women gains an importance which we have not attributed to it hitherto" (Freud, 1931b, p. 226).

60 "Little girls usually discover for themselves their characteristic phallic activity—masturbation of the clitoris; and to begin with this is no doubt accompanied by phantasy. The part played in it by nursery hygiene is reflected in the very common phantasy which makes the mother or nurse into a seducer" (Freud, 1931b, p. 232). Alternate translation: "The little girl generally finds out spontaneously her mode of phallic activity: masturbation of the clitoris, and in the first instance it is no doubt unaccompanied by phantasies. The way in which the tending of the child's body influences the awakening of this activity is reflected in the very common phantasy of seduction by her mother, her wet-nurse or nursemaid." (Freud, 1932b, p. 287).

61 "[I]n this dependence on the mother we have the germ of later paranoia in women. For it appears that this germ is the surprising, yet regular, dread of being killed (? devoured) by the mother. It would seem obvious to conjecture that this anxiety corresponds to the hostility which the child develops towards her mother because of the manifold restrictions imposed by the latter in the process of training and physical care, and that the immaturity of the child's psychic organization favours the mechanism of projection" (Freud, 1932b, p. 283). Also: "we discover the fear of being murdered or poisoned . . . already present in this pre-Oedipus period, in relation to the mother" (Freud, 1932c, p. 120).

the right circumstances since the impulses they represent are "unacceptable." Similarly, Freud investigates the possibilities generated by prohibitions on masturbation, by the implications of the bisexual nature of the
female genitals (his notion that the girl's path to maturity involves relin-
quishing the "masculine" clitoris for the "feminine" vagina), and by the
various infantile reactions to the fact of the absence of a penis in girls.
None of this, however, is explicitly linked up with hysteria, a concept
which by the end of Freud's career has become almost an afterthought in
his work.

Contemporaries of Late Freud

By 1930 psychoanalysis has gained much wider acceptance, and many
writers have weighed in with contributions of their understanding of
hysteria. The notion of a hysterical *character* is now widely discussed,[62]
signaling a departure from the equation *hysteria = conversion*.

For example, Wittels (1930) offers the following general description
of the hysterical character using Freud's new terminology from the second topography:

> The hysterical character never frees itself from its fixation on the infan-
> tile level. Hence it cannot attain its actuality as a grown-up human being;
> it plays the part of a child, and also of the woman. The hysteric person
> has no actuality; she (or he) confuses fantasy and reality, that is to say,
> allows the law of the id to enter into the ego. (p. 186)

Wilhelm Reich (1933), writing three years later, presents a more
comprehensive view of the hysterical character. The most conspicuous
characteristics of hysterics, he says, are an "importunate sexual attitude" and "a specific kind of physical agility exhibiting a distinct sexual nuance" (p. 204). Analysis reveals an underlying severe anxiety,
Reich says, which is overcome by activity: flirtations and "pseudo-pas-
sionate displays" (p. 205). But beneath these overt characteristics,
Reich posits a number of others:

---

62 Freud himself devotes some attention to character types. In "Libidinal Types," he says,
"Erotics are those whose main interest . . . is turned towards love. Loving, but above all, *being
loved*, is the most important thing for them. They are dominated by the fear of loss of love, and are
therefore especially dependent on others who may withhold their love from them" (1931a, p. 218).
He tentatively suggests that when people of the erotic type succumb to neurosis, they are likely to
suffer from hysteria.

Whereas *shyness* and *anxiousness* paired with *coquetry* as well as physical agility are conspicuous in the behavioral expressions of a hysterical
character, the additional specific hysterical character traits are concealed.
Among these we find *fickleness of reactions*, i.e., a tendency to change
one's attitudes unexpectedly and unintentionally; a *strong suggestibility*,
which never appears alone but is coupled with a strong tendency to reactions of disappointment. A hysterical character . . . can easily be persuaded of the most improbable things. By the same token he will readily
give up his beliefs when others, just as easily acquired, replace them.
Hence, an *attitude of compliance* is usually followed by its opposite,
swift *deprecation and groundless disparagement*. . . . this is related to the
exceptional capacity for *sexual attachment of a childish nature*. The *vivid
imagination* can easily lead to . . . *fantasized experiences* [that] are
reproduced and grasped as real experiences. . . . There is also a strong
tendency to embody psychic conflicts in *somatic symptoms*. (pp.
205–206)

As etiological factors contributing to the development of hysteria,
Reich (1933) cites not only (as most important) "the character of the
person most responsible for the child's upbringing," but also "the stage
of development in which the instinctual apparatus meets its most crucial frustration" (p. 204)—specifically, "the genital stage of childhood
development, with its incestuous attachment" (p. 206). While this coincides with Freud's notion of hysteria as being an oedipal phenomenon,
Reich argues that "pregenital, oral, anal, and urethral strivings form a
part of the hysterical character" though he adds that these strivings "are
embodiments of genitality, or at least allied with it" (p. 206).[63]
According to Marmor (1953), Reich posits a continuum "from pure
melancholia (depression), in which orality is predominant, to pure hysteria, in which 'genitality' is predominant"—another indication that
pregenital factors are beginning to attract more attention as etiological
factors in hysteria (p. 658). Marmor also notes that Reich emphasizes
the following characteristics in the hysterical character that could be
seen as having pregenital roots: "a compulsive need to be loved and
admired; intense feelings of inadequacy, which may be conscious or
unconscious; a strong dependency on the approval of others for self-
esteem; a powerful capacity for dramatization and somatic compliance;

63 Ferenczi (1925) suggests, in a similar vein, that "the anal and urethral identification with the
parents . . . appears to build up in the child's mind a sort of physiological forerunner of the ego-
ideal or super-ego. Not only in the sense that the child constantly compares his achievements in
these directions with the capacities of his parents, but in that a severe *sphincter-morality* is set up
which can only be contravened at the cost of bitter self-reproaches and punishment by conscience.
It is by no means improbable that this, as yet semi-physiological, morality forms the essential
groundwork of later purely mental morality" (p. 379).

and a tendency to repress aggressive feelings or attitudes, or to act them out in concealed ways" (pp. 657–658).

Fenichel (1932), on the other hand, emphasizes the Oedipus complex in his discussion of the etiology of hysteria.[64] He writes that infantile masturbatory fantasies develop into partially conscious adult daydreams that "serve the patient as substitutes for his sexual activity, which he repudiates. . . . All [these daydreams] are derivatives of his earliest Oedipus phantasies" (p. 144). Like Freud, Fenichel believes that conversion symptoms represent a "turning from reality to phantasy, a process made necessary by the repression of the Oedipus complex" (p. 149). "This is most clearly seen in types of persons whose body seems 'alien' to them," Fenichel writes, "who are inhibited both in respect to motility and sensation, and have generally speaking no proper relationship with their own body. In them the 'bodily' is repressed, because body and infantile sexuality are for them equivalent" (p. 162). Even Fenichel, however, makes reference to pregenital factors when he writes about the fantasy of fellatio, which he considers to be extremely common and important in the formation of hysterical symptoms. While he provides some oedipal explanations for this fantasy, he also says that its presence can indicate a "partial regression to the oral which follows the failure in the Oedipus complex" or "a partial incorporation of the object, which is, according to Abraham, an archaic sexual aim" (p. 163).

Klein and Fairbairn

The focus on the preoedipal origins of hysteria increases in intensity in the years following Freud's death.

While Melanie Klein does not devote much attention to hysteria per se or to its etiology, as early as the 1920s she begins urging reconceptualization of the Oedipus complex to encompass the earlier oral and anal stages.[65] Then, throughout the 1930s and '40s, she introduces a number of immensely influential concepts: the developmental stages of

---

64 "The hysterical symptom then appears to be a compromise between the repressed Oedipus complex, which breaks through in a distorted form, and the forces that are in the service of repression" (Fenichel, 1932, p. 144).

65 "I have repeatedly alluded to the conclusion that the Oedipus complex comes into operation earlier than is usually supposed" (Klein, 1928, p. 167).

the paranoid (or schizoid) position and the depressive position,[66] the notion of good and bad part-objects,[67] the use of projection and introjection from earliest infancy,[68] the pregenital sense of guilt,[69] and the drive for reparation.[70] These theories have a huge impact on psychoanalytic theory in general as well as on subsequent thinking about hysteria since they take as their starting point that the earliest infantile experiences shape all subsequent development,[71] including whatever subsequent pathology arises.[72] Though earlier in her career she espouses the

66 "During the paranoid position, that is to say during the first three to four months of life, splitting processes, involving the splitting of the first object (the breast) as well as of the feelings towards it, are at their height. Hatred and persecutory anxiety become attached to the frustrating (bad) breast, and love and reassurance to the gratifying (good) breast. However, even at this stage such splitting processes are never fully effective. For from the beginning of life, the ego tends towards integrating itself and towards synthesising the different aspects of the object. (This tendency can be regarded as an expression of the life instinct.)" (Klein, 1948, p. 119).

"I . . . attributed to the depressive position a central rôle in the child's early development, for with the introjection of the object as a whole the relation to the object alters fundamentally. The synthesis between the loved and hated aspects of the complete object gives rise to feelings of mourning and guilt which imply vital advances in the infant's emotional and intellectual life. This is also a crucial juncture for the choice of neurosis or psychosis" (Klein, 1946, p. 100).

67 "[O]bject relations exist from the beginning of life, the first object being the mother's breast which is split into a good (gratifying) and bad (frustrating) breast; this splitting results in a division between love and hate" (Klein, 1946, p. 99).

68 "[T]he relation to the first object [the mother's breast] implies its introjection and projection, and thus from the beginning object relations are moulded by an interaction between introjection and projection, between internal and external objects and situations. These processes participate in the building up of the ego and super-ego and prepare the ground for the onset of the Oedipus complex in the second half of the first year" (Klein, 1946, p. 99).

69 "[T]he super-ego is formed in the earliest stages of the child's life, being first felt by the ego as anxiety and then, as the early anal-sadistic stage gradually comes to a close, as a sense of guilt as well" (Klein, 1932, p. 229).

70 "The drive for reparation . . . can be regarded as a consequence of a greater insight into psychic reality and of growing synthesis, for it shows a more realistic response to the feelings of grief, guilt and fear of loss resulting from the aggression against the loved object. Since the drive to repair or protect the injured object paves the way for more satisfactory object relations and sublimations, it in turn increases synthesis and contributes to the integration of the ego" (Klein, 1946, p. 105).

71 "The early stages of the Oedipus conflict are so largely dominated by pregenital phases of development that the genital phase, when it begins to be active, is at first heavily shrouded and only later, between the third and fifth years of life, becomes clearly recognizable. At this age the Oedipus complex and the formation of the super-ego reach their climax. But the fact that the Oedipus tendencies begin so much earlier than we supposed, the pressure of the sense of guilt which therefore falls upon the pregenital levels, the determining influence thus exercised so early upon the Oedipus development on the one hand and that of the super-ego on the other, and accordingly upon character-formation, sexuality and all the rest of the subject's development—all these things seem to me of great and hitherto unrecognized importance" (Klein, 1928, pp. 179–180).

72 "In early infancy anxieties characteristic of psychosis arise which drive the ego to develop specific defence mechanisms. In this period the fixation points for all psychotic disorders are to be found. . . . The psychotic anxieties, mechanisms and ego defences of infancy have a profound

commonly held view that hysteria is an oedipal phenomenon,[73] using the new terminology of her later theories, Klein is able to argue that the physical symptoms of hysteria have their origin in introjected "persecutory objects," which are experienced as attacking the ego.[74]

Fairbairn, whose work is cited by Klein and who in turn cites her in his work, also advances some hugely influential—and similar—theories in the early 1940s. After years of work with schizophrenic and schizoid patients, he contends that "the paranoid, obsessional and hysterical states . . . essentially represent not the products of fixations at specific libidinal phases, but simply a variety of techniques employed to defend the ego against the effects of conflicts of an oral origin" (1941, p. 252).[75] He recommends a major reformulation:

> It would appear as if the point had now been reached at which, in the interests of progress, the classic libido theory would have to be transformed into a theory of development based essentially upon object-relationships. The great limitation of the present libido theory as an explanatory system resides in the fact that it confers the status of libidinal attitudes upon various manifestations which turn out to be merely techniques for regulating the object-relationships of the ego. (p. 253)

Furthermore, he suggests that there are far-reaching and less-than-optimal consequences for Freud's abandonment of his early notion that hysteria involves a split of the ego.[76] He contends that Freud, in shifting his focus from hysteria to melancholia and psychic structure—in par-

---

influence on development in all its aspects, including the development of the ego, super-ego and object relations." (Klein, 1946, p. 99).

73 "[I]n hysteria the primacy of the genital zone has always been attained" (Klein, 1926, p. 44).

74 "My experience has shown me that . . . anxieties which underlie hypochondriasis are also at the root of hysterical conversion symptoms. The fundamental factor common to both is the fear relating to persecution within the body (attacks by internalized persecutory objects), or to the harm done to internal objects by the subject's sadism, such as attacks by his dangerous excrements—all of which is felt as physical damage inflicted on the ego. The elucidation of the processes underlying the transformation of these persecutory anxieties into physical symptoms might throw further light on the problems of hysteria" (Klein, 1975[1952], p. 84).

75 "The conviction that this is so is supported by two facts: (a) that the analysis of paranoid, obsessional, hysterical and phobic symptoms invariably reveals the presence of an underlying oral conflict, and (b) that paranoid, obsessional, hysterical and phobic symptoms are such common accompaniments and precursors of schizoid and depressive states" (Fairbairn, 1941, p. 252).

76 "It was upon a study of hysteria that Freud originally based the concept of repression; and it was only when he turned his attention from the nature of the repressed to that of the agency of repression that he became preoccupied with melancholia. In my opinion it is a matter of regret that he did not pursue his study of the agency of repression within the same field as his study of the repressed and thus did not make the phenomena of hysteria the basis of his theory of the mental apparatus" (Fairbairn, 1944, p. 82).

ticular, to the repressing agency of the mind, the superego—created serious theoretical incompatibilities[77] that led away from potentially productive investigation of schizoid mechanisms in hysteria.[78] Fairbairn reports that his own clinical work forces him to conclude that hysteria *always* involves splitting,[79] and, furthermore, that the amount of guilt experienced by hysterics—the factor Freud deems crucial in hysteria, according to Fairbairn—is not sufficient to generate the inhibitions that encumber them.[80] He consequently concludes that the origins of repression and guilt precede the oedipal stage:

> *Repression* originates primarily as a defence against "bad" internalized objects (and not against impulses, whether incestuous in the genital sense or otherwise) . . . *guilt* originates as an *additional* defence against situations involving bad internalized objects. According to this view, guilt originates on the principle that the child finds it more tolerable to regard himself as conditionally (i.e. morally) bad than to regard his parents as unconditionally (i.e. libidinally) bad. (1944, p. 75)

The upshot of all this is that Fairbairn comes to believe "that the position underlying the development of hysterical symptoms is essentially a schizoid position" (p. 82).

---

77 "[W]hilst Freud conceived the Oedipus situation, to which he looked for the rationale of repression, as essentially a *genital* situation, his account of the origin of the super-ego, which he regarded as the instigator of repression, is conceived in terms of an *oral* situation, i.e. a situation corresponding to a stage which, according to the 'phase' theory, must necessarily be *pre*genital" (Fairbairn, 1944, p. 75; italics added).

78 "Freud's new theory turned the clinician's attention away from the realities of childhood trauma and abuse to a highly elaborated developmental schema of endogenously organized instinctual wishes and phase-specific, object-related fantasies, out of which internal conflict and the division between conscious and unconscious processes were derived. This led to a hierarchical rendering of conscious and unconscious processes, with vastly different theoretical implications and clinical applications than the model of vertical splits, organizing schemata, and multiple self-states that was described by Janet and the young Freud, and that was referred to in Fairbairn's plea that theoreticians 'return to hysteria'" (Davies, 1996, p. 559).

79 "[M]y own investigations of patients with hysterical symptoms leave me in no doubt whatever that the dissociation phenomena of 'hysteria' involve a split of the ego fundamentally identical with that which confers upon the term 'schizoid' its etymological significance" (Fairbairn, 1944, p. 74).

80 "It is equally difficult to find a satisfactory explanation of the symptoms of 'hysteria' at the super-ego level—if for no other reason than that in 'hysteria' the libidinal inhibitions which occur are out of all proportion to the measure of guilt which is found to be present" (Fairbairn, 1944, p. 75).

The 1950s and 1960s

At various times and places—notably in the late 1950s in North America and Great Britain—the diagnosis "hysteric" seems to disappear. Kris, for example, writes in 1956 that "hysteria as a clinical entity seems at this stage ever more amorphous" (p. 81), and Wisdom (1961) finds that "there is much that is obscure about the theory of hysteria."[81] Some writers even suggest that the term *hysteria* is obsolete, and that some of Freud's patients presented in his case histories as hysterics were actually schizophrenic. Reichard (1956), for example, claims that "Anna O. and Emmy von N. were schizophrenic" (p.155), and that "our psychiatric nosology [is] unsatisfactory because it is burdened with archaic elements. Outstanding among these is the term 'hysteria,' a survivor from prescientific antiquity and a catchall for a variety of dynamically unrelated symptoms, including conversions, phobias, hallucinations, and fugues. Such a diagnosis, which takes no account of the degree of ego defect involved, is obviously useless for purposes of determining treatment or prognosis" (pp. 157–158). Similarly, Easser and Lesser write in 1965 that "The terms hysteria, hysterical character, etc., are so loosely defined and applied so promiscuously that their application to diagnostic categories has become meaningless. The use of these labels for evaluation, analyzability, or prognosis has become tantamount to predicting a throw of the dice" (p. 392).

Much of the literature emerging at this time focuses on the growing interest in the analytic treatment of schizophrenia and psychosis. Indeed, Spotnitz's (1969) groundbreaking work *Modern Psychoanalysis of the Schizophrenic Patient* barely mentions hysteria—except by way of contrasting it with schizophrenia, in which he finds, despite occasional similarity of overt symptomatology, a "morbid tendency not observed in hysteria—a blocking of feelings" (p. 16). Similarly, his important *Psychotherapy of Preoedipal Conditions* (published in 1976, but composed mostly of articles written in the 1950s and 1960s) contains no references whatsoever to hysteria.

Nonetheless, a number of books and articles focusing on hysteria do appear. Many of them address the complexity and ambiguity of the disorder.

Veith, in her 1965 book *Hysteria, the History of a Disease,* writes:

---

81 "A few minutes with the literature, after the early work of Freud, reveals how unrevealing it is. It tells us little and gives the impression that the origin of the disorder is vague" (Wisdom, 1961, p. 224).

Hysteria is an extraordinarily interesting disease, and a strange one. It is encountered in the earliest pages of recorded medicine and is dealt with in current psychiatric literature. Throughout all the intervening years it has been known and accepted as though it were a readily recognizable entity. And yet, except for the fact that it is a functional disorder, without concomitant organic pathological change, it defies definition and any attempt to portray it concretely. Like a globule of mercury, it escapes the grasp. Whenever it appears it takes on the colors of the ambient culture and mores; and thus throughout the ages it presents itself as a shifting, changing, mist-enshrouded phenomenon that must, nevertheless, be dealt with as though it were definite and tangible. (p. 1)

In his comprehensive 1953 article, Marmor writes that "although hysterical *symptoms* are indeed usually among the easiest of all clinical disturbances to resolve, the underlying hysterical *character structure* is often one of the most difficult to alter" (p. 660). Noting the similarity between extreme hysterical symptomatology and certain schizophrenic reactions, the tenuous contact with reality typical of many hysterical patients (including, in particular, confusion of fantasy with reality), and the fact that under duress hysterical patients often regress to borderline or schizophrenic states, he argues that hysteria functions as a defense against psychotic regression.[82] He looks to the oral—that is, pregenital—origins of hysterical pathology to explain these phenomena, recalling that Freud's report on Dora included numerous references to overtly oral symptoms.[83] He suggests that hysterical symptoms often clear up in treatment due to transference compliance—the patient's wish to please the analyst.[84] Marmor theorizes that "the fixations in the oedipal

82 "Although it is recognized that hysterical symptoms . . . may at times be defenses against psychotic regression, the fact is . . . that the tenuous contact of the hysteric with reality is typical of him, as is his tendency at times to confuse fantasy with reality. Under extreme stress the ego of the hysteric retreats even further from reality, and the confusional states which may ensue under such circumstances probably represent transitional borderline syndromes on the road to actual psychotic regression" (Marmor, 1953, p. 661).

83 "Globus hystericus, vomiting, anorexia, and bulimia are by-words in the symptomatology of hysteria. In 'Fragment of an Analysis of a Case of Hysteria,' Freud (1905) takes cognizance of a number of oral symptoms presented by his patient, Dora, notably nausea, anorexia, gastric pains, and a history of prolonged thumb sucking in childhood" (Marmor, 1953, p. 658).

84 "The easy disappearance of hysterical symptoms under therapy, like the hysterics' suggestibility, is often a form of transference compliance, the unconscious formula being, 'If you will love and protect me, I will be or do whatever you want of me.' But this same oral dependency becomes a source of major resistance when the analysis impinges upon it directly. The patient stubbornly clings to patterns of passivity and ingratiating compliance and the working through of these and similar character traits is often one of the most difficult of analytic tasks" (Marmor, 1953, p. 661–662).

phase of development are *themselves the outgrowths of pre-oedipal fixations, chiefly of an oral nature.*[85] While acknowledging the importance of the Oedipus complex (and the castration complex) in the etiology of hysteria, he contends that those complexes are significantly colored by preoedipal developments,[86] and that the overt sexual behavior of the hysteric has *pregenital*, as opposed to genital, significance.[87]

Rangell (1959) finds that hysterical factors may be a part of a variety of pathologies, representing either vestiges of oedipal-level development from which a patient has regressed or the explanation for somatization.[88]

Easser and Lesser (1965) view the essence of hysteria as the defensive substitution of one emotion for another—a tactic they say can be employed by patients in any diagnostic category. Any emotion, they write, can be used by the hysteric as a signal (analogous to anxiety) to avoid the threat of inner psychic tension. The hysteric then changes the quality of the emotion into something more tolerable. An aura of excessive emotionality prevails, but the true affect remains hidden and unconscious.[89] They point out that this overt intensity of emotion in hysterical patients can lead to technical difficulties since "the psychoanalyst in his countertransference can be aroused by the contagion of the exaggerated affect" (p. 391).

---

85 "The kind of parent whose behavior keeps a child at an "oral" level is apt to be the kind of parent whose behavior favors the development of a strong oedipus complex. The pre-oedipal history of most of the hysterics I have seen has revealed one of two things—either intense frustration of their oral-receptive needs as a consequence of early defection or rejection by one or both parent figures, or excessive gratification of these needs by one or both parent figures" (Marmor, 1953, p. 662).

86 "[M]any of the manifestations of the castration complex in the hysteric become more meaningful when they are understood not in terms of genital anxiety but in terms of the fear of losing love or of being cut off symbolically from the maternal breast, an interpretation of castration anxiety which Freud (1926) was the first to advance in The Problem of Anxiety" (Marmor, 1953, p. 666).

87 "The sexuality of the hysteric is indeed a sham, but primarily because it expresses a pregenital oral-receptive wish rather than a genital one. The distress and surprise of the hysterical woman when her seductiveness leads to her being approached genitally is consequently understandable. She is being approached as a woman when what she really desires is to be taken as a child" (Marmor, 1953, p. 667).

88 "[B]ehind the most diverse symptomatology, or alongside it, one might find (i) a piece of a hysterical mechanism, representing the forward-won psychosexual position from which regression has taken place; and (ii) possibly also a piece, even if only a fragment, of a conversion mechanism, representing a somatic expression of the nuclear conflict, either at the forward or the regressed position" (Rangell, 1959, p. 637).

89 "One observes an impressive array of emotional behavior, emotional thought, emotional interrelatedness, and emotional use of the body. Despite its intensity, this emotionality always remains peripheral and a shield for the core affect" (Easser & Lesser, 1965, p. 398).

Shapiro, in his 1965 book *Neurotic Styles*, posits that the hysteric has a *particular style of cognition* that leads inevitably to the use of repression as a defense, and that the content of what is being repressed—sexuality, say—is not as significant as the manner in which the world is perceived.[90] He attributes to this style of cognition an array of traits he associates with hysterics: naïveté, impressionability, and excessive emotionality.

In an article recalling older themes, Zetzel (1968) warns of the possibility of hysterical symptomatology obscuring underlying depression and suggests that patients with such a condition may be difficult to analyze.[91] "True" or "good" hysterics have attained oedipal development, he says, and as a result have experienced a whole-object relationship with both parents, an accomplishment he considers to be a prerequisite for a successful psychoanalysis. He believes it is merely that in hysterics "the postoedipal relationship has been less satisfactory and more ambivalent than the relationship established in the pre-oedipal period" (p. 257).[92] He cites oedipal factors such as fear of castration and penis envy as key elements in the etiology of hysteria.

The 1970s and 1980s

The debate about whether hysteria should be considered an oedipal or preoedipal phenomenon continues during this period. Giovacchini (1976) cautions that "it is important to establish the basis one uses for making a diagnosis, since classification based purely on behavior, or the enumeration of symptoms, is extremely difficult at best. It is almost impossible when dealing with patients suffering from characterological problems" (p. 173). He finds, for example, that "Anna O. and the Wolf

90 "This lack of factual detail and sharp definition in hysterical cognition can hardly be attributed to the operation of the defense mechanism of repression. It is not a matter of the exclusion of specific ideation or emotional contents from consciousness and does not principally have to do with the contents of thought at all. It is a *form* of cognition, although, to be sure, it is a form that is often likely to result in vagueness or diffuseness—even barrenness—of clear, sharp thought content" (Shapiro, 1965, p. 113).

91 "[T]here are women whose manifest hysterical symptomatology proves to be pseudo-oedipal and pseudo-genital. Such patients seldom meet the most important criteria for analysability" (Zetzel, 1968, p. 257).

92 "It is my thesis, in summary, that the true hysteric, whether male or female, has experienced a genuine triangular conflict. The hysteric, in addition, has been able to retain significant object relationships with both parents" (Zetzel, 1968, p. 257).

Man presented . . . many bizarre features indicative of a primitive orientation, much more primitive than had been formulated for hysteria and the obsessive compulsive neuroses" (p. 176). Krohn, in his extensive 1978 monograph on hysteria,[93] recommends "classifying all hysteriform pathologies *not* based on highly structured ego functioning as 'borderline personality—infantile type' and excluding them from the category of 'hysteria'" (Rupprecht-Schampera, 1995, p. 458; italics added).

Hysteria is the topic of a panel discussion at the 28th meeting of the International Psychoanalytic Congress in Paris in July 1973. The discussants include David Beres (from New York), Alfredo Namnum (Mexico City), Eric Brenman (London), and André Green (Paris); Jean Laplanche (1974) summarizes the proceedings in the *International Journal* the following year. The changed nature of the clinical picture of contemporary hysterics and the preoedipal underpinnings of hysteria are themes of all the panelists.[94]

Beres emphasizes that not only is hysteria most likely to be seen clinically as a personality disorder (as opposed to a symptom condition), but that it is also likely to be mixed with other narcissistic pathologies.[95] But because he sees the ability to fantasize as a key element in the clinical picture presented by these patients and because they seem to relate to others as distinct objects, he finds that a certain (preoedipal) degree of structural development has been attained. "With such patients," Beres claims, "the objects to which they relate are primarily props in their fantasies which they act out, in their love life and elsewhere, fantasies that are usually totally repressed and distorted in their conscious expression. These are patients who instinctualize their mundane experience of everyday life. Every encounter evokes a libidinal or aggressive fantasy, which is usually unconscious but sometimes conscious" (quoted in Laplanche, 1974, p. 460). He acknowledges, with Freud, that these patients use repression as a primary defense, and that conversion symptoms may emerge as a result although he finds it more likely that a character disorder will develop since ego functioning may be impaired by regression.[96]

93 See Krohn, 1978, pp. 99–101.

94 "The psychoanalytic formulations of hysteria at the Panel and since have been dominated by the use of pre-oedipal concepts and, thus, by desexualisation. It was viewed more in terms of personality disorders than as a conflict or a symptom, or as one of the defences against psychosis. In both views, the key concepts were pre-oedipal, and related to the dyadic constellation rather than to Freud's original oedipal (triad) constellation" (Yarom, 1997, p. 1120).

95 "Similarly, an apparently hysterical personality may also manifest infantile, narcissistic, paranoid or schizoid traits . . ." (quoted in Laplanche, 1974, p. 460).

96 "The regression of some ego functions is of special significance. The labile emotionality, suggestibility, disturbed object relationships and diffuse anxiety can best be understood in relation

Namnum suggests that changes in the clinical picture of hysteria may have taken place as a result of the "sexual revolution" in the culture at large sparked by psychoanalysis itself. He, too, believes that the presence of hysterical symptoms is not necessary to find a diagnosis of hysterical character or personality.[97]

Brenman believes that "a severe anxiety underlies hysteria" and that while a repressed sexual conflict may be present, behind that conflict is "a more fundamental conflict which is the basis of psychotic illness . . . i.e. [the conflict] between survival and catastrophe, on the one hand, and denial of these anxieties on the other" (quoted in Laplanche, 1974, p. 464). In other words, hysteria is used as a defense against psychotic regression. "A certain kind of so-called 'whole object' relationship is made that enables clinical psychoses and disintegration to be avoided," Brenman argues, a relationship engendered by a "hysterogenic mother" (p. 463). This is a mother who is herself "overwhelmed by anxiety, unconsciously conveying that the infant's anxieties are really catastrophic" but who attempts to lull the baby into believing all is well with "excessive indulgence of the physical needs, devotion, excessive sensuous stimulation, encouraging greedy dependency," hypersexuality, and the "negation of psychic truth" (p. 464). In Brenman's formulation, the anxiety—fear of psychic catastrophe—is paramount, and repression of sexual impulses and concomitant guilt appear as superficial phenomena.

Concurring with Namnum, André Green says that "conversion is no longer considered the central feature in hysteria" (quoted in Laplanche, 1974, p. 464).[98] But differing with Brenman, he resists viewing sexuality as secondary or peripheral in the etiology of hysteria: "To refer only to orality and to consider sexuality as a defence looks more like a denial than a theoretical advance" (p. 464). However, Green suggests that it is the interplay of three factors that determine development of hysteria: sexuality, fears of abandonment or loss of love, and the degree of structural maturity[99]—thereby acknowledging the importance of the

to deviant ego functions—poor impulse control, impaired reality sense, impaired organization function and the intrusion of unconscious drive impulses on autonomous ego functions" (quoted in Laplanche, 1974, p. 460).

97 "[A] girl's reaction to a sexual encounter may be hysterical if it reflects a certain kind of conflict in a particular manner, regardless of whether she develops symptoms or not, or whether there is a tendency to conversion or not" (quoted in Laplanche, 1974, p. 461).

98 "The capacity to develop conversion symptoms has been dissociated from the hysteric character traits defining the hysteric personality." (quoted in Laplanche, 1974, p. 464).

99 "[T]he problem may lie in the relationship between sexuality, love and reaction to loss related to different ego structures" (quoted in Laplanche, 1974, p. 464).

preoedipal.[100] He also discusses the hysteric's use of fantasy as "a symbolic system whose function will be to prevent any surprise coming from the object or from the id" (p. 465), suggesting that it functions both as a container for (preoedipal) anxiety and a means of binding sexual and aggressive impulses.[101] Through "over-sexualization" and "an enormous attempt to displace guilt on to the accused aggressor," these fantasies turn despair into a sense of triumph and generate a feeling of excitement, Green says, giving rise to the sense of manipulativeness often encountered in hysterics.[102] In the end, Green agrees with Brenman, suggesting that the essential aim of the mechanism of hysteria "is a violent struggle against potential depression; a depression in which self-value is blatantly abased" (p. 465). Laplanche points out that "this fact emphasizes at the utmost the shift between Freud's hysteria—repression erected against sexual gratification—and hysteria today, in which sexuality still holds . . . but in which the struggle is against the narcissistic injury leading to depression" (p. 465).

Khan (1975) likewise finds that sexuality is an important factor, one that comes into play after breakdown at the developmental level:

> In adult life the hysteric deals with anxiety by sexualization; in object relations the hysteric employs sexual apparatuses of the body-ego in lieu of affective relating and ego functions. Both the promiscuity and the inhibitions in the hysteric's sexual experiences result from this. The hysteric tries to achieve through use of sexual apparatuses what, otherwise, a person achieves through ego functioning. This accounts for the craving for sexual experience in the hysteric, which is matched only by the hysteric's inability to sustain or be nurtured by any loving relationship. Hence, in their self-experience, the hysterics live in a perpetual psychic state of *grudge*. They feel something is either being withheld from them or their wishes are not being recognized for what they are. (p. 350)

The notion of a grudge arising from frustrated gratification of sexual impulses leads Khan to the conclusion that aggressivity is awak-

---

100 "[A]cting out . . . seem[s] in hysteria to evoke what could be called the fear of depressive insight rather than a true clash of the ego" (quoted in Laplanche, 1974, p. 465).

101 "So the fantasy . . . opposes this increase of tension by binding the id impulses and succeeds in a double operation giving some sort of satisfaction through the fantasy wish-fulfilment and freeing the individual not only from feelings of anxiety or aggression, but also from despair, hopelessness, extreme solitude, helplessness, emptiness" (quoted in Laplanche, 1974, p. 464).

102 "[A]voiding any possible surprise or any unexpected move of the object turns into an excitement, a manoeuvring which sometimes gives the feeling of a hidden triumph transforming dependency on the object into a well-known manipulation" (quoted in Laplanche, 1974, p. 465).

ened in the hysteric and becomes a key part of the hysteric's psychic makeup.[103] This dovetails with Green's reference to the "fear of loss of love" and recalls Lionells's (1984, 1986) work on hysteria.

Lionells (1984) finds in hysteria "a particular form of aggressive display in which anger is expressed as protest against the disruption of a relationship." She believes that "aggression in this instance is designed to restore a desired interpersonal connection rather than to distance or destroy" (p. 634),[104] and that there are two varieties of hysterical aggression typical of the hysteric: the tantrum or tirade and a posture of whining and complaining.[105] Writing as a member of the interpersonal school, Lionells believes that the hysteric's behavior is *always* essentially aggressive in that it involves "pressing the self against the environment" (p. 636), and that this aggressive behavior "emanates from interpersonal needs which are central to the hysteric's core experience" (p. 634). Lionells (1986) conceptualizes "hysterical behaviors as the operation of a self-system designed to obtain security and diminish anxiety in the interpersonal field, rather than as defenses against internal impulses" (p. 572). She emphasizes that "hysteria is a form of interaction regardless of its intrapsychic existence" and finds that "what differentiates hysteria is its addiction to approval-seeking as its primary mode of interaction" (p. 572). (See Nobus and Evans's comments on Lacan, below.) Sex is pressed into service as a means of gaining this approval (p. 575).

With regard to the issue of mental structure, Lionells (1986) says that "the hysteric's inner self is relatively unformed and unintegrated" (p. 576), and that "self and other remain diffuse figures in perpetual interaction but not in genuine relation" (p. 577).

The pressure of approval-seeking exaggerates identity diffusion and the sense of symbiotic merger. A solution to the loss of self is found in hysterical emotionality and rage reactions which create a whirlwind of affect, achieving relief rather than resolution. The personality is cleansed and consolidated with the expulsion of noxious unacceptable feelings. (p. 579)

103 "[T]he hysteric is not only fundamentally ambivalent and hostile toward his own innate ego capacities but is maliciously hostile and envious of any ego functioning in the loved object in adult life" (Khan, 1975, p. 351).

104 "Aggression is used to protest the object's not remaining gratifying and to reestablish the emotional bond" (Lionells, 1986, p. 579).

105 "In fact the content and meaning of these two forms of aggressive display are quite similar, the difference being that the one erupts as a temporary explosion in a basically positive transference situation while the other may characterize what seems to be a basically negative transference" (Lionells, 1984, p. 636).

1990 and Beyond

In the recent psychoanalytic literature, there has been a wide-ranging examination of the controversy surrounding the etiology of hysteria and the related implications for treatment, as well as continuing contributions specifically concerning that etiology. Halberstadt-Freud (1996) emphasizes the tendency of the hysteric to convert preoedipal anxiety into sexual excitement and to employ seductiveness in interactions with real objects as a defense against that anxiety. She warns the analyst of the possibility of being seduced by the hysteric into focusing on genital fixations at the expense of treatment of underlying narcissistic configurations.[106] Nonetheless, she believes that "early Freud was right: hysteria is based on seduction," but only "in the sense of prematurely aroused desires that have more to do with the adult's than with the child's need" (p. 987).

Laplanche (1995, 1999) provides an important reassessment of the seduction theory, Freud's earliest notion of what causes hysteria. He believes that, in a sense, a real seduction *has* taken place (and universally takes place) in a child's early life.[107] The essence of the seduction—the assault—is "a communication which is at once revealed and hidden" (Laplanche, 1974, p. 468)—the unconscious and enigmatic sexual meaning of what is proffered by the adult to the child in myriad ways even at the child's oral stage.[108] He believes that the adult's unconscious sexual fantasies are a powerful ingredient in any interaction between parent and child, and that the notion of seduction can only be

106 "In practice, hysteria is frequently misleading, tending to make the other powerless by seduction and blockage of any meaningful dialogue. Disavowal of depression and of mourning for lost love is converted into excitement. It is more fruitful to connect depression with narcissistic deficiency than with erotic elements in the transference and countertransference. The therapist must be able to withstand seduction to choose the sexual or genital level as a theme, whereas the anxieties operate in a much more primitive experiential layer of the personality" (Halberstadt-Freud, 1996, p. 991).

107 "But the crucial question is to decide whether the seduction-phantasy has to be considered merely as a defensive and projective distortion of the positive component of the Oedipus complex or whether it is to be treated as the transposed expression of a fundamental datum, namely, the fact that the child's sexuality is entirely organised by something which comes to it, as it were, from the outside: the relationship between the parents, and the parents' wishes which pre-date and determine the form of the wishes of the subject. Viewed from this angle, seductions really experienced as well as seduction-phantasies become nothing more than concrete expressions of this basic fact" (Laplanche & Pontalis, 1973, p. 407).

108 "[W]e find at the oral level and, more generally, at the level of maternal care, 'excessive sensual stimulation' (Brenman), sexual seduction and the element of passivity in which Freud persistently saw the specificity of hysteria" (Laplanche, 1974, p. 469).

understood if, in addition to the physical gestures of the adult and the fantasies of the child, the enigmatic sexual message of the adult's unconscious inherent in the reality of the imperfect communication between them is also taken into account.[109] Laplanche (1999) says that "it is the breaking in of an 'excess of message', emanating from the other, which functions like pain, originating first from the outside, *then* coming from that internal other which is repressed fantasy" (p. 211, italics added). Laplanche's formulation thereby unites key elements of the etiology of hysteria discussed in the immediately preceding decades—sexuality, object-relatedness, and preoedipal development— with elements Freud had suggested before 1900: trauma and seduction.

Developing a theme he broached 20 years earlier in the "Panel on Hysteria Today," Green (1996) emphasizes the continuing importance of taking sexuality into account,[110] even when preoedipal or narcissistic pathologies are being studied:

> The whole structure of symptoms in which sexuality seems to play a contingent role or an apparently unimportant one acts as if the other aspects—[those] not overtly genital—were meant to protect and to hide the core of the pathology. In fact, the sexual and genital fixations are like the heart of an onion covered by many layers, as the secret that the patient has to keep extremely private. In the eyes of others, patients want to appear as if these problems were non-existent or trivial. (p. 874)

Rupprecht-Schampera (1995) sees a dichotomy in the psychoanalytic literature between oedipal hysteria and preoedipal hysteria, conditions that are seen respectively as "benign and malignant hysterias, the emphasis being placed on their differing central themes (oedipal

---

109 "[T]here is a third domain of reality, which is neither the pure materiality of the gesture (assuming that this could in any case be grasped) nor the pure psychology of the protagonist(s). So we have the reality of the message and the irreducibility of the fact of communication. What psychoanalysis adds is a fact of its experience, namely that this message is frequently compromised, that it both fails and succeeds at one and the same time. It is opaque to its recipient and its transmitter alike. Put simply, seduction is neither more nor less real than a parapraxis, the reality of which is not reducible to its materiality. A slip of the tongue is no more or less real materially than a correctly pronounced word. But a slip also does not boil down to each of the interlocutors' conceptions of it, which are often incomplete and reductive. It conveys a detectable, observable message, which is partly interpretable by psychoanalysis. It is in terms of this third domain of reality and not of material reality that I persist in saying 'seduction' rather than 'seduction fantasy'. The priority I assign to it is based on the fact that the other scenarios invoked as primal have seduction as their nucleus, to the extent that they do convey messages from the other, always at first in the direction from adult to child" (Laplanche, 1995, p. 211).

110 "Over the years psychoanalysis has dissociated hysteria from the Oedipus complex, and underplayed the role of sexuality and gender identity" (Yarom, 1997, p. 1122).

versus pre-oedipal material)" (p. 458). He attempts to reconcile these positions with his concept of "early triangulation," in which he considers the role of the father in the early psychic development of the child (creating the triangle mother-child-father). Taking as a starting point Mahler's ideas about separation and individuation and Green's (1975) comment that "there is no . . . couple formed by mother and baby without the father, for the child is the figure of the union between mother and father" (p. 13), Rupprecht-Schampera argues that "the so-called third element is present in the psychic life of the child from birth and determines the very being of a human individual" (p. 460). He believes that "the future hysteric, as a child, does not, in an already conflictual early mother-child relationship, have the father sufficiently available in his triangulating auxiliary function, or does not experience him as such, so that the separation from the mother and hence the entire process of separation-individuation appears as a virtually impossible developmental task" (p. 461). Contending that a child who experiences trauma or anxiety in interaction with the mother during the course of separation-individuation will turn to the father for a response that will resolve these difficulties, Rupprecht-Schampera carefully traces a variety of possible defensive maneuvers employed by the future hysteric. In the case of a girl, he says, she may realize that she is "an erotically attractive female creature" and use this attribute as a means of attracting the father's attention—a "premature oedipalization." If this tactic is successful—if the father "can respond to the child in moderation and with pleasure"—the conflict with the mother can be modulated sufficiently to avoid developmental disruption. If it is unsuccessful, however, "if the father's reaction to the little girl is also eroticized, or if he brings frustrated sexual wishes or sexual conflicts of his own into the relationship with his daughter, the situation between the two will be potentially traumatic," resulting in powerful guilt feelings and a still-unresolved preoedipal conflict with the mother.[111] According to Rupprecht-Schampera, a whole series of further maneuvers may unfold to repress and contain the anxieties and impulses associated with this situation, leading to thought disturbances, self-attack, and withdrawal into infantility:

111 "In my opinion, *the typical hysterical personality arises if the attempt to win the father as an early triangular object by an eroticised approach results in a further negative experience with him—i.e. a disappointment in him—which now presents an additional threat to the child's psychic structure. The child is compelled to try to come to terms with the now exacerbated conflictual situation, and to develop further defences (typical of hysteria)*" (Rupprecht-Schampera, 1995, p. 462).

In this way, the female hysteric has created a fantasised oedipal scenery that superficially resembles the "normal" oedipal conflict, but which is the product of complicated defensive movements and serves to conceal and disavow the actual traumas experienced with both mother and father. Sexualisation, repression, disavowal, alteration of perception and modification of the self-image (by renunciation of individuation and withdrawal into infantility) give rise to an unstable defensive system that is constantly under threat and can provide only a mediocre guarantee of psychic functioning, because all these defensive movements may well lead back to the situation in which the female hysteric feels threateningly dependent on an excessively powerful mother, so that a neurotic cycle arises. (p. 463)

Rupprecht-Schampera (1995) also considers the problem of male hysteria and finds that the boy similarly turns to the father to resolve preoedipal conflict with the mother and, if the father is unresponsive or absent, may attempt to prematurely sexualize his relationship with his mother, yielding the risk of "a much more direct confrontation with the threatening early object, unprotected by the triangular presence of a third person." He notes that "the hysterical solution is therefore *a priori* always more difficult, and carries a greater threat, for men than for women" (p. 466).

In short, Rupprecht-Schampera (1995) attempts to demonstrate how the appearance of oedipal phenomena in the hysteric (like sexualized object relationships) can actually be the result of the preoedipal struggle for separation-individuation.[112] He further finds that the hysteric resorts to conversion—to the generation of physical symptoms—when "psychic forms of triangulation organized on a higher level collapse" (p. 467). "A real third person and that person's help are not always available when urgently needed," he says, "but the body is always there." He contends that preoccupation with the body functions as a distraction from "the threatening experience of helplessness in [a] relationship" (p. 467).

Bollas (2000) views hysteria as a complicated pathology with roots in the preoedipal period although he finds that the hysteric's "underlying sense of being is not jeopardized, certainly not as it is with the borderline, schizoid or narcissistic personality," and that the hysteric's object is a whole object (p. 12). He attributes this fact to "the mother's

---

112 "Driven by hope and disappointment, the subject constantly oscillates between pseudo-oedipal advances and withdrawals into infantility. Since this results neither in a resolution of the Oedipus complex nor in successful separation, this oscillation is perpetuated indefinitely" (Rupprecht-Schampera, 1995, p. 464).

skill in developing her infant's sense of self and other" but contends that the mother is conflicted about sexuality and conveys this to the infant.[113] In the case of the hysteric, Bollas says, a particular type of "intense, if detached, maternal love" is involved, one in which "an unconscious sense of maternal desire for the child's sexual body— especially the genitals"—is missing (p. 12). He explains that "in the presence of this primary object, the child seeks out who he or she is to the mother and then tries to identify with this object of desire and to represent it to the mother" in an attempt to win the desired sexual affection (p. 12). In the context of what Bollas describes as a "sexual epiphany" occurring around the age of three—"a meaningful intensification in sexual excitement, as biological maturation drives newly intense genital sexual sensations" (p. 13), the child opts for one of two "solutions to the anguish of sexuality: the ascetic and the precocious" (p. 79). In the first strategy, the "ascetic," the child "attack[s] the self's sexuality in order to oblate maternal desire (if it existed) and parental sexuality" (p. 79). Bollas calls this "death-drive hysteria," a masochistic renunciation of all things sexual, a "romance with the death drive" that can lead to suicide (p. 79). He describes the other alternative, "precocious" hysteria, as "a manifestation of the life drive" insofar as it leads to sexual promiscuity, but he adds that this strategy entails the construction of a "false self" with roots in the mother's tendency to eroticize parts of the body other than the genitals (p. 80). The notion of a "false self" dovetails with Bollas's characterization of the hysteric as someone who is "gifted in identifying with and representing the desire of the other," and he warns the analyst that this trait can cause great confusion in treatment since "hysterics can successfully imitate schizophrenics, borderlines, narcissists, and perverts" if they discern that those conditions are of special interest to the analyst (p. 177).

Intense concern with the desire of the other is also a configuration Lacan cites in his extensive discussion of hysteria. As explained by Nobus (2000), Lacan believes that "hysterics mold themselves into a figure which they think will arouse the Other, something which grips the Other's attention and which provokes interest, fascination, and attachment or love" (p. 30). Similarly, Evans (1996) gives Lacan's definition of the hysteric as "precisely someone who appropriates another's desire by identifying with them" (p. 79). As Nobus explains (2000), hysterics use this stance as part of a strategy to redress the feeling that they have been victimized and robbed of their enjoyment of life; they

113 "In one single respect, in her sexuality, she is insecure, and this she communicates to her infant" (Bollas, 2000, p. 12).

accomplish this by revengefully manipulating the Other into experiencing lack.[114] Since, as Lacan (1998) claims, "the hysteric's desire is not
the desire for an *object*, but the desire for a *desire*" (p. 407), the notion
of "false self"[115]—assimilating another's reality as one's own—
becomes relevant, as does the notion of impaired capacity to evaluate
reality. These concepts also emerge in Lacan's formulation of the neurotic and, in particular, the hysteric.[116] Yet, interestingly, according to
Lacan, the neurotic pairs a "passion for ignorance" (of real impulses
and desires) with a desire to understand her symptoms. Fink (1997)
notes that Lacan believes the hysteric "expects knowledge: she looks to
the Other to fill her lack of being . . . and lack of knowledge. This is
what makes it easy for her to request the analyst's help—she recognizes
her dependence on the Other—but makes it difficult for her to work
once she is in analysis" (p. 132).

> Just as she seeks and provokes, if need be, lack/desire in her partner,
> seeking to know that she is as an object of desire, so too she seeks
> knowledge about herself—'What do I have, doctor? What is the matter
> with me?'—and expects to receive that from the analyst . . . Should the
> analyst comply, attempting to supply the hysteric with knowledge about
> herself, this knowledge . . . is only momentarily gratifying to the
> analysand. It is almost immediately questioned, examined, scrutinized,
> and evaluated by the hysteric seeking the lack in the analyst's knowl-
> edge, the lacuna or gap; for this gives her the role of exception, living
> proof that she can supplement or complement the analyst's knowledge.
> (p. 132)

Similarly, Yarom (1997) finds the issue of the hysteric's relationship
to knowledge to be important in the understanding of hysteria:

> The hysteric has been characterised traditionally by "not knowing" and
> "not remembering" something essential to him or her, which has to do
> mainly with sexuality and incestuous wishes. This repressed knowledge

114 "They hold the Other responsible for their current misery and swear to take revenge on the
Other for all the harm that has been done to them. It is this hysterical accusation of the Other
which Freud initially mistook for a genuine account of sexual abuse . . ." (Nobus, 2000, p. 29).

115 "In hysteria we are not talking about falseness in the sense of Winnicott's 'false self'.
Falseness and resorting to fantasy are taken in the context of sexuality and the relationship
between the sexes" (Yarom, 1997, p. 1125).

116 "In keeping with Freud, Lacan . . . surmised that hysteria and obsessional neurosis are two
neurotic languages, whereby the obsessional idiom is a dialect of the hysterical standard. Towards
the end of his career, Lacan even adduced that the psychoanalytic treatment of all neurotics rests
upon a 'hysterisation' of the patient, which indicates that he agreed with Freud on the *hysterical
core within obsessional neurosis*" (Nobus, 2000, pp. 27–28; italics added).

activates him/her in mysterious ways, enabling the conscious mind to avoid assuming any responsibility for actions that fulfil unconscious wishes. . . . In analysis, the aim of knowing comes up against the major defence of not knowing and thus encounters resistance. In hysteria, the forbidden knowledge, which received thing- and word-representations, can be expressed in disguised ways, through the body and action, in dramatic externalisation of relevant content and affect. . . . In families of hysterics, forbidden knowledge leads to pervasive collusion among family members to deny perceptions, thoughts and feelings around certain areas involving a taboo. Direct verbal reference to those areas is denied because that would necessitate doing something about them. (p. 1175)

Phyllis Meadow (2003) summarizes the issue of "not knowing" in hysteria by relating it to the drives: "We can think of ego defenses as attempts to weaken the power of life and death urges by robbing ideas of their affects. In hysteria, one renders ideas harmless by transforming them into somatic symptoms. A conversion may appear as a motor enervation or as a hallucinatory sensation" (p. 28).

Discussion

It appears that in the psychoanalytic investigation of hysteria, *what* is being investigated is not clearly agreed upon, and certainly the theoretical orientation used to evaluate what is being investigated is not agreed upon either. The very language and terminology used to discuss the phenomenon have evolved through numerous permutations. An investigator using terms like "repression of unacceptable ideas" or "unconscious sense of guilt" might have difficulty communicating with investigators using the terms "split-off part objects," "drive for reparation," "desire of the Other," or "triangulation."

Yet even though all the various points of view seem to offer some advantage for theoretical clarification, Freud's contributions to the understanding of hysteria still seem supremely relevant—especially when all his theoretical shifts are taken into account. While not providing a complete explanation, his early notion that traumatic experience of some sort involving the future hysteric's parents (or other important figures in the child's life) can figure into the development of hysteria seems to be generally accepted. Fantasies arising from these interactions or—alternatively or additionally—fantasies arising from the universal experience of the child's struggle to build mental structure in the context of powerful inner urges and interaction with powerful enigmatic objects are also germane, especially when unacceptability of the fantasies and concomitant repression of the fantasies are factored in. That these fantasies involve unacceptable sexual impulses seems clearly borne out by the totality of clinical experience represented in the literature. In my view, this does not contradict the notion that unacceptable aggressive impulses are involved as well. In the example given above of the young girl who was groped by shopkeepers, Freud's (1895) emphasis on Emma's sexual arousal was based on his early libido theory, but one could also assess the incident emphasizing forbidden reactive rage, which would be more in line with his later dual drive theory. Whether the unacceptability arises from a superego imposing moral constraints against incestuous wishes (or indecorous violent behavior) or from a primitive ego attempting to ward off projected fantasies of annihilation (or the real threat of retaliation), Freud's idea that the energy attached to the fantasies must be discharged in some way still holds. Conversion into physical symptoms or particular behavioral patterns is the result in hysteria. It is conversion—the substitution for what is unacceptable by something tolerable but distorted, excessive, detrimental, and inefficient—that gives hysteria its mysterious quality and makes it difficult to decipher. Substitution of something distorted for what is "real" is also the element that gives rise to a break with reality, the quality associated with the preoedipal pathologies, schizophrenia and psychosis.

Yarom's suggestion (1997) comes to mind: "that we preserve Freud's original constellation of hysteria: conflicts with regard to sexuality and gender (the oedipal level *and* the pre-oedipal), the major defence mechanism (repression) and the way in which the repressed makes its return (conversion)" (1121–1122). The combination of factors delineated by Green also seems relevant: "the relationship between sexuality, love, and reaction to loss, [all] related to different ego structures (quoted in Laplanche, 1974, p. 464)." Though I agree with Namnum's contention[117] that hysteria is an entity which has changed and will continue to change with the culture (since the hysteric is concerned about the fantasy of the other—about the other's desire—and will therefore continually reconfigure himself or herself in an attempt to please or become desirable), I believe that the manner in which the hysteric relates to other people will always be determined by the interaction of a few key (but admittedly nebulous) factors: innate constitution and inherent strength of the drives;

117 "Hysteria has changed and is likely to continue to do so, from epoch to epoch, because it takes the form that is especially appealing to those—priests, physicians or psychotherapists—whose attention it seeks" (quoted in Laplanche, 1974, p. 462).

preoedipal structural development; preoedipal experience, including trauma and resulting defenses; and the oedipal experiences.

My survey of the psychoanalytic literature on hysteria readily provided an explanation of how my analyst and my supervisor could have had such different assessments of my patient's state: their assessments were not so different after all. One could say that they were merely responding to distinct, but equally valid, aspects of her psychological makeup or, alternatively, that they were merely applying different terminology to the same phenomena. Certainly the literature lends weight to the notion that preoedipal and narcissistic elements are woven into the fabric of the hysteric's character structure, just as it could be argued that the literature corroborates the notion that a narcissistic or borderline personality might very well encompass hysterical elements.

The question then arises as to the importance, if any, of these distinctions. For me, it all comes down to a question of technique—what to do in the consulting room if one suspects one's patient is (or is not) a hysteric. The only sensible approach would seem to be an open-ended one that allows and enables the patient to progress from whatever fixation point predominates in the moment. The technique Spotnitz has suggested—one of waiting for contact, not "leading" the patient, avoiding the infliction of narcissistic injury, inviting the patient to put into words whatever is in his or her mind at the moment, and working indirectly by using emotional interventions (informed by countertransference feelings) designed to remove the patient's blocks to telling his or her life story in an emotionally significant way—is the only one that really makes sense. Using this flexible technique, the analyst is not boxed into a stance that may constrain the patient into an area of character or a pattern of response that precludes access to deeper but still relevant psychic configurations. Even if, for example, a patient oscillates within the space of one analytic session between preoedipal and oedipal configurations, an analyst schooled in the technique of Spotnitz can provide interventions that are responsive to the patient's emotional state in the moment, fostering progressive communication.

REFERENCES

Bollas, C. (2000), *Hysteria*. London: Routledge.
Davies, J. M. (1996), Linking the "pre-analytic" with the postclassical: integration, dissociation, and the multiplicity of unconscious process. *Contemporary Psychoanalysis*, 32:553–576.

Easser, B. R. & S. R. Lesser (1965), Hysterical personality: a re-evaluation. *Psychoanalytic Quarterly*, 34:390–405.

Evans, D. (1996), *An Introductory Dictionary of Lacanian Psychoanalysis*. New York: Routledge.

Fairbairn, W. R. D. (1941), A revised psychopathology of the psychoses and psychoneuroses. *International Journal of Psychoanalysis*, 22:250–279.

Fairbairn, W. R. D. (1944), Endopsychic structure considered in terms of object-relationships. *International Journal of Psychoanalysis*, 25:70–92.

Fenichel, O. (1932), Outline of clinical psychoanalysis. *Psychoanalytic Quarterly*, 1:121–165.

Ferenczi, S. (1925), The psycho-analysis of sexual habits. *International Journal of Psychoanalysis*, 6:372–404.

Fink, B. (1997), *A Clinical Introduction to Lacanian Psychoanalysis*. Cambridge: Harvard University Press.

Freud, S. (1888), Hysteria. *Standard Edition*. London: Hogarth Press, 1:41–57.

Freud, S. & J. Breuer (1893a), On the psychical mechanism of hysterical phenomena: preliminary communication. *Standard Edition*. London: Hogarth Press, 2:1–18.

Freud, S. & J. Breuer (1893b), On the psychical mechanism of hysterical phenomena: preliminary communication. *Early Psychoanalytic Writings*. P. Rieff, ed. New York: Macmillan.

Freud, S. (1893c), Case histories. *Standard Edition*. London: Hogarth Press, 2:19–182.

Freud, S. (1894), The neuro-psychoses of defense. *Standard Edition*. London: Hogarth Press, 3:43–70.

Freud, S. (1895), Project for a scientific psychology. *Standard Edition*. London: Hogarth Press, 1:283–398.

Freud, S. (1896a), The aetiology of hysteria. *Standard Edition*. London: Hogarth Press, 3:189–224.

Freud, S. (1896b), The aetiology of hysteria. *Early Psychoanalytic Writings*. P. Rieff, ed. New York: Macmillan.

Freud, S. (1897), Letter to Wilhelm Fliess, September 21, 1897. *The Complete Letters of Sigmund Freud to Wilhelm Fliess 1887–1904*, J. M. Masson, trans. & ed. Cambridge, MA: Harvard University Press, 1985.

Freud, S. (1908a), Hysterical phantasies and their relation to bisexuality. *Standard Edition*. London: Hogarth Press, 9:155–166.

Freud, S. (1908b), Some general remarks on hysterical attacks. *Standard Edition*. London: Hogarth Press, 9:227–234.

Freud, S. (1912), The dynamics of the transference. *Therapy and Technique*. P. Rieff, ed. New York: Collier Books, 1963.

Freud, S. (1914a), From the history of an infantile neurosis. *Standard Edition*. London: Hogarth Press, 17:1–124.

Freud, S. (1914b), On the history of the psycho-analytic movement. *Standard Edition*. London: Hogarth Press, 14:17–18.

Freud, S. (1916–1917), Introductory lectures on psycho-analysis. *Standard Edition*. London: Hogarth Press, 16.

Freud, S. (1920), Beyond the pleasure principle. *Standard Edition*. London: Hogarth Press, 18:3–64.

Freud, S. (1923), The ego and the id. *Standard Edition*. London: Hogarth Press, 19:1–66.

Freud, S. (1925 [1924]), An autobiographical study. *Standard Edition*. London: Hogarth Press, 20:1–70.

Freud, S. (1926), Inhibitions, symptoms and anxiety. *Standard Edition*. London: Hogarth Press, 20:75–176.

Freud, S. (1927a), Some psychological consequences of the anatomical distinction between the sexes. *Standard Edition*. London: Hogarth Press, 19:241–260.

Freud, S. (1927b), Some psychological consequences of the anatomical distinction between the sexes. *International Journal of Psychoanalysis*, 8:133–142.

Freud, S. (1931a), Libidinal types. *Standard Edition*. London: Hogarth Press, 21:215–220.

Freud, S. (1931b), Female sexuality. *Standard Edition*. London: Hogarth Press, 21:221–243.

Freud, S. (1932a), Libidinal types. *Psychoanalytic Quarterly*, 1:3–6.

Freud, S. (1932b), Female sexuality. *International Journal of Psychoanalysis*, 13:281–297.

Freud, S. (1932c), New introductory lectures on psycho-analysis. *Standard Edition*. London: Hogarth Press, 22:1–182.

Giovacchini, P. (1976), Ego pathology: diagnostic and treatment implications. *Contemporary Psychoanalysis*, 12:173–185.

Green, A. (1975), The analyst, symbolization and absence in the analytic setting. *International Journal of Psychoanalysis*, 56:1–22.

Green, A. (1996), Has sexuality anything to do with psychoanalysis? *International Journal of Psychoanalysis*, 76:871–883.

Halberstadt-Freud, H. C. (1996), Studies on hysteria one hundred years on: a century of psychoanalysis. *International Journal of Psychoanalysis*, 77:983–996.

Khan, M. M. R. (1975), Grudge and the hysteric. *International Journal of Psychoanalysis*, 4:349–357.

Klein, M. (1926), Infant analysis. *International Journal of Psychoanalysis*, 7:31–63.

Klein, M. (1928), Early stages of the oedipus conflict. *International Journal of Psychoanalysis*, 9:167–180.

Klein, M. (1932), The psycho-analysis of children. *International Psycho-analytic Library*, 22:8–379.

Klein, M. (1946), Notes on some schizoid mechanisms. *International Journal of Psychoanalysis*, 27:99–110.

Klein, M. (1948), A contribution to the theory of anxiety and guilt. *International Journal of Psychoanalysis*, 29:114–123.

Klein, M. (1975[1952]), Some theoretical conclusions regarding the emotional life of the infant. *International Psychoanalytic Library*, 104:1–346.

Kris, E. (1956), The recovery of childhood memories in psychoanalysis. *Psychoanalytic Study of the Child*, 11:54–88.

Krohn, A. (1978), *Hysteria: The Elusive Neurosis*. New York: International Universities Press.

Lacan, J. (1998[1957–58]), Formations of the unconscious. *The Seminar of Jacques Lacan, Book V*. Paris: du Seuil.

Laplanche, J. (1974), Panel on "Hysteria Today." *International Journal of Psychoanalysis*, 55:459–469.

Laplanche, J. (1995), Seduction, persecution, revelation. *International Journal of Psychoanalysis*, 76:663–682.

Laplanche, J. (1999), *Essays on Otherness*. London: Routledge.

Laplanche, J. & J.-B. Pontalis (1973), *The Language of Psycho-Analysis*. D. Nicholson-Smith, trans. New York: Norton & Co.

Lionells, M. (1984), Aggression as a hysterical mechanism. *Contemporary Psychoanalysis*, 20:633–642.

Lionells, M. (1986), A reevaluation of hysterical relatedness. *Contemporary Psychoanalysis*, 22:570–597.

Mahler, M. S., F. Pine, & A. Bergman (1975), *The Psychological Birth of the Human Infant: Symbiosis and Individuation*. London: Hutchinson.

Makari, G. (1997), Dora's hysteria and the maturation of Sigmund Freud's transference theory: a new historical interpretation. *Journal of the American Psychoanalytic Association*, 45:1061–1096.

Marmor, J. (1953), Orality in the hysterical personality. *Journal of the American Psychoanalytic Association*, 1:656–670.

Meadow, P. W. (1989), Object relations in a drive theory model. *Modern Psychoanalysis*, 14:57–58.

Nobus, D. (2000), *Jacques Lacan and the Freudian Practice of Psychoanalysis*. London: Routledge.

Rangell, L. (1959), The nature of conversion. *Journal of the American Psychoanalytic Association*, 7:632–662.

Reich, W. (1933), *Character Analysis*. New York: Simon & Schuster, 1945.

Reichard, S. (1956), A re-examination of "Studies in Hysteria." *Psychoanalytic Quarterly*, 25:155–177.

Rupprecht-Schampera, U. (1995), The concept of "early triangulation" as a key to a unified model of hysteria. *International Journal of Psychoanalysis*, 76:457–473.

Shapiro, D. (1965), *Neurotic Styles*. New York: Basic Books.

Spotnitz, H. (1969), *Modern Psychoanalysis of the Schizophrenic Patient*. New York: Grune & Stratton.

Spotnitz, H. (1976), *Psychotherapy of Preoedipal Conditions*. New York: Jason Aronson.

Veith, I. (1965), *Hysteria, The History of a Disease*. Chicago: University of Chicago Press.

Wisdom, J. O. (1961), A methodological approach to the problem of hysteria. *International Journal of Psychoanalysis*, 42:224–237.

Wittels, F. (1930), The hysterical character. *Medical Review of Reviews*, 36:186.

Yarom, N. (1997), A matrix of hysteria. *International Journal of Psychoanalysis*, 78:1119–1134.

Zetzel, E. R. (1968), The so-called good hysteric. *International Journal of Psychoanalysis*, 49:256–260.

16 West 10th Street
New York, New York 10011
Srg1@earthlink.net

Modern Psychoanalysis
Vol. XXXI, No. 2, 2006

Oedipus Rex Revisited

PATRICK LEE MILLER

This paper argues that psychoanalysts must revisit Oedipus Rex *to extract its deeper lessons. Although Oedipus does demonstrate genuinely oedipal desires, his tragedy stems not so much from them as from a narcissistic rage over his original mutilation and abandonment by his parents. But Oedipus is not only the object of our analysis; he is a prototype of the psychoanalyst, as Freud himself recognized. Sophocles thus appears to diagnose the dangers of psychoanalysis. Whatever hope exists in the midst of these dangers is then inferred from his prophetic sequel,* Oedipus at Colonus.

Freud first read Sophocles' drama in 1873. Revisiting it in 1897, Freud (1954) attached the name of Oedipus to the now famous complex, writing in a letter to Wilhelm Fliess that he had deciphered the "gripping power" of Sophocles' play in its portrayal of the secret desires of every child: to possess one parent and annihilate the other (Letter 71, pp. 221–225).[1] Indeed, in "The Interpretation of Dreams," Freud (1900) went further and rejected the canonical interpretation of the play as a tragic conflict between human will and divine destiny (pp. 261–263). Instead, he wrote, the legend's power "can only be understood if the hypothesis I have put forward in regard to the psychology of children has an equally universal validity" (p. 261). Thus, according to Freud, psychoanalysis illuminated the power of the play, rather than the other way around. Sophocles' tragedy, however, hides dark lessons for psychoanalysis itself. In order to unearth these lessons, we must begin by attending to the peculiar inconsistencies of the text, especially those within the puzzle of Oedipus himself.

1 Cf. Freud (1954), Letter 64, pp. 206–210. See also Rudnytsky (1986), pp. 11–12.

© 2006 CMPS/*Modern Psychoanalysis*, Vol. 31, No. 2

Traumatic Knowledge

The text of this play presents many inconsistencies, but one is so odd that it has persuaded an esteemed philologist (Ahl, 1991) to claim that Sophocles' Oedipus neither murdered Laius, nor married his mother— that the tragedy is his mistaken conclusion that he did both. How many men obstructed Laius at the crossroads and killed him? The answer seems obvious: one—namely, Oedipus. This at least is the version that prevails by the end of the play. But according to the version first told by the king's slave, the one survivor from his retinue, there were many. "This man said," tells Creon, "that the *robbers* they encountered were *many* and the hands that did the murder were *many*; it was *no single man's* power" (122; italics added).[2] Moreover, this version agrees with Creon's own report from his trip to the Delphic oracle: "let some one punish with force this dead man's *murderers*" (107; italics added).

But we must not take Creon's report of the oracle as the word of Apollo himself, or even of his inspired priestess. That word was notoriously obscure and ambiguous. For instance, Croesus, the Lydian king, consulted the oracle about his plans to attack the neighboring kingdom of the Persians. Delphi returned the answer that he would destroy a great kingdom, and Croesus mistook these ambiguous words as approval of his plan. He failed to consider a darker possibility: that the kingdom he would destroy would be his own.[3] Similarly, Creon may hear at Delphi as much what he expects to hear as what Apollo actually says. And like everyone in Thebes, Creon would have assumed for all these years that several men killed his former brother-in-law. Jocasta and the Chorus—who, as so often in Greek tragedy, represent inherited and conventional wisdom—both speak in the plural of "murderers" (292, 715).[4]

In immediate response to Creon's report, and speaking of it later, Oedipus too accepts this conventional version (109, 307). Why wouldn't he? It's what the only eyewitness said. However, on five other occasions during his investigation he speaks of *one* killer (124, 139, 225, 230, 296). Most remarkable of these occasions is the last. The Chorus has just informed Oedipus: "It was said that he was killed by certain *wayfarers*" (292); in the very next line Oedipus replies: "I heard that

---

2 Unless otherwise noted, citations from *Oedipus Rex* are taken from Grene & Lattimore (1991).

3 Herodotus 1.53.

4 At 277 the Chorus says, "I neither killed the king nor can I declare the *killer*." But, significantly, their lapse into the singular follows a 60-line speech of Oedipus.

too, but no one saw the *killer*" (293). More remarkable still is that Oedipus, at some level, is aware of the discrepancy. In the midst of the confusion he declares with heavy dramatic irony: "Upon the murderer I invoke this curse—whether he is one man and all unknown, or one of many" (246). According to Dawe (1982), the most recent editor of the Greek text, this is not Oedipus committing a parapraxis, a Freudian slip, but instead a technique Sophocles uses to prolong the inquiry and, thus, the dramatic excitement. What goes unexplained is why Oedipus is the one who most often uses the singular. Were it a slip, though, we would know why: he knows that it was one man—himself.

When he has revealed to his audience, and in some ways to himself, that he once killed a rich man and his attendants at a crossroads, he then, significantly, begins to analyze the ambiguity between singular and plural: "You said that he spoke of highway robbers who killed Laius. Now if he uses the same number, it was not I who killed him. One man cannot be the same as many. But if he speaks of a man traveling alone, then clearly the burden of guilt inclines towards me" (840). Despite the validity of his analysis, however, there is no awareness in it of his own persistent reversion to the singular. Oedipus the Wise cannot analyze himself, which has of course been his problem from the very beginning, for there are fundamental questions that Oedipus, solver of the Sphinx's riddle, ironically never asks—questions, that is, about himself.

His name, for instance, is one such question. In Greek it is *oidipous*. Two etymologies are possible since the *oid*- prefix is the root of two Greek verbs: *oida*, "to know," and *oideo*, "to swell." *Pous* means "foot."[5] *Oidipous* as a name therefore means at once "swollen-foot" and something like "knower-of-feet." The latter meaning is especially appropriate for the solver of the riddle of the Sphinx: What walks on four feet in the morning, two in the afternoon, and three in the evening?[6] The answer is man, an answer that is obvious once it has been discovered. But only Oedipus was able to divine it, and without any divine help. "I solved the riddle by my wit alone," he contemptuously tells Teiresias, priest of Apollo. "Mine was no knowledge got from birds" (398–399).

Oedipus was born to answer that question. His knowledge came not from birds but from iron. Before Laius and Jocasta sent him off to

5 The genitive of *pous* survives into English as the prefix in "podiatrist," healer of feet. Sophocles plays upon the Greek etymologies in several places. For instance, at line 43 he ends a line with *oistha pou*, which not only mimics *oidipous*, but also means "you know, perhaps."

6 "Two-footed" in Greek is *dipous*. The riddle has several variants. The shortest version can be found in Apollodorus 3.53–4.

Mount Cithaeron to be exposed, they had the tendons of his feet pierced and fettered (717, 1034). Exposing deformed children—monsters, as they were once known, since *monstrum* in Latin means sign, in this case a bad one[7]—was an accepted, even common, practice in antiquity. Plato recommends it in his *Republic* (5.460c). Oedipus was no physical monster—not yet anyway. It was the Delphic prophecy received by Laius, that worst of all signs, that destined Oedipus to perform monstrous deeds. But the staples now deformed his feet, which became swollen. He truly became *oidipous*, the swollen-footed: "so that from this," says the Corinthian messenger who once received him into his arms on Cithaeron, "you're called your present name" (1036). Oedipus says poignantly, "My swaddling clothes brought me a rare disgrace" (1035).

While he was fettered, furthermore, his two feet were one. The morning of his life, then, was not spent on four feet, but on three. In the evening of his life, after he has blinded himself, he will be guided by his faithful daughter Antigone. Lear (1999) has pointed out that he then walks on four feet.[8] Oedipus thus inverts the usual course of a human life encoded by the Sphinx's riddle. Destined not to know that course in his own case, Oedipus nonetheless knows it of others: "the Sphinx came upon him," says the Chorus in gratitude, "and all of us saw his wisdom and he saved the city" (510). This is the riddle of Oedipus, swollen-footed, knower-of-feet, who does not know until too late why his own feet are swollen. "How terrible to have wisdom," says Teiresias, "when it brings no profit to him who is wise" (357). He is speaking of himself, but he might equally well be speaking of Oedipus.

Their tragic wisdom is not all they share.[9] It is not long before they will share blindness. Oedipus will deprive himself of sight because of what he has learned—even, we should add, because of what his wisdom has brought about. Teiresias also lost his sight because of what he learned. According to legend, Zeus and Hera debated the question of who enjoyed sex more, the man or the woman, each insisting that it was the other. To solve their debate, they enlisted Teiresias as judge, who had spent seven years as a woman for striking copulating snakes with his staff. His answer to them was: the woman. Hera was so angered by his siding with Zeus that she blinded him. Zeus, on the other hand, was

---

7 The Greek is *teras* (whence "teratology") and means the same as the Latin.

8 The interpretation, while irresistibly clever, sits uneasily with Teiresias's parting prophecy that Oedipus will end by "tapping his way before him with a stick" (457).

9 Their similarities will be undeniable in *Oedipus at Colonus*, the belated sequel to the *Oedipus Rex*. Goux (1993) points out their salient differences (p. 92).

so pleased that he compensated Teiresias for the loss of his sight with prophetic vision of the future.[10]

"Darkness!" cries Oedipus (1314). "Why should I see whose vision showed me nothing sweet to see" (1334–1335). When he had vision, there were crucial facts he never saw. For example, after Creon has returned from Delphi with the oracle's instructions that the murderers of Laius must be found and punished, Oedipus asks: "Was it at home or in the country that death came upon him, or in another country travelling" (112–114)? Apparently then, Oedipus has never inquired into the death of his predecessor on the throne, not to mention his wife's former husband.[11] When he learns from Creon's mission to Delphi that he must finally do so, he also learns that there was a witness to the crime; but, as Voltaire (1877, pp. 18–28) first noticed, he doesn't summon the man for another 700 lines (860)—nearly half the play. According to Dawe (1982), this neglect, like his original failure in enquiring, arises *dramatis causa*: "Sophocles does not throw away the thrill of discovery in a few brief seconds," Dawe writes, "when he has it in his power to bring his audience to a peak of excitement for an appreciably longer time" (p. 15). Dawe thinks Sophocles is using the same dramatic technique in postponing Oedipus's realization that he has killed his father and married his mother. By line 1076 Oedipus has, according to Dawe, learned six facts that would have enabled him to draw this inevitable inference: it was virtually certain that he had killed Laius; Laius had once received an oracle that he would be killed by his son; he, Oedipus, was destined to kill his own father; Polybus and Merope were not his real parents; Laius and Jocasta had exposed a baby after mutilating its feet; and finally, he himself has had mutilated feet since infancy (p. 21).

As if these facts weren't clear enough, especially for the one who solved the riddle of the Sphinx, Teiresias has already told him everything in no uncertain terms: "I say you are the murderer of the king whose murderer you seek" (363) and "I say that with those you love best you live in foulest shame unconsciously" (367). For all his pretense to be an uncompromising seeker of truth (1076 ff.), however, Oedipus has already shown himself systematically unable to learn the truth about one thing—himself. Moreover, while quarreling with Teiresias, his alter ego, and thus his fiercest enemy, Oedipus was hardly in a state

---

10 The story can be found in Ovid's *Metamorphoses* 3.318–338.

11 No less amazing is Jocasta's ignorance of both men. She has never made serious inquiry into Laius's murder, and apparently she has never heard the story of Oedipus's Corinthian past—even though she has borne him four children! Oedipus and Jocasta share a mutual neglect of the past and of one another. For a discussion of Jocasta, see Stimmel (2004).

of mind to believe such truths stated so baldly. Insight into this state of mind, a state that appears to be the *modus operandi* of Oedipus, is what psychoanalysis can contribute to the philological interpretation whose resort to *dramatis causa* appears increasingly unsustainable.

Oedipus takes so long to learn the truth about himself not because Sophocles is drawing out the excitement—as if tragedy were a roller-coaster ride with an especially long incline—but because, like Jocasta, at some level he already knows what it is. And knowing it already—with its fetters and abandonment, drunken humiliations and divine trickery, impulsive rage that destroyed what he wished he could have loved, and blind love that consorted with what he wished he could have destroyed—he'll do everything he can to hide it from himself.

Knowingness

According to Lear (1999), the way Oedipus hides the truth about himself—his mechanism of defense—is "knowingness." This pretense to knowledge earns Oedipus rebukes from both Teiresias and Creon. "Do you know who your parents are?" asks Teiresias. The question is rhetorical, and Teiresias answers it himself, as we have seen: "Unknowing" (415). By contrast, Creon admits, "I don't know; and when I know nothing, I usually hold my tongue" (568). Even the Corinthian Messenger, who has known Oedipus the adult for only a few moments, says presciently: "you don't know what you are doing" (1008). Despite these many boasts of knowledge, and more, it is not until the very end of the tragedy that Oedipus admits to his daughter that he is a father "seeing nothing, knowing nothing" (1484). By this time, of course, it is too late.

There is considerable debate among philologists about what Aristotle means by *hamartia*—literally, "missing the mark"—when he writes that every tragedy must have an instance of it (*Poetics*, 1453a10). Neoclassicist literary critics interpreted it as the "tragic flaw," which generations of school kids were then trained to see not only in Shakespeare, but also in Attic tragedy. Dodds (1966), the great English philologist of the last century, argued forcefully, in a paper with the provocative title "On Misunderstanding the *Oedipus Rex*," that Oedipus has no tragic flaw—he is the victim of destiny. *Hamartia* for Aristotle is ignorance of a particular fact, he added, not a general flaw of character (reprinted in Bloom, 1988, pp. 35–47). But the distinction is academic, at least in the case of the Oedipus. Oedipus is ignorant of a fact—his parentage—because of his character flaw, his knowingness.

Oedipus knew the solution to the riddle of the Sphinx—he even learned it by himself—and so he knows everything else too. How else to explain the fact, noticed by Lear (1999), that "on the few occasions when someone challenges Oedipus's claim to know already—Teiresias, Creon, and the Messenger—Oedipus explodes with anger and suspicion" (p. 43)? These rival claims to knowledge threaten Oedipus's confidence that *he* knows. Ironically, this confidence in knowledge stems from a wish to ignore; more ironically still, this wish to ignore stems from a deep but dim knowledge. Knowingness is thus allied with ignorance, and ignorance masks knowledge. Motivating these convolutions is the darkness of that basic knowledge.

"But how," protests the philological skeptic, "can Oedipus's unconscious knowledge of the truth be proven? All we have is the Greek text, and we must be faithful to it." In reply, our position is not much different from that of the analyst, who has little more than the text of daily meetings from which to reconstruct the invisible dynamics of a mind. Many of the same clues are available: word choice, metaphors, slips, ambiguities, inconsistencies. Just as the analysand is destined to act out his conflicts in the consulting room, so too is Oedipus destined to act out his conflicts, and thus his dimmest recollections, in the text of the play. Lear (1999) offers an example of this acting out in Oedipus's extreme reaction to the insult of "bastard." "It is one thing to be contemptuous of a drunk's appalling behavior," Lear writes, "it is quite another to lose control of one's thoughts and emotions" (p. 48). Why would Oedipus have taken the insult so seriously unless he knew at some level that it was true?[12] His adopted parents certainly do, and their reaction is every bit as defensive. As he retells it: "they took the insult very ill from him" (783). More significant is his reaction to this knowledge: he leaves home never to return. According to Lear, "Oedipus here acts out his abandonment" (p. 48).

The idea is worth pursuing a little further, the idea that Oedipus reveals his unconscious knowledge of his traumatic abandonment by repeating rather than remembering. Beside the acting out of his abandonment, to which we will return below, there are other ways in which Oedipus reveals his unconscious knowledge of the truth about his life. As we shall see, the richest of these ways is dramatic irony, of which the ambiguity of language is a particular example.

---

12 This knowledge seems also to inform the one time he takes Teiresias seriously—when he prophesies about his parentage. "Who are they of all the world?" exclaims Oedipus (437).

All of these ways support Freud's (1900) claim—made in "The Interpretation of Dreams" but substantiated neither there nor anywhere later, to my knowledge—that

> The action of the play consists in nothing other than the process of revealing, with cunning delays and ever-mounting excitement—a process that can be likened to the work of a psychoanalysis—that Oedipus himself is the murderer of Laius, but further that he is the son of the murdered man and of Jocasta. (pp. 261–262)

The action of the play is a process that can be likened to the work of a psychoanalysis, and this action is Oedipus's investigation. In the beginning he investigates the murder of Laius, but eventually he is revealed to have been investigating, we might say analyzing, himself. Freud's affinity for Oedipus, who anticipated him in performing a relentless self-analysis, thereby becomes immediately understandable. Whether or not they both solved the riddle of the Sphinx—whose answer, as we have seen, was Man—still remains to be determined.

Dramatic Irony

In some cases, the analysand says something that is opaque to himself but clearer to his audience, i.e., the analyst. It is the analyst's job to detect dramatic ironies. In the same way, we serve as analysts to Oedipus. For instance, all the many curses that he invokes against the unknown murderer of Laius will be fulfilled, as we know, by himself (236, 243, 246, 250–251). There are important wishes disclosed by this dramatic irony. On one level, he wishes to assert his innocence: "What I say to you, I say as a stranger to the story, as a stranger to the deed" (219–220). But there is also another wish—to bring upon himself these very curses he feels he deserves. "When I drive pollution from the land," he says, "I . . . act in my own interest" (138–139).

As for Oedipus's true relationship with Laius and Jocasta, through the repeated use of dramatic irony Sophocles reveals that Oedipus has some knowledge of it. While prosecuting the investigation of Laius, Oedipus says, "I fight in his defense as for my father" (264). While speaking of the king's sad fate, he muses, "Had his line not been unfortunate we would have common children" (261–262). On the surface he does not yet know that he is Laius's only child. We know better. They do indeed have children in common—Oedipus's own children: Antigone, Ismene,

Eteocles, and Polynices—who are also, as Sophocles never loses an opportunity to remind us, his own brothers and sisters.

There are many other examples of dramatic irony, of which we should mention five obvious ones. First, Oedipus says that he is an ally to Apollo and Laius (244–245), but he scorns the first and kills the second. Second, he says that he looks at every story (292), which is no more true now, when he ignores Teiresias, than it has been during all his years in Thebes when he seems never to have asked the most basic questions. In the same spirit, third, he says to Teiresias, "Your life is one long night so that you cannot hurt me or any other who sees the light" (374–375). As with every reference to sight in this exchange, it is Oedipus who is really blind, not Teiresias, who alone sees the truth. Fourth, he claims never to have seen the shepherd before, but this man saved his life as a baby (1110–1111). Finally, Oedipus accounts himself "a child of Fortune, beneficent Fortune" (1080–1081). After only another 20 lines he will be unable any longer to hide from the horrible truth of his life. In isolation, each of these instances may appear to be a simple mistake; taken together, they reveal a pattern of self-deception.

The ambiguity of language is the most specific element of Oedipus's investigation that can be likened to the work of psychoanalysis. This is, however, merely a special case of dramatic irony. When Oedipus says, for example, that he holds the bed of the former king as well as a *homosporos* wife (260), the word is significantly ambiguous. "Held in common" may be the meaning he consciously intends, but "kindred" seems to be what he means at some deeper level. We are once again in the position of the analyst, perceiving the subtext of his words, waiting for them to become manifest. A reader, however, can appreciate the ambiguity only by hearing Oedipus speak in his own language. At this point, then, the philologist can come to the aid of the analyst. Here are three other examples of the phenomenon.

When Oedipus begins his investigation he says *egō phanō* (132), which can mean either "I will show" (who the criminal is) or "I will appear" (to be the criminal). By now we know which he intends and which reveals a hidden voice. When Jocasta wishes to tell Oedipus, "A messenger has arrived from Corinth to announce that your father, Polybus, is no longer"—is no longer alive, that is—she unconsciously uses an awkward word order that could also mean: "A messenger is here to announce that Polybus is no longer your father" (956). Finally, when the shepherd reports the prophecy that Laius once received, the prophecy that frightened him and Jocasta enough to have the baby Oedipus exposed, he uses a particular grammatical construction that could mean either that Oedipus would kill them or that they would kill Oedipus (1176). The construction is the accusative and infinitive, the same grammar used by Delphi to trick Croesus into invading Persia.

Abandonment, Betrayal, and Expulsion

Having seen so many instances of unconscious meaning, let us turn now to the most important group of them: those concerning the themes of abandonment, betrayal, and expulsion.

First, when Teiresias withholds the terrible truth from Oedipus, Oedipus immediately suspects him of plotting with Creon to depose him: "And now you would expel me," he says with mounting rage (399). "My friend Creon," he adds of his brother-in-law, "friend from the first and loyal, thus secretly attacks me, secretly desires to drive me out" (387). Teiresias cooperates in the enactment: "A *deinos*-footed curse . . . shall drive you forth out of this land" (418). *Deinos* is ambiguous in Greek and can be translated into English as "terrible" or "clever"—both of which signify something important here. A terrible-footed curse has certainly followed Oedipus from the moment his ankles were pierced. So too has he been followed by a clever-footed curse since he first used his native wit to solve a riddle about feet, thereby winning his mother's hand in marriage.[13]

Most telling of all references to expulsion are those of Oedipus once he has recognized his patricide and incest. He desires to be totally isolated from the world, to "wall up my loathsome body like a prison" (Fagles [1977] 1520; cf. Grene [1968] 1388). With the same self-loathing he exclaims: "Light of the sun, let me look upon you no more after today!" (1182). Sunlight often stands for life, as opposed to the dark mist of Hades. Here Oedipus may be asking to be expelled to the place where his parents originally sought to send him—to death, or he may be anticipating his self-blinding. After all, one reason he gives for this act is that the eyes that saw such crimes as he committed cannot look upon his people (1385). His self-mutilation is thus a self-banishment, just as his parents mutilated him in order to abandon him.

---

13 Teiresias is not alone; the play is steeped in covert references to feet and expulsion. On feet: "A time when first our feet were set secure on high" (49); "at the feet of a king" (128); "at our feet" (130); "with a stronger foot than Pegasus" (468–9); "lonely his feet" (479); "its feet are no service [*ou podi*]" (877); "the laws living on high [*hupsi-podes*]" (866); "the joints of your feet will be witnesses" (1032).

Like the themes of abandonment, betrayal, and expulsion, the metaphors of light and sight run throughout the play, but they cluster here as he takes the brooches to his eye-sockets. The Greek for eye-sockets is *arthra* (1270), the very same word used for ankles.[14] He thus pierces these *arthra* with the gold brooches of his mother, the woman who long ago allowed his other *arthra* to be pierced by iron. As he blinds himself, he says, "I will never see the crime I have committed or had done upon me" (1272). The blinding thus condenses a punishment for his own crimes and a reenactment of his parents' crime. At the very least he has turned passive into active. What Oedipus was doomed to repeat unconsciously is now in his conscious mind. "Leave me live in the mountains where Cithaeron is," he laments, "that's called my mountain, which my mother and father while they were living would have made my tomb" (1451–1454). He now knows consciously what he knew at some level from the beginning: his home is abandonment, the love he knew from birth was betrayal, and the expulsion that Creon will not impose upon him he requires of himself. "I beg of you in God's name hide me somewhere outside your country, yes, or kill me, or throw me into the sea, to be forever out of your sight" (1410–1412).

The Complex of Oedipus

How does this reading of *Oedipus Rex* inform our understanding of the Oedipus complex? Oedipus appears to have known for a long time, at some level, both that the old man at the crossroads was his father and that the queen of Thebes was his mother. Since he killed the one and married the other, it is arguable that Oedipus was indeed oedipal.[15] But the oedipal constellation of desires is not the constellation that determines his action throughout the play. Aggression, as we have seen, characterizes him throughout, but in the end this aggression is directed equally against Jocasta: entering the room where Jocasta has hung herself, he begs, "Give me a sword . . . to find this wife no wife, this mother's womb" (1255–1256). This passage is hard to square with unmixed love of the mother, and it is not surprisingly ignored by Freud and by other psychoanalytic critics.

14 The word survives into English in "arthritis."

15 By contrast, Lear (1999, pp. 38–39), Vernant (1988, p. 110), and Bloom (1988, p. 1) believe that Oedipus was not oedipal. Their position is now taken for granted in philology.

Oedipus is thus enraged with both parents, and with good reason. More influential than his so-called oedipal desires are the wounds in his feet. More determinative than his desire to possess his mother and annihilate his father is his longing—first conceived as a prophecy, then reconceived as a conspiracy, but finally recognized as a destiny—to be alone on Mt. Cithaeron where he belongs, and where indeed he will wander the rest of his life. This longing is his deepest "complex," one more preoedipal than oedipal, born not of forbidden desire but of pain and abandonment.

No wonder he was dangerously proud of solving the Sphinx's riddle by himself, without help from gods or men. Both abandoned him long ago, and he will prove that he can make it without them. This independence is as evident in his pains as in his pleasures. Proudly ignorant of priestcraft, he has become king of Thebes by answering the Sphinx's riddle himself. In one famous image, in fact, he points to himself.[16] When he investigates the plague that afflicts his people, he does so for the most part alone, ignoring the warnings of others. Eventually he learns that he is the pollution, and as a result, he pokes out his own eyes. He is thereby prosecutor and defendant, judge and executioner. Still proud of his independence, he says of this self-punishment, "the hand that struck my eyes was mine, mine alone—no one else—I did it all by myself!" (Fagles [1977] 1469–1471; cf. Grene [1968] 1331–1332). French philosopher Jean-Joseph Goux (1993) has summarized Oedipus's story tersely:

> [An] autodidact who has become an autocrat through an autoreferential response, pursues an investigation that will become more and more autobiographical, in which he himself will discover that he is the guilty party, after which he will inflict punishment on himself. (p. 135)

Oedipus and Narcissus

In the light of such a summary, how could psychoanalysts have ignored Oedipus the narcissist? How have they overlooked the oscillation, so typical of narcissism, from the grandiosity of "I count myself the son of Chance, the great goddess" (Fagles [1977] 1188–1189; cf. Grene [1968] 1080–1081) to the abasement of "for the love of god, hide me somewhere, kill me, hurl me into the sea where you can never look on me again" (Fagles [1977] 1543–1546; cf. Grene [1968] 1410–1412)?

---

16 The Vatican plate; cf. Goux (1993), p. 135.

The mythic parallels between Oedipus and Narcissus are inescapable and deserve their own treatment. Suffice it now to mention only that the tragedy of each is a tragedy of self-knowledge. In Ovid's version of the Narcissus story, for instance, a prophet is asked whether Narcissus will live a long life, and the prophet declares that he will, *so long as he never knows himself* (Ovid, 3.348). As we have seen, Jocasta speaks nearly identical words to Oedipus before she departs to kill herself: "I pray you never know the man you are" (1068). Less than 20 lines later he will know himself in a way that can no longer be denied, and it will ruin him. The self-knowledge that dooms Narcissus is of course the sight of his own reflection in the still pool, and the prophet who warns his mother is none other than Teiresias. The blind seer thus knows that Narcissus will be ruined by seeing himself; the same blind seer knows that Oedipus will lose his sight by knowing himself—or, paradoxically, for seeing that he has never before recognized what he has somehow known about himself. The intricate similarities and differences between Narcissus and Oedipus deserve further examination, to be sure, but the question remains: why have they so often been ignored by psychoanalysts?

Narcissism has posed a challenge to Freudian psychoanalysis since Freud himself first tried to explain it in his 1914 paper, "On Narcissism." His engagement with it then was deep enough to provoke new developments in his metapsychology, developments that even Ernest Jones described as "a disagreeable jolt to the theory of instincts on which psychoanalysis hitherto worked" (cited in Gay, 1988, p. 341). According to some, though, the jolt was not disagreeable enough. The depth of the challenge has been recognized since at least Kohut's (1971) *Analysis of the Self*, and it is this: to which conflict is narcissism a solution? While answers have been tendered—some more orthodox than others—none has been universally accepted. Metapsychological solutions are not the object of this paper, but metapsychological difficulties may help explain the shortcomings of orthodox analytic interpretations of Oedipus. In order to develop a less-than-orthodox interpretation, then, allow me to return us to the historical context of *Oedipus Rex*. Perhaps the perspective afforded by this return will allow us to elicit from the tragedy a fresh answer to the question it poses once again to psychoanalysis.

Politics and Philosophy

The Greek title of Sophocles' play is *Oidipous Turannos*—Latinized slightly, *Oedipus Tyrannus*. Despite their inescapable popularity, both the fully Latinized title *Oedipus Rex* and the English *Oedipus the King* are bad translations; neither captures the notion of usurper inherent in the Greek *turannos*. Hewing to this connotation, Knox (1957) argued that the character of Oedipus condenses Sophocles' prophetic vision of fifth-century Athens, the so-called enlightenment it helped advance, and the revolutionary anthropology first articulated by this movement's philosophers.

These usurping philosophers began to seek wisdom without deference to gods, their priests, or ancestral tradition. Of Heraclitus, for instance, it was said that he was nobody's pupil but that he had "inquired of himself and learned everything from himself" (Diogenes Laertius 9.5). This particular autodidact was supposed to have said, "the knowledge of the most famous persons . . . is but opinion" (Diels & Kranz, 1959, 22B28). Some said he did have a teacher, Xenophanes, who introduced the skepticism that would become the posture of many subsequent philosophers. "No man has seen nor will anyone know," he wrote, "the truth about the gods and all the things I speak of" (21B34). The specific target of this skepticism was the polytheism of traditional Greek religion. If oxen and horses and lions had hands with which to draw, he argued, they would fashion gods in the image of oxen and horses and lions (21B15). So likewise, he argued, do we project our own images and call them gods: "Ethiopians say that their gods are flat-nosed and dark, Thracians that theirs are blue-eyed and red-haired" (21B16). Freud's "The Future of an Illusion" would follow Xenophanes' lead 2,400 years later.

For all his skepticism, though, even Xenophanes believed in a single, omniscient, and omnipotent god; this god was simply beyond human understanding. Piety could still be found in the philosophers of the sixth century. In the fifth, however, the Sophists took this skeptical posture one step further, subverting even Xenophanes' purified monotheism. Protagoras famously claimed that "Man is the measure of all things," making of every pretense to truth a mere projection. Herodotus effected the same end for conventional wisdom in his *Histories* by recounting stories of foreign customs, stories that implicitly subverted the credibility of local tradition. As for god and customary guarantees of divine punishment for wrongdoing, Critias claimed that one wise man invented the divine in order to guarantee obedience to the laws (Diels & Kranz, 1959, 88B25). Such a projection would be especially useful to a *tyrannus*, and Critias became one himself for a short time after Athens had lost the Peloponnesian War.

This war of almost 30 years cost the Athenians dearly. By the end of it, in 404, they had lost not only their empire and their independence, but more than one generation of young men. But even in 427—the year Sophocles staged the *Oedipus Rex*—the war had already exacted a high price from them, exacerbating the gruesome plague described by Thucydides (2.47–54). Whose fault was it? Blame is no more easily placed for the plague in Athens than for the plague in Thebes. The mythic plague was in a way the fault of Oedipus, for committing his crimes and polluting the city; then again, Apollo was to blame—for sending it in the present, but in the past for dooming Oedipus to those same crimes. Similarly for the real plague in Athens, it was the fault of the gods; but in another way Pericles was to blame.

Pericles was a student of Anaxagoras, who was the first great philosopher to reside in Athens and also the first of all Greek philosophers to be tried for impiety. Among other blasphemies, he called the sun a hot stone (Plato, *Apology* 26d). (As we read in Sophocles, the Sun was considered divine and was indeed associated with Apollo.)[17] Schooled by Anaxagoras, Pericles devised an eminently rational strategy and sold it to the Athenians with irresistible rhetoric: stay within the walls and allow the Spartans to ravage your fields; rely upon your navy alone and think of Athens as an island. But Pericles never foresaw the irrationality that his rational war would unleash. Neither did he foresee the plague. Once it entered through the port, it spread through Athens so quickly that "the bodies of dying men lay upon one another, and . . . the sacred places also in which they had quartered themselves were full of corpses of persons that had died there" (Thucydides, 2.52.2–3). So begins the *Oedipus Rex*: "a deadly pestilence is on our town, strikes us and spares not, and the house of Cadmus is emptied of its people while black Death grows rich in groaning and in lamentation" (27–30). Similarities between Oedipus and Pericles, or more broadly between Oedipus and Athens, are legion, and Knox (1957) has documented them thoroughly in *Oedipus at Thebes*.[18]

No less rich are the similarities between Oedipus and Socrates, the quintessential philosopher, who more than any other represents the innovations of the fifth century.[19] Like Oedipus, he too receives a puzzling response from Delphi, as Race (2000) has noted.[20] Unlike

17 At 765–767 (Fagles [1977]; cf. Grene [1968] 660–661) the Chorus shouts: "Never—no, by the blazing Sun, first god of the heavens." "Sun" here translates *Halion*, or Helios.

18 See especially p. 77.

19 Aristophanes' *Clouds* (423) accordingly used Socrates to condense a century of intellectual innovation.

20 Race (2000) claims that Socrates and Oedipus, "(1) both receive an enigmatic oracle from Delphi; (2) both devise logical plans to avoid fulfilling it; (3) both ironically fulfill it in the very act of trying to avoid it; (4) both discover in the process the limitations of human knowledge; and (5) both become *paradeigmata* for their fellow human beings" (pp. 102–3).

Oedipus, *pace* Race, Socrates does not try to avoid fulfilling this response although he does investigate it critically. Instead, he tries to find out what his oracle means in order that he may discharge his duty to Apollo (Plato, *Apology* 21b). By his attempt to do so, however, and by the oddly similar quest for self-knowledge that his attempt becomes, he likewise ends by fulfilling the prophecy in a tragic way—or at least in a way that seems tragic to those, like his friends, who consider death an evil. Socrates, by contrast, sees death as a liberation, the aim of all philosophical training. In the end, then, he willingly administers the hemlock to himself, just as Oedipus willingly administers the brooches (Plato, *Phaedo* 63e–64a). Additionally, both go to places they consider their proper home: Socrates to the afterlife, where he can discuss philosophy with the heroes; Oedipus to Cithaeron, where he can wander alone. Sophocles' Oedipus thus seems to condense not only Pericles but also Socrates. With Knox (1957), then, we may say that Oedipus represents the political and philosophical facets of the Greek enlightenment.

Initiations

This condensation comes into even clearer focus when we notice how different is the story of Oedipus in Sophocles' hands from the formulaic legend of other mythic heroes who undergo the rite of initiation into manhood. The stories of Jason, Perseus, and Bellerophon are examples of this "monomyth," as Goux (1993) calls it. Simplifying the analysis somewhat, we may say that they must leave home, slay a monster, and receive a bride. But their trials are physical, requiring violence. Oedipus, by contrast, solves the Sphinx's riddle with words alone. The most famous image of his story—incidentally, the very image Freud received on a medallion when a group of his adherents celebrated his fiftieth birthday by commemorating his achievements— has Oedipus seated calmly before her.[21] Compare this equanimity with the canonical images of these other heroes: Bellerophon stabbing the Chimaera with a lance, Perseus slicing off Medusa's head with a dagger, or Jason being disgorged by the Dragon he has slain from within. Oedipus utters just one word: Man. Thereupon the Sphinx kills herself, Thebes is free of her depradations, and, just like the other heroes,

21 For an account of the medallion incident, see Rudnytsky (1986), pp. 4–6 and Gay (1988), p. 154.

Oedipus receives a bride for his exploits. She turns out, of course, to be his mother. In *Oedipus, Philosopher,* Goux (1993) argues that Sophocles intentionally perverted the monomyth in order to diagnose the Greek enlightenment. By trading violent deeds for clever words, in short, the hero is never really initiated. As a result, he never leaves his mother and *must* kill his father. So-called oedipal desires are therefore the price to be paid for enlightenment, Greek or otherwise.

When the results of all these studies are taken together—Lear (1999), Knox (1957), Race (2000), Goux (1993) as well as the other textual evidence we have canvassed—Sophocles appears to have fashioned his Oedipus as a complex political, philosophical, and psychological lesson. Just as Oedipus, the autodidact *tyrannus,* suffers for his knowingness, so too will Athens, both tyrant of Greece and school to its proud philosophers, suffer for its own pride. Furthermore, just as Oedipus, the intellectual hero who fights with words, will never really be initiated and escape the curse of his family, so too will the Greeks, who have traded the archaic world of tyrants, warriors, and mythical monsters for a new one of law, democratic debate, and skeptical philosophy, find themselves facing the old tyrants, monsters, and force—only now deep-seated within each person, in a place yet without a name.

Psychoanalysis as Trauma

But what importance does this historical lesson have for psychoanalysts today? To conclude, let me offer a few hypotheses. Oedipus's knowingness stemmed from the trauma of his original abandonment by parents and gods. To find the roots of Athenian knowingness, then, we should diagnose their particular wound. Taking the parallel literally, we should ask, by whom were *they* abandoned? Following our brief history of skepticism, two culprits emerge: by custom and the divine—in short, like Oedipus himself, by their parents and the gods. After philosophical enlightenment, the Greeks were left alone to fashion a brave new world. The arrogance of an Empedocles—who began his celebrated poem "I go about you as an immortal god" (Diels & Kranz, 1959, 31B112)— may therefore be analyzed as a grandiose fantasy, compensation for the pain of abandonment.

There are testimonies that one philosopher of the fifth century, the Sophist Antiphon, offered psychoanalysis and dream interpretation for a fee. "He founded an art to cure griefs," claims one ancient source, "analogous to that one which among physicians serves as a basis for the treatment of diseases; in Corinth, near the marketplace, he arranged a place with a sign, in which he announced himself able to treat the grief-stricken by means of discourses."[22] He himself is known to have written that "the mind leads the body into health or disease or anything else" (Diels & Kranz, 1959, 87B2) We can only imagine how he helped the mind accomplish this or what his analyses involved, but we can be sure that the man who claimed that there was no natural justice would have abjured traditional pieties (87B44). Perhaps we should expect a philosopher who had contributed to the climate of disenchantment also to have developed techniques to manage the new anxieties he may very well have helped to produce. In both capacities, he anticipated Freud. As did Plato. After all, the *Republic* first develops a tripartite model of the soul and places the monsters of mythology where they still remain: in the lowest of the three parts. "It doesn't shrink from trying to have sex with a mother," Plato writes, "it will commit any foul murder, and there is no food it refuses to eat" (*Republic* 9.572c–d). His philosophy and the ascetic practices it recommended were the techniques he developed to tame this inner monster. Philosophy itself thus became the Greek enlightenment's rite of initiation.

We have inherited this philosophy whether we would wish to or not, even whether we know it or not. Like a Delphic prophecy, then, this philosophy, our philosophy, cannot be escaped. Among its many legacies for us are the esteem of doubt over deference, theories over stories, inanimate over animate causes, and a cosmos ordered according to scientific laws over one ruled by divine caprice. Like Xenophanes and his successors, we cannot help but recognize our projections as such. If we fail, psychoanalysis is ready to disabuse us: spirits are really inner objects, the self is but an assemblage of identifications, and romantic love is only a transference. Fortunately, this brainchild of Plato also helps us to manage the disenchantment it encourages, to tame the monsters it now locates within the soul. But how successful can it be?

Sophoclean Hope?

Looking to the text of *Oedipus Rex* alone, we seem to receive a lesson that psychoanalysis has ignored to the letter: simultaneously disenchanting the world and hoping that initiation can be achieved through

22 Pseudo-Plutarch (*Vitae Decem Oratorum*, I, 18), cited in Lain-Entralgo (1970), p. 97–98.

talk will only make matters worse. Behold Oedipus. But we should no more look just to the text of this one play than did Sophocles and the Athenians who viewed his tragedies at the Greater Dionysia. By widening our view first to this festival and then to the sequel Sophocles would not live to see performed there, we can distinguish two reasons for some hope.

The Athenians saw not a character alone but a whole performance in the context of a whole festival, a religious festival in honor of Dionysus. Oedipus made the mistake of seeking self-knowledge alone; Sophocles offered it to the Athenians collectively. If there is hope for analysis in Sophocles' first prophecy, it may be found here—not on the page, but in the communal rite of pity and fear (Aristotle, *Politics* 1341b32ff). While apparently an individual practice—some critics would say a solipsistic one—psychoanalysis is nonetheless communal: a small community of two, to be sure, but a community nonetheless. Like Oedipus, Freud analyzed himself. Ever since, though, the analysand and the analyst participate in the analysis together. If psychoanalysts are to decide for themselves whether this community is enough to manage the anxiety of disenchantment and achieve modern initiation, all without paying the price of Oedipus, they should revisit this play.

For Sophocles, however, such reflection seems to have been only the beginning. In the final year of his life, he wrote a sequel to *Oedipus Rex*, a play neglected by many philologists, not to mention most analysts: *Oedipus at Colonus*.[23] Whereas Oedipus brashly entered the stage of the earlier play, styling himself a savior, and left the same stage blind but no less jealous of his independence, he enters the later play led by his daughter, reminding even her, "We're outsiders. We need guidance" (12–14). Whereas the younger Oedipus was confident of his knowledge, sought to escape the oracle by applying it, and took responsibility for his crimes when he could not, the older Oedipus excuses his past many times by claiming ignorance of facts and impotence before fate. Of Laius, he protests, "I never knew who he was" (548); of his fate, "the gods know I had no choice" (523). Whereas once he was irreverent, now he is pious—even scrupulous. Arriving in a sacred glade, home to unfamiliar gods, Oedipus urges a local, "tell me their names so I may pray to them" (42). Finally, whereas he once advanced his intellect as remedy to Thebes's ills, he now makes an unusual offer to protect Colonus. "I have a gift to give you," he says vatically, "my own broken body—not much to look at, but appearances can deceive, and it has

---

23 All citations of this play are taken from the translation by Peter Meineck (Meineck & Woodruff, 2003).

the power to bring you great good" (576–579). Thus putting humility before arrogance, destiny before choice, and his body before his mind, Oedipus receives the summons of a god and disappears (1627–1629).

Sophocles himself was a native of Colonus, not far from Athens. After a lifetime in Athens, absorbing the innovations of the Greek enlightenment, he returns in his final play to his childhood home. The grave he has Oedipus leave there to protect the inhabitants of Colonus may therefore represent his own. Not a hero but a tragedian, his apotropaic legacy is not a tombstone but his plays. Heeding one of them, and despairing, we ought to investigate its sequel if we are to understand Sophocles' final word and find in it any hope. "We cannot choose between two Oedipus figures," advises Goux (1993), "the philosopher-king of Thebes and the dispossessed saint of Colonus" (pp. 206–207). Following him, we must depart from Freud, who seems nowhere to have mentioned Colonus. Studying the philosopher-king alone, his assessment of Oedipus remained limited, as limited as were his roughly contemporaneous studies of two other interrupted cases: Bertha Pappenheim (Anna O.) and Ida Bauer (Dora). If we are to achieve a fuller understanding of Sophocles' Oedipus, whether as psychoanalysts or as philologists, we must consider his character in all its phases and postures: the old man alongside the young, the suppliant alongside the king, the saint alongside the sinner. "We must think them through together, as the tension that constitutes the Occidental subject in its tragic dimension" (pp. 206–207).

Whatever does this mean? Let us approach this strange conclusion by another route, summarizing our argument before seeking again some small glimmer of hope in this dark story. Using the work of several scholars, we saw how Sophocles seems to have used the Oedipus of *Oedipus Rex* to represent the pitfalls of the Greek enlightenment: not just arrogant knowingness, the pretentious effort to make everything clear, but also the disenchantment of the world through talk. If the story of Oedipus remains to psychoanalysis what it seems to have been for Freud—a paradigmatic story, a prophetic myth—it dooms analysis to tragedy. The cost of the self-knowledge that is sought in psychoanalysis, in other words, would appear to be tragic if it is sought in the manner of Oedipus the king. Demanding complete transparency, this Oedipus is analogous to the Freudian demand to make the unconscious conscious, the irrational rational.

But if the tragedy of *Oedipus Rex* is somehow redeemed by the events of *Oedipus at Colonus* and if we believe that Sophocles had wider lessons for all who seek self-knowledge, its final cost must be tallied against the peculiar triumph of Oedipus the suppliant. In his resignation to fate, his humility before ancestral traditions, and the gift of his body rather than the deductions of his imperious reason, this Oedipus could be analogous to a more deferent attitude to the unconscious and irrational. Taking seriously our inability to fathom the unconscious in the rational terms of conscious life, such an attitude not only respects the inherent limits of reason, it goes so far as to value the unfathomable guidance of its internal other. Wisdom, Sophocles could be saying to us, is not to be found in the life of pure reason, the fantasy of the totally analyzed analyst, but instead in a compromise—brokered uniquely by each person in consultation with another—between psychoanalytic inquiries, the recognition of their limits, and a wary esteem for what must always remain beyond them.

REFERENCES

Ahl, F. (1991), *Sophocles' Oedipus: Evidence and Self-Conviction*. Ithaca, NY: Cornell University Press.

Bloom, H., ed. (1988), *Sophocles' Oedipus Rex (Bloom's Modern Critical Interpretations)*. New York: Chelsea.

Dawe, R. D. (1982), *Sophocles: Oedipus Rex*. New York: Cambridge University Press.

Diels, H. & W. Kranz (1959), *Die Fragmente der Vorsokratiker*. Berlin: Weidmann.

Dodds, E. R. (1966), On misunderstanding the *Oedipus Rex. Greece and Rome* 13:37–49.

Fagles, R., trans. (1977), *Sophocles: The Three Theban plays*. New York: Viking.

Freud, S. (1954), *The Origins of Psychoanalysis: Letters to Wilhelm Fliess, drafts and notes: 1887–1902*. M. Bonaparte, A. Freud & E. Kris, eds. New York: Basic Books.

Freud, S. (1900), The interpretation of dreams. *Standard Edition*. London: Hogarth Press, 4–5.

Freud, S. (1914), On narcissism: an introduction. *Standard Edition*. London: Hogarth Press, 14:67–102.

Freud, S. (1927), The Future of an Illusion. *Standard Edition*. London: Hogarth Press, 21:1–56.

Gay, P. (1988), *Freud: A Life For Our Time*. New York: Norton.

Goux, J. (1993), *Oedipus, Philosopher*, C. Porter, trans. Stanford, CA: Stanford University Press.

Grene, D. & R. Lattimore, eds. (1991), *Sophocles I*. Chicago: University of Chicago Press.

Kohut, H. (1971), *The Analysis of the Self: A Systematic Approach to the Psychoanalytic Treatment of Narcissistic Personality Disorders.* New York: International Universities Press.

Knox, B. (1957), *Oedipus at Thebes.* New Haven, CT: Yale University Press.

Lain-Entralgo, P. (1970), *The Therapy of the Word in Classical Antiquity*, L. J. Rather & J. M. Sharp, trans. New Haven, CT: Yale University Press.

Lear, J. (1998), *Open Minded: Working Out the Logic of the Soul.* Cambridge, MA: Harvard University Press.

Meineck, P. & P. Woodruff (2003), *Theban Plays.* Indianapolis: Hackett.

Race, W. H. (2000), The limitations of rationalism: Sophocles' Oedipus and Plato's Socrates. *Syllecta Classica*, 11:89–104.

Rudnytsky, P. L. (1986), *Freud and Oedipus.* New York: Columbia University Press.

Rusten, J. (1990), *Sophocles: Oidipous Tyrannos.* Bryn Mawr, PA: Bryn Mawr University Press.

Stimmel, B. (2004), The cause is worse: remeeting Jocasta. *International Journal of Psychoanalysis,* 85:1175–1189.

Vernant, J. P. (1988), Ambiguity and reversal: on the enigmatic structure of *Oedipus Rex. Sophocles' Oedipus Rex (Bloom's Modern Critical Interpretations).* H. Bloom, ed. New York: Chelsea.

Voltaire, (1877), *Théatre.* Vol. 1, *Œuvres Complètes de Voltaire.*

Department of Philosophy
Duquesne University
Pittsburgh, PA 15282
millerp2212@duq.edu

Modern Psychoanalysis
Vol. XXXI, No. 2, 2006

Writing as a Protective Shell: The Analysis of a Young Writer

ALINA SCHELLEKES

This paper focuses on the use of writing in the life and analysis of a young woman, beginning with a presentation of the analysis and ending with a discussion of the role of writing in the patient's life and in her analysis. The author demonstrates how the analytic process helped to free the woman's writing from its autistic function and facilitate its transformation into a builder of identity rather than a substitute for it.

Instead of teeth he has words in his mouth. He chews with them. They never fall.

Elias Canetti (1989)

On a winter day in 1997, Tamar telephoned. She asked without any urgency about beginning an analysis, but her tone, half hasty, half restrained, conveyed that she was in great distress. Tamar came to our first meeting dressed in a potpourri of clothes that seemed to have been gathered for the sole purpose of keeping her as warm as possible. As she began peeling off layers, I found myself fascinated by her powerful presence: her black, burning, engulfing eyes looked as if she were pouring herself through them. When she'd finished undressing, she immediately started telling me, as if we already knew each other and with no reservations concerning or examination of her interlocutor, the reasons she was seeking analysis. She had been suffering from severe backaches, was suffocating in her life, and could no longer stand herself or the world she was in contact with. She felt subjected to countless demands and expectations, even more so because of the way she

© 2006 CMPS/*Modern Psychoanalysis*, Vol. 31, No. 2

positioned herself vis-à-vis the world. She felt compelled to be attentive to others and their needs; she felt flooded and invaded, so much so that in the past few weeks she withdrew from social life—did not take phone calls, did not leave home, and used her husband as a buffer to mediate and block the invasions of the external world. She spent most of her time in bed in a sort of self-regulated home hospitalization. Despite her embarrassed little smiles and giggles, there was something in her fierce gaze and the flow of her speech that told me she was on fire, burning from within, in desperate need of human contact.

She said she was a writer and immediately gave me two of her books. In spite of her professional success she felt as if she were a whore, supplying others' needs through her writings, and then again drained, emptied into those who lived emotionally through her writing and thus at her expense. She also felt she had no core identity of her own since she was deeply influenced by her husband's values and tastes as if she were a mere copy of him. As a child she also functioned, in her perception, as an extension of her mother, who used to force her into listening to things she had written or to her flood of speech. She remembers that she felt compelled to absorb mental substances, which were much beyond her emotional understanding, even if intellectually she was able to express meaningful opinions. One can assume that her talents, which had been outstanding from an early age, and her compliance became catalytic agents for emotional abuse by her mother who, she said, "thrust herself into me, all bleeding and wounded." For the last eight years she had had no contact with her mother because she could no longer tolerate being related to as if she were not a separate person with a life of her own.

In the first months of analysis the frequency of sessions grew gradually up to five per week based on Tamar's own pace. I considered it vital that the intensity of our contact grow from within her, as opposed to her past where her environment had been in complete disparity with her needs.

Tamar was 34, married, with an eight-year-old son. In spite of her abilities and education (she earned a masters degree *cum laude*), she was not involved in any professional activity and cleaned offices to earn money.

She had been born in a small town where, the third of six sisters, she spent the first years of her childhood. Her parents were of Sephardic origin; both had successful careers in the humanities. When Tamar's mother was eight months old, her mother (Tamar's maternal grandmother) had been hospitalized in a psychiatric hospital with no clear diagnosis, probably some form of schizophrenia. Prior to her hospitalization this grandmother had had severe difficulties in taking care of her two little children, and Tamar's mother had been frequently found covered in her own excrement. No contact was maintained with this grandmother, and the family assumed that she died years later in the hospital. With the grandmother's hospitalization, Tamar's mother and her elder brother were moved to the care of their paternal grandmother until her death when Tamar's mother was 16. After her grandmother's death, Tamar's mother lived with various relatives, including her father who tried to abuse her sexually, and stayed for a while in a boarding school until she met Tamar's father, who was 15 years her senior and successful in his profession. After this desperate search for a home and not because of love, the 17-year-old married. Soon she had several daughters who became a much heavier burden than she could bear. Tamar's mother attempted suicide more than once, and Tamar's father saved her again and again. The marriage was full of tension and quarrels, each parent mocking and criticizing the other in front of their daughters. The father mobilized his daughters to take care of his "mad" wife or to find her when she ran away. The mother confided to her daughters about the deep repulsion she felt toward her husband, especially toward his "disgusting" sexual manners. Tamar became her mother's chosen secret partner, compelled to listen to all her experiences, including intimate ones concerning menstruation, defecation, etc. Chaotic boundaries and complete lack of separation and privacy characterized not only the parents' relationship, but also that of the daughters, who had no separate belongings. Today Tamar has meaningful contact only with her youngest sister. She feels deeply identified and concerned with this sister, whose chronic mental disease is felt by Tamar to be a pipe through which all the family pain is drained and discharged. Academically Tamar has always been a brilliant student. Socially, in spite of longstanding friendships, she has always been frustrated and disappointed. She always felt her family to be "inferior" because of its economic neediness, Sephardic origin, dark skin color, and, especially, the unsettled family environment.

For many years Tamar lived in a state of emotional chaos and confusion. Her relationships were marked by a desperate search for contact and sense of belonging. In her twenties she met her husband. A few years her senior, he was an introverted man who had himself struggled with extreme emotional circumstances and at present is a prominent and very successful figure in his own artistic field. They fell quickly in love with each other, married soon after they met, and shortly thereafter had a son. Feeling immature and unfit to become a mother, Tamar wondered if she had given birth to her baby only for her husband's sake. Throughout her son's early childhood she felt terribly overburdened, like a child compelled to rear a child. She felt she needed to completely erase herself to make sure she did not pour herself into the boy's soul in the way her mother had done to her. When her son was one year old, her parents got divorced and soon thereafter she broke off contact with her mother. She has maintained a relatively stable relationship with her father, today an old man still trying hard to mend the never-ending rift among his daughters. After ending the relationship with her mother, Tamar began to pour her energy into writing and studying literature. She is aware of her professional successes, but they fade away soon after they occur. Similarly, she has a hard time with words, her primary mode of expression. She expresses herself with unusual richness and precision but feels she evaporates through her words at the moment they reach the other person, and she becomes "a mouthpiece serving the identification needs of those who read" her writings.

In our first analytic encounter, Tamar placed books she had written on my table so I "could know her through them." I read a bit and was struck by the quality and intensity of her writing, but I also felt bombarded by the emotional content that pulled me into her world—but not as part of our real encounter and not at the same pace. I felt I had been assigned the role that little Tamar had played vis-à-vis her mother when she was exposed prematurely to a mother who was flooded, almost at the point of bursting. I put the books aside waiting to feel the ripe moment for such reading, which indeed came a few months later.

An Emotional Deluge

During this initial phase Tamar filled the sessions by talking continuously. Always on the verge of exploding, she could hardly wait for the session, hungry to have the contact with me again. I also felt an intense need to enter her world but wondered at the speed with which Tamar was pulling me into her soul, with no reluctance or reservations, probably with no real capacity to choose. In one of the first sessions she told a dream from the previous night:

> My husband, my son, and I are all at a picnic. My motorcycle helmet and my son's have been totally crushed whereas my husband's is lost. . . . We're looking for it and asking if anyone has seen it. . . . A neighbor thrusts tomatoes into my husband's ears.

The dream was told as an association to a feeling of emotional abuse she experienced in every interaction. "You ask a question, and you get shit in your ears." Tamar felt extremely unprotected, continuously under the threat of being flooded emotionally from within and by the aggressive and undifferentiated intrusions of any meaningful person with whom she interacted. Her talk was articulate in its way—but poetic, figurative in very eccentric ways (some examples will be quoted in this paper); I experienced it as if it were a sort of high fever, a painful symptom of a long-lasting emotional deluge and minimal containment. Her endless loquacity required me to be a receptacle into which she discharged her suffocating emotional torrents, but also functioned as a barrier that warded off my potentially intrusive interventions.

"It seems extremely frightening to you to open yourself up and trust that I will realize the extent of your distress and yet not be terrified by your abundance and aggressively attack or flood you in return," I said. "I feel that my talk is meant to satisfy you," she responded, tearfully. "When talking, I lose track of my ideas and become alienated from them."

A similar process occurred in her writing. She knew that her texts were very clear and created an intense emotional impact on her readers, but she felt that "the text creates a contour out of which I fall forever, as if evaporating through my words." As a writer, Tamar invested much care in constructing precise forms, which reflected a wish to feel defined and demarcated. However, she perceived this as a miserable effort to hide herself from the "obscure messages that dictate themselves endlessly." Her writing style is not obscure but vivid, but she feels when she is writing as though she is "throwing herself into the other person's retina like a frozen set of keys." This odd figure seemed to me to represent her ideas as keys that her readers can use to open their own souls as they learn about themselves; they are "frozen" because their source, Tamar, is left cold and barren.

Frequently I felt that Tamar's intense presence in our sessions demanded both that I enact the role she'd played with her mother and also that I contain, process, and regulate her torrent of communications to reduce it to a consumable flow. Many times I felt as if I were a revolving door moving continuously between these two different existences, but the oscillation between them enabled me both to enter her internal world and to get out of it and walk by her side. In this way I was gradually able to accompany her non-intrusively, which counteracted the emotional rape she had experienced throughout her life.

A Perturbing Dream

Right before one of our first sessions she met another patient who had just left my office. She excitedly related this incident while immediately trying to reassure me: "I am used to having no privacy."

The following night she had a very perturbing dream:

> I climb up stairs leading to a party; I'm in between a number of young women. The girl in front of me bows, and her vagina and rectum are exposed. I insert my hand into this girl's holes, as if masturbating her, until a white, thick vaseline-like fluid comes out from her rectum. I also come. The following scene is in your office. While we are talking, my eldest sister, Daniela, looks at us through the window. [Daniela is described by Tamar as competing with the youngest sister, Nina, who is considered more mad.] Daniela is trying to talk with me through the shut window. I do not hear her and try to drive her away. Daniela does not give up. She vomits a white thick fluid and says that the solutions against madness are on the bookshelves in your room. She has to enter and take them. I try to stop her from entering the room, but Daniela bursts into the room, and I start fighting with her. Our father appears and tries to separate us. I voicelessly shout and bite Daniela's hand.

She woke up in a panic and had another dream:

> You and I are talking in your kitchen while two other girls are also there. . . . I do my best to ignore them, but it doesn't work. . . . Suddenly a butcher covered with blood comes out of the kitchen.

In great turmoil, Tamar could hardly separate the dream from her associations and mixed them together into a stormy narrative. I felt overwhelmed by the flood of emotions and information. Though stormy and diffuse sexual contents were evident, I thought mainly about her sense of being broken into and invaded, about her confusion and difficulty differentiating between individuals, between parts of herself, between inner and outer life, between various affects, between concrete and symbolic, between the various body orifices through which her contents were expelled. I thought about the dream image of girls climbing the stairs in front of and behind her, revealing a suffocating and adhesive sisterhood in which madness represented the only right to territory, privacy, and concern.

In responding, I chose to emphasize how unbearable it was for her to have never had a room of her own and how she now feared the same could happen in analysis. I added, "You feel you might not have the right to be in analysis since other family members who define themselves as more mad than you would invade our space." In the second dream again she could not be in a private situation since other girls (my children?) interfered with and stole our intimacy. Finally I talked about how she felt she was exploding or leaking out. She cried softly, saying she was tired of all human contacts and would like to disconnect from the world and just come to analysis.

Will I Write Myself to Death?

After months of no creative activity, she felt more relaxed and started to write again, but she was afraid that no one would read her and that she might again "write [herself] to death since words are created where one cuts oneself off." She remembered that she had started to write soon after breaking off with her mother and had written a lot about that relationship in the hope that it would enable her to initiate a different dialogue with her. But this hadn't happened.

More relaxed, she became preoccupied with the ways I was carrying her in my mind. She wondered, "What makes it possible for you to have enough internal space for me, your other patients, and your children?" Thus my capacities as mother/analyst with many children were thoroughly and anxiously scrutinized.

"You need to check my ability to carry simultaneously inside myself various but separate worlds," I told her. In response she recalled numerous situations in which she had felt a complete lack of personal territory and of differentiation. She described how mad she used to get every time she saw the neighbor's window that was facing her garden, how stressed she felt seeing a carpenter mending something in my garden. I said, "Every presence becomes a terrible invasion that erases and annihilates you."

Soon after this I noticed she was wearing an unpleasantly heavy perfume. I imagined that with this pungent smell she was trying to build a strong sense of presence in place of her blurred and fragile self; with it she could penetrate and occupy me beyond the concrete time we spent together. I talked about her need to enter the other and thus feel present within him and thoroughly perceived, but I chose not to relate this insight directly to the perfume.

Soon Tamar felt she could move a bit more in the external world as if, she said, "I have released myself from the hanging rope I have put around my neck." As she became calmer, I started to feel extremely

tired, probably a belated sign of my concentrated investment and concern over all these months. It seemed that only when Tamar was more
relaxed could I allow myself to feel all my feelings.

Tamar wondered to what extent I could understand her without her
becoming exhausted in the endless efforts she had always used to make
herself heard and understood. I said that she was not sure I could manage by myself (without her having to explain herself endlessly). She
smiled and was moved by the possibility that someone might be able to
manage without her investment and support. She was used to seeing her
mother's needy face whenever she tried to take a step on her own, as if
she could never move without first taking care of her mother.

Tamar started to write for a newspaper, but after the initial enthusiasm, she felt intensely frustrated by having to write reviews that examined and promoted other writers at the expense her own work. "Again I
feel that I am a provider of services. If I hadn't had writing abilities, I
certainly would have become a whore."

Depositing Herself in the Analyst's Mind

The conflict between her need to dwell in her internal world (analysis)
while also functioning in her life (relating to her husband and her son
and meeting people) became one of the main issues in analysis. She
explained that her gradual ability to become involved in various activities in the outside world was possible only because she, "skinless, like
a broken reed," deposited herself into my mind. With no clear sense of
having a defined form, she borrowed my shape, using me as a mediating and regulating agent, a sort of transitional object that was simultaneously internal and external, enabling her to move between the two
poles.

I began to be aware that my presence had a special quality in the sessions: my existence seemed to take the form of a silent background figure absorbing, remembering, patiently waiting, and reacting gently
with only minor interferences. I molded my speech much less in terms
of content and more by modulations of tone and rhythm of speech, a
soft, slow, enveloping speech that reminded me of how I used to talk to
my children when putting them to sleep or comforting them when they
were in distress. Many times Tamar recalled words that I had said in
passing although I hardly registered them as potentially having any
meaningful impact. She processed and absorbed my words to construct
an internal presence, a psychic skeleton of clear and definite form. At

the same time Tamar described her position on the couch as part of an inverted sort of birth process: in her perception I was sitting on the chair and she, reclining, head toward me, was coming out of me, legs first.

After six months of analysis, Tamar renewed her relationship with her mother, but the contact was confusing. She complained that others created and defined her and made use of her, as if, she said, "a soft and warm sweater is being knitted from my flesh."

I Will Leak to Death

When I cancelled one of our sessions because of illness, she experienced it as a trauma, which gave birth to a dream in which I came to her house, stole her bed, slept in it, and did not agree to leave it. In response I said that my sickness transformed me into a needy person who robbed her (as her mother used to) while she would have liked so much not to leave my bed/couch. Tamar expressed the fear that she might have burdened me too much and that as a result I might wish to maintain distance from her. This fear was soothed, in my opinion, in the dream's language by my refusal to leave her bed, which vicariously fulfilled her wish that I stay close to her. Facing a short vacation I was about to take, she became anxious that her back would be in pain again and that she would not be able to come to our sessions. She brought up many associations about having been stolen by others. When I noted that in illness I seemed to vanish, she calmed. I added that when I faded away, she "felt crumbly" and lost her own sense of shape. She confirmed that she would "slowly, slowly leak to death"—by which she seemed to be evoking not bleeding but dissolving.

One day she came to the session very agitated and confused, saying that the day before (when we did not meet) she had completely collapsed into a brief psychotic episode.

"While I was not with you," I responded, "you felt as if you were losing your sense of form and were going mad." I told her how my absence had caused her to leak out completely. Tamar felt that the terribly lonely experience and the resulting short psychosis made sense now as if her breaches had now been healed.

In one of her texts she wrote how painful it was for her to feel that my face belonged to me. Thus, the pain of my being separate hit her with all its intensity. She did enjoy her ability to write again, but she was frustrated that all she could do was "describe in an amazing way my non-existence." The writing was the only space in which she felt she could move, whereas in real life she felt disconnected even when she was functioning reasonably well. She said she would like to break off with everything in order to start from the beginning, to be reborn. The fantasy of breaking off was comforting, but also terrifying, since it was clear that many parts of herself felt lost when she was disconnecting from others.

Between sessions she wrote to me often, a written accompaniment that was to go on for years. Every now and then she gave me what she had written, and I later read it. These pages became a very important channel of expression, an intermediate connection between us that kept me present inside her and her within me, that built a sense of continuity, and that sometimes contained experiences that she found difficult to bring up in the sessions. Many times I talked about things she'd written but could not directly express in our meetings. She was surprised that I volunteered to touch upon things that, she feared, could burden me.

Tamar started to miss her childhood home and wished to have some of her sisters as guests and to see her mother more often. She seemed less confused and more differentiated. She felt a renewed need to study, saying: "I would now like to *catch* knowledge as it feels I can now take in much more," as if knowledge, until then, had been experienced by her as intrusive. The use of the phrase "to catch" reminded her of shoplifting when she was an adolescent and of the fear that she might be caught. I wondered aloud to what extent these thefts had expressed not only the dread of being caught, but also the wish to be caught—that is, to be seen—so that the strong needs lying behind the act of theft could then be revealed. (In Hebrew the word "to catch" has a double meaning: to acquire/to get and, also, to perceive.)

"In one of our sessions I was afraid that you were recording me, but it might have been fun," Tamar said. "Maybe if I'd been recording," I replied, "you would have feared that I was listening to you stealthily, but in such case I would also have 'caught' every bit of you in my mind without having to rely on my memory, which can lose parts of you."

Tamar seemed embarrassed that I guessed her wish and spoke again about her need to acquire new knowledge. "You need me to put new food into you, like a feeding parent who does not leave the infant to self-feed," I told her. "I am used to devouring my own flesh until I am completely emptied," replied Tamar, "except when, following our sessions, I leave feeling calm as if my stomach was full."

To Live in My House, in My Body

Enthusiastically, Tamar bought seeds from a shop next to my house and planted them in her garden. She dreamt that my house was "an old and warm wood house with a carriage and hunting dogs coming out of it." She wanted me to adopt her so that she could live in my house, in my body. She would like to be on my couch all the time and do nothing while I guessed everything that happened inside her. Instead she felt compelled to talk. She felt that her words were created for my sake, like a ladder or bridge by means of which I could reach her.

I talk about her wish to dwell inside my mind and thus be understood without having to make so much effort and about her deep hunger (hunting dogs) that she feels as frighteningly aggressive (they become more benign Dalmatians). She says that she feels envious of everyone, as though she were destitute, even homeless—her house does not seem really to be hers. Her wish to be fed by me also arouses guilt, as if it would be theft. I assume this is how she felt whenever she expected her parents to relate to her warmly, givingly. I wondered aloud to what extent she experienced me as stealing from her, as resembling those who possess things because they rob others, who then become destitute. Tamar conceded, with some embarrassment, that she did perceive me in that way (among other ways).

The more frequent our sessions, the greater was Tamar's anxiety regarding the breaks in between. She felt she was held tightly by me and was disturbed when I fell sick and had to cancel a few sessions. In my absence pain flared up in her back. She felt that she did not have "a house to contain everything she created." People appreciated her, but did not really read her writings. Was she referring to me because I had failed to hold together all her parts and had postponed reading her books?

Because I thought she needed me to enter into her world on a deeper level, I decided to read her books. My reading, and our subsequent discussion, was very meaningful to her because she usually felt that nobody really wanted to encounter her inner layers.

The need to have a house for all she bore inside herself became intensified as my summer vacation approached. In the last session before the summer break she was desperate, feeling that her world, and especially her biography, would never change and that there was nothing left to express in her writings; she feared being in close interaction with me and thought she was testing what she felt toward me, i.e., what I meant to her.

"Maybe if you were to look at your feelings toward me, you might discover a lot of anger related to my vacation," I said. Tamar rejected my interpretation and struggled to conceal her neediness especially since I was the one who was going to inflict pain on her.

A Desperate Separation

When I came back from my vacation, I found two burning-with-pain letters, imbued with intense longing and subtle signs of anger. My answering machine bore two desperate messages in which she declared she was on the verge of getting herself hospitalized. Tamar felt as if she were cracking into pieces, in a terrible state of restlessness, and "bearing a toxic pregnancy, bursting with accumulated internal fluids." Highly concerned about her state, I called her before our scheduled session. The sound of my voice immediately soothed her. I instantaneously became the container she so desperately needed. When I met with her, she looked terribly pale and in pain. Hardly stopping for a moment, she recalled that all through our break she had been flooded with memories of being used and invaded by her sisters, "annihilated by their expectations and a prisoner of extraneous definitions" (marriage, motherhood, writing). During my absence her back pain reappeared in its full intensity. She felt like a breathless child in need of artificial respiration, while in reality she had to function as mother to her own son. I talked in various ways about myself as a mother who had left her small daughter unprotected, flooded from within and from the outside. Later I related her feelings about me to those she used to have toward her mother. During the session Tamar gradually became calmer and regained color in her face, and in one day her back pains completely disappeared. My presence and my tone of voice seemed to constitute an immediate soothing agent, joined by my words, which defined the impact my absence had on her. The back pains seemed to represent both an expression of the emotional burden she had felt and an attempt to organize herself through a clear and defined sensation, i.e., pain. With my presence, her restored sense of being held in my mind became her emotional spine, its support relieving her back pains.

Keeping the Light of Your Room inside Me

Approximately a year after beginning analysis, Tamar quit her job (cleaning offices) and felt much more able to function in roles that fit her qualifications and capacities. She felt I was the "space" into which she could "pour herself," enabling her to participate in various public, professional events without losing her own identity. When I told her that I'd watched her in a TV interview, she felt I had been mediating between her and the outside world so that the two seemed less disconnected. She described how she went to professional meetings, keeping the tone of my voice and the light of my room inside her. Because I safeguarded the two opposite poles of her experience, inside and outside, she felt able to move back and forth between these poles without losing anything.

Often Tamar feared that things she expressed in these public forums became lost to her, untethered, as it were, the moment she put them into words, but she felt that I could reconnect them to her, and that was my responsibility. I did this many times, especially trying to connect our sessions and her writings. I assume that the feeling of disintegration and estrangement that accompanied the "birth" of her writings was a repetition of her experience of having been born to be in the service of her mother, with the resulting failure to establish a firm sense of self-existence.

Tamar was afraid people would expect her to be always strong and functioning, but what she wanted most was to be my baby, just lying quietly and listening to my "soft, enveloping voice." Her yearning was sharpened by the experience of having grown up with a baby/orphan/mother, who had felt all *her* life like an "abandoned baby surrounded by feces." Tamar perceived her father as overburdened by the need to care for his wife and five daughters, but still, unlike her mother, capable of loving beyond his own person. She felt toward her mother both compassion and anger; she conceived of her mother as a "lump of flesh oppressed by the tyrannizing memories of a terrible childhood." She felt that her mother experienced herself as never having grown, aged, matured—only her appearance had—her skin, which Tamar had felt responsible for caressing in order to comfort her mother.

Tamar had a dream in which she "stole a flower from a neighbor's garden while the family were celebrating their son's birthday." The idyllic family scene portrayed in the dream was painful, especially since she felt growth required stealing from others. Embarrassed, she told me she had started to read with fervor Winnicott's writings but worried she was stealing from me. Whenever she received something from another person, she felt a tremendous emotional debt, which became a terrible burden. She became tense when I smiled at her as if she were compelled to give me something in return. Similarly, she feared that when people enjoyed her writings, they expected to get more and more of her.

During this period my verbalization of her feelings had a powerful impact. Tamar felt that my words "unloaded bomb loads" that were about to explode inside her every minute. She felt "lighter" and able to "move outside." She started to cook for the first time, describing to me what she bought and prepared. She dreamt that my daughter was her sister, which made me, of course, her mother. The dream and the ensuing associations came after incidentally meeting in the street my light-skinned daughter playing with her dark-skinned friend. Tamar concluded that if I allowed my daughter to befriend a Sephardic girl (like Tamar), then it might be a sign of my readiness to accept her too. Of course, this train of feeling immediately brought to the surface the dramatic and painful differences between the two of us she experienced: I am light-skinned; she is "black" (with all the status connotations she attached to this difference). I live in a house "full of children"; she is abandoned in the street, compelled "to buy a womb" (her house). She was filled with feelings of envy, experiencing me both as a containing and a robbing mother. She became afraid that I would not be able to tolerate her envy and her neediness and that I would compel her to behave in a mature way. If she detected any signs of wavering in my ability to tolerate her, she would expect me to rob her of "the little girl inside herself," which usually survived with great efforts of concealment.

Tamar was surprised that I was able to explain these dynamics to her without her having to explain herself extensively. Every time she felt understood by me it moved her deeply as if she existed for the first time, was seen and understood by another person without needing "to sculpt [me] as [her] rearing environment."

A Break in Understanding

Tamar told me she had a defect in her sex organs, that "the internal lip was bigger and sticking out." She was considering having a surgical intervention to fix the defect. I was extremely worried by the intensity of her anxiety and by the rather psychotic thinking that might drive her to self-destructive action. I summarized to her the sequence of events as I understood them at the moment: how she felt I had robbed her and threatened to steal the little child part of herself; how she felt an intense emotional hunger and neediness, which she tried to satisfy by grabbing and stealing (for example, she abused her right to receive books from a publishing house); how she felt so ashamed, ugly, and defective when the hunger (the internal world) stuck out that only a sharp knife would be able to fix her. I finished this session worried and exhausted, perhaps similarly to how a surgeon feels after a long and dangerous operation.

Following this session Tamar had a dream:

I am traveling in a car and have just stopped. I see myself in the driver's mirror and wonder whether he sees me too, whether he is aware of my existence. Immediately the driver reminds me of you.

I asked, "How have I not seen you?" She said she'd wanted us to speak concretely about the terrible defect in her sex organs. "There is no need to translate this defect into any other language since it is the origin and basis of all my other experiences."

Again I became very worried, feeling that "the internal language was sticking out" or, in other words, that her ability to think metaphorically had broken down completely and that her insistence that we talk only in a physical and concrete way was an expression of her internal breakdown. My attempt to translate her talk into another language brought back her back pains and the emotional pain felt whenever one did not speak her internal language. "You will always be a foreign body that allocates me limited moments of togetherness and abandons me in the end," she said.

Tamar and I explored the sequence of events that occurred between us in sessions and the burning impact any experience of separateness and boundary had on her. The end of a session was often experienced as if it were the end of the analysis. The intervals between sessions became "hatchets cutting her body" so deeply that she lost any sense of wholeness and identity, not knowing anymore who she was, what she felt, whether to continue writing, etc. My failure to talk in a concrete language was a cutting and separating hatchet, which left her feeling as if she'd been vomited on and dismantled. At this stage she felt alive only when she could psychically lodge herself inside me. Anything that implied physical or emotional separateness could disorganize and annihilate her very existence. I tried to describe as precisely as I could my understanding of what went on inside her and gradually, after a few sessions, her back pain disappeared, and she became calmer.

Retrospectively, I believe I had the chance to experience in the transference her very early feeling that she was not understood within herself but had to speak only the other's language. In her writings she struggled to express with precision her internal world and thus to save whatever the early interpersonal relations had damaged. When words and language failed, the physical pain, with which she had come to analysis, recurred, and the image of the physical defect appeared. This image constituted her most internal language and needed no translation. Only when I ceased trying to translate the image and spoke with few simple and exact words, did she feel I was speaking from within herself. Her pains faded away and so did the mental breakdown expressed in the image of the internal lip that was sticking out and needed to be cut. Throughout, I avoided any interpretation in terms of more classical castration anxieties, which I found only partially captured her deeper anxieties.

Wondering about the Other

Tamar started to wonder hesitantly about my feelings and judgments about her. Until then, ignoring me had been vital in enabling her to create a space in which she could move freely, whereas any piece of practical or emotional information about me felt as if it were compelling her to react to and to accommodate my presence and needs. Now she felt more able to tolerate information about me and was even curious. I hesitated as to how to react to her. On one hand, I felt that through her questions she did not really try to know me but expressed the need to maintain contact with parts of herself that she had deposited within me that might otherwise have become estranged. On the other hand, many of Tamar's qualities touched and moved me, but I worried that were I to relate to them, she would interpret that in her internal language as a way of deriving enjoyment for myself from those aspects of her—which would constitute exploiting her and would at the same time render those parts of her dead to herself. I shared my thoughts with Tamar. She was surprised that I thought about her in this way. She added that her questions now expressed her wish to play with desires and ideas, as opposed to all the years in which she felt her mother had not given her permission to be in the world as a separate subject with a right to experience and express herself freely, but rather kept her as a subject in the service of others. For example, from an early age she felt her mother had focused on Tamar's superior ability to understand and evaluate literature, including texts that she (her mother) had written, without showing any interest in Tamar's own writings and her need to express herself. I talked about the love-hate feelings that Tamar experienced when she wrote critical essays about other writers, and I wondered to what extent she had tried, when she asked me to evaluate her, to deposit the hated critical function into me in order to free herself from the constraint to react to others' needs and thus to express her autonomous self.

Digestion or Invasion

Tamar felt calmer and started talking about herself as highly demanding toward others. She felt she interpreted others in strange ways as if they were aggressive and violently intrusive. She described how people were hurt by her and consequently avoided contact with her. She experienced with deep pain the discrepancy she was now aware of between how she perceived herself and how others perceived her. Any gift she was given was perversely interpreted by her emotional mirror as a sign of being robbed, abused, or competed with. She felt compassion toward her husband and remorse for her own frequent harshness toward him, but she wanted him to be able to absorb her "poisoning acids" without becoming hurt and turning her "into a murderer in his internal world." She felt compassion for her mother's pain, for her mother who had not had the chance to experience "a mother absorbing her feces." She herself was "undoing [making up for] an early deprivation" by trying "to pour [her] feces upon others while they absorb it and get dirty."

For many years she had been erasing herself to provide her son with a different mother from the one she had experienced, but the effort to raise him was made without any real emotional maturity. Actually she was angry at anyone who assumed that she could be a mother and that included me. She was angry that I assumed she could get from her house to mine, that she could rise from the couch at the end of sessions when in reality she felt incapable and without existence.

These feelings got stronger as we approached a few days' vacation I would be taking. Before our break her writings were full of anger. Tamar wanted to be incessantly in my mind-body, in my house, in my professional theory. She would like me to guide her in the Ph.D. studies that she contemplated beginning. She felt she'd found a home in the psychoanalytic literature, as if the texts she'd started reading mirrored her experience of analysis. She seemed to attain definition and identity through this swallowing of me and my fields of interest. Yet, she was afraid of losing herself inside me and felt guilty for reading writings that belonged to my work though her guilt seemed also to conceal a pleasure. I thought about the dyad in her childhood in which she felt stolen by her mother. Now for the first time in her life, she was part of a dyad in which the two participants could co-exist without one annihilating the other.

I wondered aloud to what extent her words described a different feeling: to what extent she perceived *me* as stealing from her—her analysis when I was absent, her money, her identity. Tamar was startled by this interpretation, but her writing revealed that she was taking it in:

I am afraid I will find myself deeply immersed in a story which is not mine, but another's. Somewhere in the middle of the way, it turns upside down, it becomes monstrous, what used to be for my sake becomes against me, negates me as a result of intrusion, confused identity, too much copying until I become a stranger to myself, vomiting all my contents, even my own body, which is controlled by invaders whom I myself have invited to enter my world. Every meaningful encounter becomes one of invasion, every meaningful person becomes a rapist.

In the following sessions Tamar reacted with great pain and anger to anything real or imagined that she experienced as distancing me from her. During one session she heard a baby cry. Tamar immediately perceived me, "as expected," as an unavailable person, an absent mother, and burst into tears. I tried to put her feelings into words: how she felt that the external world had entered our room in a very intrusive and painful way exactly when she needed to be my tearful baby. Gradually she felt comforted and observed that the crying baby represented the cry that might accompany her in my absence during the coming brief holiday.

The World Opens

In spite of our shared apprehension, the days of vacation passed quietly. She registered for her academic studies, and when we met again, she told me with excitement that for the first time during an absence of mine she had not lost her sense of having a form. Instead she feared her involvement in her new studies might result in losing her ability to write; it was as if her experience of theft, annihilation, and competition had shifted from the interpersonal realm to an internal one, where one part of her struggled against and threatened to erase another one.

Tamar's style of writing became more airy, as an expression of her growing ability to wait for our sessions in order to share her thoughts and of her feeling able to carry me inside her for longer periods of time. At the same time, after nine years, Tamar renewed the relationship with her mother and with her son and became a bit closer to her mother, in spite of many frustrations. The mother–daughter relationship became the renewed focus between the two of us as well: she needed me to think continuously of her, and she wondered to what extent I could bear her inside me without collapsing under the weight, a burden she herself carried in relation to her son. When Tamar imagined me carrying her within me, she felt lighter, not "exploding with overweight." I could "hold" Tamar the writer, allowing her more assertively to participate in public professional activities.

Hesitantly, she expressed the fantasy that I too would write, that we would "become one writing entity." She wondered to whom the story written by this entity would belong. I said she had a powerful need to merge in order to hold together all the parts of her personality. The more Tamar dared to get involved in the world, the more she felt separated from me. In spite of her clear enjoyment of new activities, she feared that both of us would lose connection to her little girl parts. In anxiety she clung to the fantasy of merger with me and, sporadically, reduced some of her public activities so as to safeguard her more basic needs. I added that she felt as if every move or success of hers threatened me and was inciting me to steal from her or humiliate her, which in turn compelled her to suppress her strength. Tamar was moved and burst into tears.

Another Separation

With my approaching summer vacation I thought about ways of maintaining contact with Tamar to avoid the disintegration of that first summer vacation. I suggested we speak on the phone at prearranged times. Tamar was quite relieved by my suggestion, which confirmed that she didn't have to fight to get me to understand and respond to her needs. During my absence we talked twice a week at very regular times. These were short conversations in which she told me how she was doing. Mostly, she sounded all right. The phone calls seemed to provide both a structure for her internal and outer worlds and a thin membrane preventing intrusion and pain, while enabling her to make small steps in the outside world. For instance, during my absence she enlarged and renovated her room's window so that the view of the outside world became much larger, and she met with university teachers to talk about her Ph.D.

When I returned, Tamar asserted that she was feeling all right, as if we had had no break, but in her writings during my absence she expressed anger relating to my travel. In the next session I referred to things in writing that she had not dared to express aloud. Tamar was surprised that I "wanted" her anger. Gradually she let herself express frustration at the lack of fit between us. She said I was stronger than she. The fact that I came from a different background and had been born abroad meant that I would never truly be her mother since my mother tongue would always be different from hers. Now all prior feelings of intimacy crumbled; I became a stranger, a rejecting foreigner who aroused feelings of envy.

Perhaps I didn't sufficiently contain the storm; Tamar stole a cheap garden water faucet from a shop close to my house. When I interpreted her feeling of being thirsty, of being deprived by me to such an extent that she had to steal for herself, something in her voice and muscle tension softened. She expressed an intensely wishful fantasy that I envelop her with my great desire for her presence. I observed that during my vacation her certitude that I wanted her had been shattered to such an extent that now she did not know if I had any interest in her at all. The rhythm of her speech slowed down, and she said how much she would like to feel she becomes a burden for me, to feel I am a tired, but happy, mother. "Your voice is like a hammock in which I swing like a baby, but a baby with a big woman's disgusting body."

When I asked her about the disgust, she was flooded with memories of her mother's sharing with her daughters everything about her bodily functions. Her mother used to lie in her bed, gazing into a mirror through which she could see her daughters walk by her bedroom and catch their eyes. "It seems," I said, "that all through your childhood you felt as if you were an inverse mirror, that you had to take care of your mother as if she were a baby whose excretions are a natural and central part of any mother's care." Tamar started to cry and said, "I want to be your baby."

The Space We Share

During the following sessions Tamar noticed for the first time various things in my room: where the window ended, the size of the table, the pictures on the walls. She talked about the unpleasant discovery that the pictures did not suit her taste and represented the many differences between us. She was curious to know who I was, what characterized me. She was afraid she would be disappointed, but with less anxiety than before. I sensed that she was starting to treat space in a different way, in a three-dimensional way that had been missing. In parallel to my thoughts, Tamar said that during my absence she, together with someone else, had started to work on a new book, feeling that there was enough space for two persons, that neither would asphyxiate nor negate the other.

However, in our sessions Tamar talked about her need to occupy all the space between us. I became aware of feeling a huge burden inside myself, as if it were a delayed reaction to holding Tamar so long in my mind and body in a sort of osmotic way. I then had the following dream:

> I was looking for an apartment to rent, but it was difficult to find one. Finally I found it and was happy to have a corner and furniture of my own. Tamar became my apartment mate. I was wearing a dressing gown [in Hebrew the same word is used for a dressing gown and something which is divided], and Tamar said how much she was in need of, and would have liked to have, such a dressing gown.

Following the dream, I thought about the feeling, in Tamar's life and in mine, of lacking a place of one's own, about her envy in the dream, and about her wish to have more from me, which I could not and did not wish to give her. Beyond my fatigue and burden, I thought how exactly my feelings echoed the relationship between Tamar and her tired, exhausted parents, who did not have enough energy to see to her needs. Thinking about all this gradually made my fatigue go away and made me wonder to what extent the more humorous tone that now appeared in Tamar's writings was also meant to raise my spirits.

A Separating Membrane

Tamar's publication of a new book occupied us for weeks. After the initial enthusiasm, she found it difficult to let the book be printed and to participate in the festive evening that celebrated its "birth." The events compelled her to be present and to be the center of attention. While reading the book, which she gave me, I was impressed with the delicate, subtle, and yet powerful way in which she expressed herself, along with the other artists whose works were part of the book. I told Tamar I enjoyed the book a lot and felt her very special presence throughout.

My words became a cruel barrier between us, turning me into a person who was "born to disappoint [her] again and again." My reaction became a way of not relating to her. She needed me not as someone who reacts to her, but as someone within whom she can live. She felt my words had been inaccurate and separated us painfully. This only heightened her need to "stick to me." The book itself became an object that forced her to admit her independent existence since the act of writ-

ing the book was done in my absence. Soon she felt she had lost any
sense of having a form of her own, that she did not know any longer
who she was, and that she could no longer write since every word was
experienced as "thickening the separating membrane."

Though we had already been through similar experiences, I found
it painful to see again how quickly she could disintegrate upon hand-
ing over her writings. In such cases she became very angry. I did my
best to put into words the sequence of feelings that led to her disintegration, the terror that accompanied this state, and the anger pent-
up inside her. The more clearly I described her feelings, the faster their
terrifying intensity diminished, enabling her to return to her activities
(teaching and participating in conferences) and to enjoy them. Later I
added that, by talking about her book as separate from her, I seemed
to become a literary critic in her mind, thereby arousing all the hate
she felt toward her own role as critic. I said when she reviewed others' writings, she felt she functioned as a mother to them, whereas she
identified herself as a little girl in her own creative writing. This line
of interpretation affected her deeply, and she began to write again after
a long cessation.

Every act of mine that brought to the fore my separate existence
(cancellation of a session, change of perfume, change of a decoration
in my office) created in Tamar a feeling of internal collapse, fluidity,
and loss of form. In such cases, I usually tried to describe, in as few and
as exact words as I could, the relationship between my moves and her
experience of disintegration. Tamar was only sometimes aware of this
relationship, but even when she was, what affected her was *my* being
aware of *my* impact on her emotional oscillations. Understanding alone
was usually not enough. She needed me to feel deep down in my bones
how I had deserted her and caused her collapse. Many times, I
expressed just this.

Other events in our interaction offered fertile ground for seeing and
understanding how her sense of having a form of her own came into
being or, alternately, collapsed. For instance, she gave me Bernard
Malamud's (1998) short story "Talking Horse" about the relation
between the tyrannical owner and his money-earning, talking horse—a
man imprisoned in the body of a horse. Tamar was very surprised when
I observed that the owner was deaf-mute. I said that from a very early
age Tamar functioned as the interpreting voice for her mother until
finally she lost any sense of having a voice of her own. I connected this
to the narrator's transitions in the story between first and third person
as expressing, in my view, the feeling of self-loss (the man–horse–narrator's) that develops when one is imprisoned or controlled from with-

out. Tamar started to cry, moved that I had pressed my ear close to her heart, and read the story over and over again.

I wondered if her interest in the story was also linked to a one-week break during which I would travel out of town. Again I had decided on an event apart from her, thus becoming the deaf-mute tyrant, whereas Tamar was dependent on and imprisoned in my decisions. Tamar, not unexpectedly, expressed intense merger needs: she would like to become "a project for cutting through [her] genes and biographical-genetic history." She would like me, in spite of my evident light Ashkenazi coloring, to be her mother, to take care of all her needs, to protect her with my body, and to prevent her from falling. She wished she could be more important to me than I was to myself, in which case I would obviously give up my travel. At the same time, she wondered whether her needs robbed me completely. She oscillated between feeling herself carried in my mind-body and feeling my absence that now, before the one-week break, made her so angry. I humiliated her by living my life apart from her. She described herself as a "flesh puddle with no borders or contour." She wondered whether my travel was an attempt to run away from her because she was such a burden. She fluctuated between despair—with a wish to stop analysis and to kill herself—and an obsessive need to absorb and decode my form and contour. She studied what I wore, what drove me to react the way I did, where I came from, and how I managed to fulfill various roles in my life. Knowing me in a more palpable and concrete way stablized her sense of me and allowed Tamar to borrow a sense of my form and purpose.

As our break approached, I recalled the separation difficulties my daughter had had during her first days in kindergarten and how having a small picture of me on a necklace had helped her. While I was having the idea of giving Tamar a picture of me, she, coincidently, fantasized that we exchange pictures. She said she would like to have a very small picture of me to put in her purse and carry anywhere she went so that my absence would cause less of a "self-cessation." I told her my fantasy. The fact that it was my own independent fantasy, rather than one formed in response to one of hers, was especially meaningful to her. My words moved her as a "renewed light in a burnt-out bulb." We exchanged pictures. Hers was to be with me only for the duration of my absence, but she carried mine permanently. During my travel we talked twice. My calls, at exactly specified times, prevented her from evaporating into the terrible internal void. In one of the phone calls she asked me for the first time, "How are you?" All these experiences and communications had created in her for the first time a confidence that I really would return.

A Zygotic Matrix

When we met again, Tamar focused on the difficulties she encountered in her writing. I, as a reader, had become a vital part of the process. She perceived her writing as a "zygotic matrix" where, though I was passive in the shadowy background, my presence was nonetheless vital. When she'd given me her picture, she'd written, "It is the first time in my life I give you a picture of my face and not of my longing. For the first time the empty space is filled with my face and not with words looking and longing for a face." For a long time she had felt that her writings stemmed from a dead core, and now she wanted to write from a different source. She wanted to engage in more careful composition. This shift would entail planning the text, fantasizing about it, and advancing slowly and coherently toward the goal, whereas Tamar's writing had been more an act of fast and efficient vomiting of poisonous and painful material into highly structured texts. Although Tamar did not change her style of writing, she did find that more varied alternatives were now at her disposal.

One morning, much earlier than our session, she saw the car of a family member of mine leaving the parking space. She was sure that at such an early hour it was because my baby girl (she was sure I had two daughters) was sick and needed medicine. Tamar said she was frequently preoccupied with the presence in my house of a baby who cried at times while I sat behind Tamar impatiently waiting for the session to end so that I could tend to my baby girl. Tamar imagined I was the kind of mother who knows how to hold her baby, that I had huge amounts of internal space for this baby who had priority over anything else, whereas she, Tamar, was compelled to live as a partial presence in my life. Simultaneously, she perceived me as a mother who abandons her baby to be with Tamar or abandons Tamar for the baby's sake. Tamar worried that I, exhausted and hungry from so much work, must hate the sticky, transparent, sick baby who is Tamar. I interfered very little with these fantasies, not correcting the inaccuracies. We spoke about the sick baby girl who concealed the presence of an abandoning/rejecting/killing other.

The sick-baby fantasies also related to my own back problems, which had necessitated the cancellation of a few sessions. I was, after all, a sick and needy mother abandoning her sick baby daughter. Tamar recalled many memories of her helpless father coping with his sick, vulgar, moaning, needy baby-wife. Tamar described her mother as a "destroyed subject," while her father was a weak man who had spent his life trying to help his wife function and taking care of his daughters, who also became his aides in caring for his wife. My back problems, which partially resembled the ones Tamar had when she came to analysis, made her again wonder about the extent to which her burden might have broken my back, transforming me into a sick baby. Of course, her fear of breaking my back concealed an aggressive wish that my back would indeed break as well as the guilt that followed this wish. It also concealed a desire to be reassured that she existed continuously and profoundly within me via our similar symptoms.

Only after many sessions did Tamar start to question whether I had a baby. When, ultimately, I made it clear that the baby's cry she had once heard had been that of a guest and that my children were much older, she felt cheated by me. By not immediately correcting her, I had humiliated her. Here was additional proof of the painful differences between us: unlike her, I had a family that received guests; I had two children, male and female, whereas she had an only son; I was good looking, whereas she was a "dark cloud of flesh." She again lost any sense of having a stable form and described herself as a "huge meat growth disconnected from any organizing column. Any column that exists is exterior to my body. I have a back but with no spinal column." As opposed to this perception, she envisioned me as organized around my identity as an analyst, a house owner, and mother of two children. Gradually she came to feel ashamed to have shown me all her envy and her distorted perceptions.

Through elaborate processing, it became clear that when her back was in pain, it made her feel she had a back. Tamar wondered to what extent I functioned as her external spinal column, enabling her to move without fearing that every step would cause her to lose her form. This was why, in her view, it had been necessary not to know anything about me. If I were static, she could be the one who moved and changed; if I changed, I ceased being an object for her "free use."

Toward Separation

Tamar's anxiety about being separate from me was now less overwhelming. To some extent, she even expressed a need for some separation. She now seemed to move more flexibly between the two impossible poles of her life: that of living in a "dense, condensed, formless, sticky, envious family dough" and that of being dropped and emotionally abandoned. She could experience some moderate degree of separateness without the simultaneous feeling of abandonment. Tamar felt that the analysis had become her home, a space where she came into being with a "lively contour" and that she wrote herself "on my heart's board." In spite of many oscillations between hope and despair, many of which were a direct result of my failure to contain her tightly enough, Tamar continued to create and fantasized writing a book together with me. Her writings between sessions became less about me and our sessions and more a diary (space) where she processed her experiences and her other writing.

After giving a lecture and receiving many appreciative comments, she came to our session very excited, but her satisfaction soon faded away. Enthusiastic remarks about her writings were, she felt, similar to the enthusiasm "a hungry person feels about the meat he is about to barbecue." "Your writing is very penetrating," I said. "You want your texts to be understood and to enter deeply into your readers' minds. But at the same time, when the texts are clear, they become a sort of public barbecue, as if each reader were roasting your flesh, using your contents for his personal needs, and thus making you feel exploited and devoured."

Tamar was very moved by my use of the term public barbecue, probably because of its close connection to "fleshy" terms she uses in her writings to express her experiences in an intense and raw way. She could not risk sending her writings into the world without being sure that they would be understood. Thus, she treated them like small children to whom an interpreting parent must be attached, right in the body of the text. "You find it difficult to believe that there will be a parent out there in the world who will know how to take care of the texts," I observed.

Tamar said she feared I, too, would not understand things she was telling me, that I would get confused. She was surprised every time someone was able to translate her without her own mediating efforts. The more she perceived me as holding her in my mind, the more she felt able to move between her internal world and the external one. At the same time, she feared her burden would break me. She feared that differences between us would make me misunderstand her. She tested every word of mine as potentially expressing the limits of my thinking ability. She hated her dependence on me and my mobility; she hated me for not being her biological mother. If I had been, I wouldn't have moved an inch away from her. Many times, extremely worried by the intensity of her internal violence, I was afraid she might become suicidal. In the end, we were both saved, it seemed, by my ability to tolerate her anger without abandoning her, giving up, or becoming vengeful.

Where We Are Now

Despite the many sharp oscillations in her feelings throughout her analysis, Tamar increasingly feels that her husband loves her deeply. She has progressed extremely fast in her Ph.D. studies, has taught and has been highly appreciated by her students, and has been involved in more interpersonal relationships without feeling abused, exploited, or misunderstood. She remains very sensitive to rejections and abandonment but can now absorb into herself much more readily the positive regard she receives. She feels more in synchrony with others, realizing that separateness is not only a threatening possibility, but also a potential for growth.

Tamar's increasing involvement in social and professional life is accompanied by frequent fluctuations between hope and despair, between having an identity and feeling formless. She oscillates between active involvement and feeling that everything is frozen and dead, that it is useless to live, create, and write. In spite of these stormy fluctuations, which I too experience, the recovery is faster, perhaps in part, because I feel less anxiety living through these fluctuations. One may say that we both have a clearer knowledge that every collapse does not necessarily imply annihilation and death, that my going away also implies my coming back, that separateness and differences between us do not deny intense attachment and connection.

Discussion

From the beginning Tamar filled the room with words. It was clear from the start that language and writing were at the center of her life. Our encounter started with a common recognition that this analysis would bring Tamar, a person with very sophisticated and personalized knowledge of the Hebrew language, into contact with myself, a person analyzing in a language that was not her mother tongue. Tamar had absorbed the verbal richness of her mother, but language had become both a loved and hated medium as if its acquisition implied for Tamar a process of being swallowed by her mother's world. My different native language (Romanian) confirmed symbolically my inability to ever become Tamar's mother and thus represented unbearable separation.

After breaking off relations with her mother, Tamar had begun to write fervently. This act, expressing both her identification with and distancing from mother (Boulous & Walker, 1998), represented an attempt to create a new mode of contact with mother without drowning forever in her mind (Kristeva, 1982). In *The Pleasure of the Text*, Barthes (1975) writes: "The writer is someone who plays with his mother's body," producing through the text a sort of new birth, in which one reestablishes the primary contact with mother's body. Ogden (1998) views writing, and its specific linguistic modalities, as a means of enabling the experience of otherness and a new look at human relations.

I will describe a few characteristics of Tamar's use of language and writing that became evident during the analysis. Encountering her weighty barrage of speech, I frequently found myself wondering how to communicate with Tamar in a way that would penetrate her sophisticated language and touch her in a more primitive, wordless manner. On reflection I find that in the first phase of her analysis I spoke minimally and quietly, using simple words whose sonorous qualities were as significant as their content.

Writing as a Protective Shell

One of the aspects of Tamar's writing that fascinated me was the discrepancy between the mathematical precision of the emotional and verbal structure of her texts, as opposed to the chaotic emotional flooding in her life. Such a discrepancy may seem surprising, but it is not when we consider Tamar's underlying mental structure. Feeling completely formless, Tamar habitually adopted the identity of the proximal significant other, almost as if she were engulfed within the other's mind. In my view, her early writings did not mirror her internal world but, by means of a very precise and geometrical use of verbal images and structures, created a protective shell (Tustin, 1990), which forestalled fragmentation and loss of identity, while functioning as constructions able to organize her and give her a sense of form and contour otherwise lacking in her experience. She sculpted her words and rhythms, played with sounds and syntax, and built precise formations. In her diary, Sylvia Plath (1982) describes writing as a way of structuring and restructuring the chaos of experience, as an "ordering, reforming, relearning and reloving of people as they are and as they might be. A shaping which does not pass away" (pp. 270–271). In a similar way, T. S. Eliot (Berman, 1993) observes that the process of writing poetry encompasses the need to control emotion and the chaotic parts of human experience. He emphasizes that poetry is not "a turning loose of emotion, but an escape from emotion; it is not the expression of personality, but an escape from personality" (Kermode, 1975, pp. 42–43).

Building a Structure Within

As the analysis progressed, Tamar's writing became less an escape from her personality—an autistic shield—and more a part of a breathing, interpersonal dialogue through which she built her emotional spinal column. Her writings gradually were able to function not only as protective shells lending her the shape of every specific text, but also as meaning-assigning containers that alleviated experiences of object loss (Brink, 1977, 1982; Martin, 1983; Jones, 1997) and internal flooding, while enabling her to build, in the context of the intense transference relation, her own "I-ness" (Tustin, 1986) to stratify the various layers of her mental and emotional life. Similarly, Ogden (2001) and especially Bollas (1999) describe how the artist creates, through his work, a new mental reality that transforms and reshapes the self. The artistic product is not merely a mirror of the writer, but a new and different essence of the writing-self. According to Bollas, the creative self transubstantiates itself into the place/shape/body of the artistic creation, which absorbs, changes, and presents the self, living now in the creation. The creative product does not represent an existing structure but presents something that did not exist before, the self that has been changed while entering into the object of art and its laws. By means of her writing during the analysis, Tamar has continuously struggled to create symbolic expressions/texts that contain and transform her emotional experience.

When Tamar regressed into states in which the danger of falling and dissolving was great (Tustin, 1986; Schellekes, 2005), the symbolic quality of her creations often weakened. In such cases, she no longer experienced her texts as symbols, but, again, as concrete, real, autonomous objects, which either comforted or annihilated, depending on the degree to which she still experienced them as part of her. When their symbolic quality weakened, their function as containers collapsed, and she experienced them as body parts evaporating or being devoured by others. The collapse of the symbolic function at the end of the creative process has been emphasized by McDougall (1997) and Bergman (2000), who describe how various artists destroyed their creations as if they were concrete and pain-inducing objects. Although Tamar did not physically destroy her writings, she sometimes lost emotional contact with her texts and experienced them as concrete products (not in a transitional space), stolen from her by readers who abused them freely. Paradoxically, the more she succeeded in expressing herself through her writings, the more successfully they affected her readers, who, through their enjoyment, were transformed in Tamar's imagination into the devouring and suffocating mother. In these moments her ability to write and think symbolically temporarily collapsed, only gradually to coalesce as I reconstructed in clear words the internal process that had made her lose these capacities. The connection between my emotional, sensory, and verbal presence and her ability to write became evident. The more she experienced me as continuously present in her mind, the more she was able to write and to use the writing in a symbolic way, which helped her strengthen her own sense of having a well-defined and complex mind-self, or I-ness.

Fear of Being Swallowed

So far I have described the dialectics of writing as it expresses both an identification with a primary object and a means of distancing from that object. Tamar's writing functioned sometimes as an autistic object meant to protect against unbearable primitive anxieties and sometimes as a new emotional essence capable of containing and organizing chaotic and disintegrating internal processes, while also building new emotional abilities.

I would like now to add a few remarks about the anxiety of disintegration and loss of identity the patient experienced when threatened with the danger of being swallowed into the object.

Tamar came to analysis like a flooded and leaking baby (Tustin, 1990) with no sense of a boundary capable of holding together all her mental contents (Mitrani, 1996). She was desperate to pour herself into a container until she was able to establish a differentiated form of her own, as if then she would experience a sort of rebirth. It isn't incidental that I began this paper with Tamar's first call as I attempted to establish an organizing axis to contain the sense of flooding she created. Her presence, her clothes, her speech, her way of glancing, and her first dreams expressed intensely how unable she was to keep all her thoughts and feelings together. She did not feel she had any encircling psychic envelope (Bick, 1968; Anzieu, 1989; Houzel, 1990) that could function as a filter, regulator, and border between internal and external world. Tamar was born into a family that for generations lacked the experience of a containing parent who could adapt to a child's needs. Her mother was the child of a mentally ill mother who from infancy neglected her physically and emotionally, leaving her flooded, hungry, and needy forever, unable to serve as a container for her own daughters (Bion, 1957, 1959, 1962). Having won her mother's love and even become her favorite daughter, Tamar felt compelled incessantly to attend to her mother's primitive anxieties, serving as a reversed container while drowning in her mother's oceanic needs. The imperative to respond so prematurely to her mother's needs created a permanent perception that environment intruded on her being (Winnicott, 1949) and forced her prematurely to take care of herself. In such a state, the body and the mind split, and the psyche-soma, which is supposed to exist in an integrated mode (Winnicott, 1949), collapses either in physical symptoms or overdevelops a compensatory cognitive structure (mind), functioning as a secondary skin (Bick, 1968, 1986). In my understanding, Tamar overly developed her inborn intellectual capacity, especially her facility with language, so that it functioned as the main tool for connecting with and containing her mother and herself. These tools, as any secondary skin, became an integral part of her sense of self and made her feel internally held. However, her literary and linguistic abilities acquired qualities of an autistic object (Tustin, 1986) to which Tamar was adhesively attached (Bick, 1986; Mitrani, 1994) in the absence of the needed containing relation. Her writings calmed her temporarily but left her with internal terrorizing holes. She was very successful intellectually but felt no form or structure of her own. The more she succeeded as a writer, the greater this gap became. Moreover, her mother's similar talents made Tamar feel that her writing abilities were natural to her, but also poisonous and hated. This duality became one of the main paradoxes in the analytic work: how to enable Tamar to diminish the autistic use of her writing and its identification with the devouring mother while she continued to write.

When she came to analysis, Tamar was in a state of total collapse. Having succeeded in a demanding professional project, she felt she had lost contact with herself. She no longer felt a clear differentiation between internal and external reality, and every interaction with significant people in her life hurt her intolerably. Her ability to use writing as a secondary skin/autistic object had collapsed. Additionally, the physical symptom of severe back pains developed. This symptom was, in my view, a new attempt to drain the terrifying loss of form into a defined pain. This symptom resulted from the parental failure to create a bodily experience of holding as a basis for the development of self (Freud, 1923; Ogden, 1989; Dale, 1997; Aron, 1998). The pain functioned as an unconscious defense, creating the illusion of holding and continuity. Symington (1985), Anzieu (1989), McDougall (1989), Mitrani (1996), and Lombardi (2002) describe, each in his specific language, the development of the psychosomatic symptom and of physical pain as an omnipotent attempt to hold the self together when it is not held by any significant other and is in danger of disintegration. In such a state the physical pain is "preferable" to the experience of annihilation, leaking, and dissolving into an endless abyss (Tustin, 1990, 1986).

The state of being swallowed into mother's psyche is similar to what Mitrani (1996) describes as a "state of at-one-ment" in which there is no sense of internal space (and three-dimensionality) that makes possible the experience of separateness. In this state, the mode of relating is based on adhesive identification (Bick, 1968), imitation (Gaddini, 1969), and adhesive equation (Tustin, 1990) in which the dependency on the object is total and the anxiety of losing it huge. The separation from the object leaves the self completely helpless and ruined, as if leaking and evaporating (Tustin, 1986, 1990, 1994; Dale, 1997), falling into a void (Winnicott, 1949, 1956, 1962, 1963; Ogden, 1991) that lacks any name or meaning (Bion, 1962) and in which any sense of temporality or space is lost (Grotstein, 1990). Such a dramatic state occurred during my first summer vacation. Tamar lost the sense of being held in my mental womb and felt as if she'd disintegrated into nothingness. In my absence, she clung to her back pains as a somatic container that simultaneously represented the lack of separation as in her fantasy her pain became my pain and a punishment for causing abandonment.

I would like to emphasize that, by adhering to the object, the mind develops the illusion that the object does not exist (since it is experienced as part of the self) and consequently the self may deny its dependence on the object or the danger of losing or destroying it (Modell, 1984). In the first phase of analysis Tamar longed to merge with me, appropriate my form and substance since she felt no sense of her own, and ignore my separate existence, enacting what McDougall (1989) calls the osmotic transference. Any awareness of our separateness would have forced Tamar to attend to my needs while giving up her own existence, as so often happened in her childhood when she and her mother had been chaotically merged. She wanted my soul to become pregnant with her and give birth to her in a new and different way. (She imagined herself emerging from my body with legs first and head last—another attempt to put the "mind" aside.) Thus, her yearning to merge with me both mirrors the terrible confusion between her and her mother and, at the same time, aspires to create a merger with completely different qualities in which I become a mother who is absorbing her and is preoccupied with and totally adapted to her needs. It seems that through this yearning Tamar tried to satisfy a very early developmental need to be completely dependent on an object able to contain her (Winnicott, 1956; McDougall, 1989).

Although in the early analysis Tamar's dependence on me was total, it was accompanied by a clear need to feel she would not be swallowed, but rather contained. Tamar needed me to help build a protecting membrane with primitive, sensuous, comforting qualities. She wrapped herself tightly in the blanket on the couch, creating a cocoon typical of the autistic-contiguous mode (Ogden, 1989) in which sensuous features such as light, contact, and sounds define a sort of autistic shape (Tustin, 1990). She felt tremendous anxiety about losing contact with my face and my eyes when she lay on the couch. My voice replaced my gaze and became a sound object (Maiello, 1995), a sort of acoustic womb (Harris, 1998; Lecourt, 1990), protecting against intrusion and dispersal. During these months it was of vital importance that I modulate myself according to her rhythms, remaining mostly silent, absorbing, remembering, and waiting. Much of my talk acted as a sort of enveloping interpretation (Keinan, 1995), a touch by means of words that gradually enables the internalization of a holding presence.

Defining the Self Within

Finally, I would like to examine the processes through which Tamar built her sense of continuity and form as well as her ability to endure separation with less pain or, in her language, with less "self-cessation." Her increased sense of having an internal structure enabled her to use writing not as a secondary skin or autistic object, but rather as something enhanced by these internal changes and, in turn, as a process through which her self was increasingly strengthened and expressed.

For a time at the beginning of analysis, Tamar dwelled inside me, adhering to and borrowing parts of my identity (Meltzer, 1986, 1992; Steiner, 1993), but without making me feel robbed or vengeful. Tamar sculpted her contour out of feelings she had in my presence and out of my words. Along with the sensuous qualities that were so important during the early stages of the analysis, Tamar valued my ability to formulate with precision her internal experience. In spite of her loquacity, *my* ability to assign meaning and name her internal processes (Britton, 1998) moved her deeply as if with my words something came into being that had never been felt before. Whenever my interpretations grasped her mental essence, her sense of having a solid internal existence was strengthened.

Later in the analysis, my ability to know her depths, without explicit help from her (Bach, 2001), and to hold her in my memory beyond the time and place of our concrete encounters were crucial in the development of a sense of self. Every accurate interpretation of mine was felt as good nourishment coming from another person. The consistency of my thoughts and decisions about her, with no demand that she take care of their existence, influenced the development of a defined sense of being. And yet she was shattered any time she perceived me as failing to speak her "internal language." My interpretation of such experiences, however, turned gradually into a healing factor of its own.

My attention to Tamar's public and professional activities enabled her to feel less terrified and invaded by the external world since I functioned as a sort of transitional object (Modell, 1993). I was a protecting power with almost concrete features when I watched the TV program in which she'd participated, when she carried the small picture of me in her purse, and when we talked on the phone during breaks in analysis. Bergman (2000) emphasizes the need many artists have that their analysts relate to their products not only as an integral part of themselves, but also as separate entities. Similarly, reading what Tamar wrote to me during the analysis seemed to make possible the very act of her writing. My reading assigned and expanded the meaning of her texts for her. Writing to me and knowing I would read all she wrote added another layer of continuity between the two of us, an additional medium through which I could look for and find her, follow the entirety of her reactions, and discover experiences she was unable to bring to the sessions and verbalize.

Gradually Tamar could tolerate that I had a personal history, tastes, and characteristics of my own. My existence, separate from her projections (Bollas, 1989, 1999; Ghent, 1989; Benjamin, 1995; Lombardi, 1998), gradually came into being through numerous fluctuations between omnipotent control of the other and acknowledgement of her existence as a separate subject. The breaks in analysis had a special impact since through them I moved away from and back to Tamar, eventually making possible the birth of a transitional space that results from sequences of loss and finding of the object, destruction and reparation (Winnicott, 1971). These dialectics were especially powerful when she had intense rage reactions. Through my ability to stand them without abandoning, giving up, or becoming vengeful, the symbolic destruction that becomes a declaration of separateness took place and with it the passage from object-relating to object-use (Winnicott, 1971).

During her analysis Tamar established a sense of having a private space independent of me. She could bear the feeling that I didn't know everything about her, that I "did not find" her always (Modell, 1993, 1997). Separation was no longer felt as an unbearable pain, but as an experience that enhanced life, play, and creativity. Tamar still has many difficult moments but lives with fewer breaks in her self-experience and continues to write in a softer and more delicate tone, needing less to be defined by the structure of her texts. She continues to write herself on "the board of my heart," symbolically creating and firming her sense of I-ness, her psychic existence as an alive and separate person with a voice of her own.

REFERENCES

Anzieu, D. (1989), *The Skin Ego*. New Haven, CT: Yale University Press. French edition, 1985.

Anzieu, D. (1993), Autistic phenomena and the skin ego. *Psychoanalytic Inquiry*, 13:42–49.

Aron, L. (1998), The clinical body and the reflexive mind. *Relational Perspectives on the Body*. L. Aron & F. S. Anderson, eds. Hillsdale, NJ: The Analytic Press, Inc.

Bach, S. (2001), On being forgotten and forgetting one's self. *Psychoanalytic Quarterly*, 70:739–757.

Barthes, R. (1975), *The Pleasure of the Text*. New York: Hill and Wang.

Benjamin, J. (1995), *Like Subjects, Love Objects: Essays on Recognition and Sexual Difference*. New Haven, CT: Yale University Press.

Bergman, M. V. (2000), *What I Heard in the Silence: Role reversal, Trauma, and Creativity in the Lives of Women*. Madison, CT: International Universities Press, Inc.

Berman, E. (1993), Introduction. *Essential Papers on Literature and Psychoanalysis*. E. Berman, ed. New York: New York University Press.

Bick, E. (1968), The experience of the skin in early object relations. *International Journal of Psychoanalysis*, 49:484–486.

Bick, E. (1986), Further considerations on the function of the skin in early object relations. *British Journal of Psychotherapy*, 2(4):292–301.

Bion, W. R. (1957), Differentiation of the psychotic from the non-psychotic part of the personality. *International Journal of Psychoanalysis*, 38:266–275.

Bion, W. R. (1959), Attacks on linking. *International Journal of Psychoanalysis*, 40:308–315.

Bion, W. R. (1962), *Second Thoughts*. New York: Jason Aronson, 1967.

Bollas, C. (1989), *Forces of Destiny: Psychoanalysis and Human Idiom.* London: Free Association Books.

Bollas, C. (1999), *The Mystery of Things.* London and New York: Routledge.

Boulous Walker, M. (1998), *Philosophy and the Maternal Body.* London and New York: Routledge.

Brink, A. (1977), *Loss and Symbolic Repair: A Psychological Study of Some English Poets.* Hamilton, Ontario: Cromlech Press.

Brink, A. (1982), *Creativity and Repair: Bipolarity and its Closure.* Hamilton, Ontario: Cromlech Press.

Britton, R. (1998), *Belief and Imagination: Explorations in Psychoanalysis.* London and New York: Routledge.

Canetti, E. (1989), *The Secret Heart of the Clock.* New York: Farrar, Straus and Giroux.

Dale, F. M. J. (1997), The Absent Self. *Encounters with Autistic States: A Memorial Tribute to Frances Tustin.* T. Mitrani & J. L. Mitrani, eds. Northvale, NJ: Jason Aronson Inc.

Freud, S. (1923), The ego and the id. *Standard Edition.* London: Hogarth Press, 19:3–68.

Gaddini, E. (1969), On imitation. *International Journal of Psychoanalysis*, 50:475–484.

Ghent, E. (1989), Credo: the dialectics of one-person and two-person psychologies. *Contemporary Psychoanalysis*, 25:169–211.

Grotstein, J. S. (1990), Nothingness, meaninglessness, chaos and the "black hole": I. The importance of nothingness, meaninglessness and chaos in psychoanalysis. *Contemporary Psychoanalysis*, 26:257–290.

Harris, A. (1998), Psychic envelopes and sonorous baths: siting the body in relational theory and clinical practice. *Relational Perspectives on the Body.* L. Aron, ed. Hillsdale, NJ: The Analytic Press.

Houzel, D. (1990), The concept of psychic envelope. *Psychic Envelopes.* D. Anzieu, ed. London: Karnac Books.

Jones, A. A. (1997), Experiencing language: some thoughts on poetry and psychoanalysis. *Psychoanalytic Quarterly.* 66:683–700.

Keinan, N. (1995), The skin as essence and as interpretation: envelope and growth. Lecture given at the Israeli Psychoanalytic Association.

Kermode, F., ed. (1975), *Selected Prose of T. S. Eliot.* New York: Harcourt.

Kristeva, J. (1982), *Powers of Horror: An Essay on Abjection.* New York: Columbia University Press.

Lecourt, E. (1990), The musical envelope. *Psychic Envelopes.* D. Anzieu, ed. London: Karnac Books.

Lombardi, K. L. (1998), Mother as object, mother as subject. *Subject Relations: Unconscious Experience and Relational Psycho- analysis*. N. G. Rucker & K. L Lombardi, eds. New York and London: Routledge.

Lombardi, R. (2002), Primitive mental states and the body. *International Journal of Psychoanalysis*, 83:363–383.

Maiello, S. (1995), The sound–object: a hypothesis about prenatal auditory experience and memory. *Journal of Child Psychotherapy*, 21(1):23–41.

Malamud, B. (1998), *The Complete Stories*. London: Vintage.

Martin, J. (1983), Grief and nothingness: loss and mourning in Robert Lowell's poetry. *Psychoanalytic Inquiry,* 3:451–484.

McDougall, J. (1989), *Theatres of the Body: A Psychoanalytic Approach to Psychosomatic Illness*. London: Free Association Books.

McDougall, J. (1997), The artist and the outer world. *The Inner World in the Outer World: Psychoanalytic Perspectives*. E. R. Shapiro, ed. New Haven, CT: Yale University Press.

Meltzer, D. (1986). The conceptual distinction between projective identifi- cation (Klein) and container-contained (Bion). *Studies in Extended Metapsychology*. Pertshire, Scotland: Clunie Press.

Meltzer, D. (1992). *The Claustrum: An Investigation of Claustrophobic Phenomena*. Pertshire, Scotland: Clunie Press.

Mitrani, J. L. (1994), On adhesive-pseudo-object relations–part l: theory. *Contemporary Psychoanalysis* 30(2):348–366.

Mitrani, J. L. (1996), *A Framework for the Imaginary: Clinical Explorations in Primitive States of Being*. Northvale, NJ: Jason Aronson.

Modell, A. H. (1984), *Psychoanalysis in a New Context*. Madison, CT: International Universities Press.

Modell, A. H. (1993), *The Private Self*. Cambridge, MA: Harvard University Press.

Modell, A. H. (1997), The private self and relational theory. *The Inner and the Outer World: Psychoanalytic Perspectives*. E. R. Shapiro, ed. New Haven, CT: Yale University Press.

Ogden, T. (1989), *The Primitive Edge of Experience*. Northvale, NJ: Jason Aronson.

Ogden, T. (1991), Some theoretical comments on personal isolation. *Psychoanalytic Dialogues*, 1:377–390.

Ogden, T. (1998), A question of voice in poetry and psychoanalysis. *Psychoanalytic Quarterly,* 67:426–448.

Ogden, T. (2001), An elegy, a love song, and a lullaby. *Psychoanalytic Dialogues*, 11:293–311.

Plath, S. (1991), *The Journals of Sylvia Plath*. T. Hughes & F. McCullough, eds. New York: Ballantine Books.

Schellekes, A. (2005), The dread of falling: between breaking one's back and breaking through. *Psychoanalytic Dialogues*, 15(6):897–908.

Steiner, J. (1993), *Psychic Retreats*. London: Routledge.

Symington, J. (1985), The survival function of primitive omnipotence. *International Journal of Psychoanalysis*, 66:481–488.

Tustin, F. (1986), *Autistic Barriers in Neurotic Patients*. London: Karnac Books.

Tustin, F. (1990), *The Protective Shell in Children and Adults*. London: Karnac Books.

Tustin, F. (1994), The perpetuation of an error. *Journal of the American Psychoanalytic Association*, 42:1307–1308.

Winnicott, D. W. (1949), Mind and its relation to the psyche-soma. *Through Paediatrics to Psychoanalysis: Collected Papers*. London: Karnac Books, 1992.

Winnicott, D. W. (1956), Primary maternal preoccupation. *Through Paediatrics to Psychoanalysis: Collected Papers*. London: Karnac Books, 1992.

Winnicott, D. W. (1962), Ego integration in child development. *The Maturational Processes and the Facilitating Environment: Studies in the Theory of Emotional Development*. London: Hogarth Press, 1982.

Winnicott, D. W. (1963), Dependence in infant-care, in child-care, and in the psycho-analytic setting. *The Maturational Processes and Facilitating Environment: Studies in the Theory of Emotional Development*. London: Hogarth Press, 1982.

Winnicott, D. W. (1971), *Playing and Reality*. New York: Basic Books.

18 Landau St.
Qiryat Ono 55559, Israel
shalin@smile.net.il

Modern Psychoanalysis
Vol. XXXI, No. 2, 2006

Suppose There Were No Mirrors: Converging Concepts of Mirroring*

ROBERT J. MARSHALL

Evidence from several realms of knowledge, scholarship, and psychoanalytic practice informs us that emotional communication is a function of mirror neurons and the process of mirroring. In fact, mirroring may provide an overarching framework to comprehend and integrate knowledge from diverse disciplines to understand human communication. Major psychoanalytic constructs such as transference, countertransference, projective identification, and induced feelings take on additional validity in light of these studies. The implications for understanding these constructs are examined.

The minds of men are mirrors to one another.

(Hume, 1739–40)

When I'm with a group of people and they start talking, I study the unconscious communication—what's going on among them and what they're trying to tell each other symbolically.

(Spotnitz, 1981)

But I have had good reasons for asserting that everyone possesses in his own unconscious an instrument with which he can interpret the utterances of the unconscious in other people.

(Freud, 1913)

*The author wishes to thank the following for their assistance in the development of this paper: Milton M. Berger, M.D., Gerald W. Vogel, M.D., Murray Sherman, Ph.D., and the Research Committee of the Center for Modern Psychoanalytic Studies.

I predict that mirror neurons will do for psychology what DNA did for biology: they will provide a unifying framework and help explain a host of mental abilities that hitherto remained mysterious and inaccessible to experiments.

(Ramachandran, 2000)

The significance of mirroring was dramatically driven home to me by Lisa, an intelligent and talented woman who had been treated by three modern analysts in individual and group therapy. She had made considerable progress but still felt depressed and desperate. Her major complaint was that no one ever understood the magnitude, severity, and complexity of her inner confusion, alarm, and rage. After years of work wherein I tried to understand Lisa's communications and Lisa did her best to express to me her plight, she wrote me a letter in which she queried, "Suppose you were raised in a home where there were no mirrors?"

That powerful question and metaphor, which continues to reverberate within me, helped me become more attuned to Lisa's description of the seeming complete lack of emotional communication between her and her family. Her self-image was rarely validated. Whenever she began processing her impulses and feelings, she felt she was met with a smashing demolition of her nascent self. She frequently felt she did not exist and always felt she was wrong. However, her experience with peers and teachers gave her a flickering glimmer of who she felt she was.

I concentrated on ego-syntonic mirroring and joining because any other interventions drove her into rages, depression, and missed sessions. The precision with which she had to be joined reminded me of Ekstein and Caruth's (1971) distinction between mirroring and echoing. An echo is a virtual replica of the original sound, whereas a mirror is likely to reflect not only one's image but also any background images—and, in our context, the projection of infantile impulses. This concept is strikingly illustrated in a bronze statue entitled "Le Miroir" in which a lovely nude is holding a mirror at an angle that would not reflect her face to her but is focused on an unknown object/person behind her.

For the most part Lisa could not tolerate any background images—she had to perceive her inner self in me. Nor could she tolerate any confrontations or interpretations. She demanded that I not act like an analyst, but be "real." This was an impossible conflict that perhaps reflected her own inner dilemma. When I was "real" and said what was on my mind, she was left without an echo or an exact replica of her feeling state that frequently led to a catastrophic reaction or her storming out of the office. The manifest demand of the parents came across as, "Be yourself." When Lisa tried to conform, the latent parental response was, "This is not you, and if it is you, you are bad. Be what we want you to be, and then you will be good. Moreover, there is no discussion because we are right." The reader no doubt perceives Bateson's (1972) double bind in this communication.

I found it difficult to process her unconscious and conscious demolition of me, much as she could not defend herself against her parent's attacks. Agreeing with her attacks on me sometimes alarmed, but frequently soothed her. When I validated her misgivings about me, she was fearful that I might abandon her.

Over time, Lisa concluded that though well-intentioned, I did not have the time, ability, and patience to hold that mirror directly in front of her. With supervisory assistance, I found the ability to join Lisa's feelings about me, which were, "You are more interested in yourself than you are in me, and that is your defect, not mine. And I do deserve to be with a person who is more understanding and giving." She had projected many of her unwanted parts into me, was less self-attacking, and maintained a commitment to pursuing health and treatment. I have the impression that my mirroring Lisa's negative feelings about me had therapeutic value that allowed her to move on to another stage of therapy.

The Importance of Mirroring in Spotnitz's Work: The Functions of Mirroring

In a classic article Margolis (1986) attempts to differentiate among mirroring, joining, and psychological reflection. Spotnitz himself (2004) attempts a differentiation.

> Joining and mirroring are both ego-modifying techniques. They are employed to deal with preverbal resistance patterns, usually those containing aggressive impulses that were stultified. In joining a resistance, the therapist agrees with the patient's words or his conscious or unconscious attitudes. In mirroring the therapist operates as a twin image. The patient wants to make contact with agreeable, similar objects, and will attack a dissimilar, disagreeable object if he feels it is safe enough to do so. The formula seems to be as follows: If you are enough like me and like me enough, it will be safe to attack you if I am convinced I will not be injured in the process. (p. 264)

Oversimplifying for purposes of the present paper, mirroring, joining, psychological reflection, ego-reinforcement, and similar words describe a spectrum of processes that create in the patient the experience that the therapist is like her. The word mirroring will be used to connote those processes. Various words describe this experience of sameness, for example, resonance (Meadow, 1991), symbiosis, fusion, twinness, merger, synchrony, or attunement with another person. The patient comes to know that you are "in his shoes." As we will see, other disciplines use words such as imitation, contagion, empathy, and even mind-reading that encompass the same underlying process.

The main function of mirroring is to mobilize early feeling states (i.e., establish the narcissistic transference) and create an atmosphere wherein the patient is enabled to come to sessions, discharge aggression, and resist the main treatment goal of "saying everything." The patient sees in the analyst those aspects of himself (drives, affects, defenses, etc.) that are unacceptable and rejected. The narcissistic defense of self-attack is deflected onto the analyst. Mirroring also allows for the mobilization of parental imagos in the transference. The analyst's experience of these projections constitutes the countertransference via the mechanism of projective identification. The patient may be both alarmed at and relieved to see that the analyst accepts these projections, withstands all feelings, and reliably returns to sessions despite the projected flaws. In Lisa's situation, I grew weary of the attacks, but was careful not to counterattack. I learned to be especially careful toward the end of sessions because ending the session mobilized feelings of rejection and abandonment, which, in turn, produced rage.

According to Spotnitz (2004), "Joining and mirroring do not cure." They do calm the patient and facilitate the first stage in the treatment. Indeed, Spotnitz referred to mirroring as "taking the wind out of a patient's sails" and frequently referred to ego-dystonic mirroring as facilitating something like "a whale blowing off steam." This discharge or catharsis is not curative. It is a stage in the treatment where the patient learns that verbal expressions of aggression are acceptable. Mirroring techniques are employed when the patient is in a preverbal period. If mirroring is used when the patient is beyond the preverbal stage, the sessions may be pleasant, but the therapy may be compromised and prolonged. When conflicts and/or trauma stem from post-verbal stages (e.g., anal, phallic, oedipal, latency), the interventions for the neurotic (clarification, confrontation, interpretation) are the techniques of choice.

Mirroring techniques may be used whenever the analysand slips into preverbal states. As Gilhooley (2005) and others have demonstrated, cycles of regression and integration occur throughout the course of a single session as well as over the course of treatment. Mirroring techniques, therefore, must be used in a timely manner and with discretion.

What do we mirror? This question occurred to me in my first modern psychoanalytic class with Lia Knoepfmacher. When I asked it, she thought I was being the class's wiseguy. After extensive discussion we determined that there was no clear answer. When I posed the same question to Spotnitz at different times, his response was, "Do whatever works to keep the patient talking." Spotnitz (2004) indicated that the strategy employed "depends on what the therapist has to do to appear like the patient" (p. 263).

The best answer that I can provide is simple: One may mirror everything. Originally, Spotnitz talked about the use of mirroring and joining to support flagging defenses. But when I study his interventions, particularly those in his early audiotapes and *Festschrift* (Sheftel, 1991), I see that he mirrors drives, impulses, feelings, sensations, physical reactions, thoughts, etc. at different levels of consciousness and unconsciousness. On a structural level, he mirrors the id, ego, and superego.

Depending on one's theoretical orientation, clinicians may mirror different aspects of the patient and for different reasons. For example, Kohut (1971) focuses on reflecting the idealizing, narcissistic aspect of the self that had not received sufficient confirmation. Rogers (1946) tends to reflect feeling states, but hesitates to link his technique to theory. Other analysts may use mirroring techniques without regard to theory.

The phenomena of mirroring are not limited to modern psychoanalytic sessions.

Anthropological Studies

One of best known uses of mirroring is described by Fossey (1970, 1971) in her studies of the upland gorillas. She found that by systematically imitating their sounds and movements she could approach the beasts in relative safety. "I tried to elicit their confidence and curiosity by acting like a gorilla. I imitated their feeding and grooming, and later, when I was sure what they meant, I copied their vocalizations, including some startling deep belching noises. The gorillas responded favorably" (1970, p. 51). In a dramatic and touching scene, Fossey (1971) imitated her favorite gorilla, not knowing "who was aping whom" (p. 577), whereupon the gorilla reached out and touched Fossey's hand. Some of Fossey's students who did not follow her directions were charged and attacked by the gorillas.

Cultural studies have demonstrated that imitating nonverbal behavior such as maintaining the customary physical distance between people facilitates cooperative relations. That explains the old adage: "When in Rome, do as the Romans."

Ferenczi (1955) was impressed by the mirroring efforts of a skilled blacksmith in shoeing an untamed mare in a well-publicized event. The blacksmith, Joseph Ezer, began by speaking to the horse in a calm manner. When the animal reared violently and neighed, Ezer simultaneously tightened the reins, roared, leaped into the air, and struck the horse on the nose. The horse collapsed. When she whinnied and reared again, Ezer sprang up and bellowed. During a period of calm, Ezer spoke soothingly until the horse bucked and neighed again. After two hours of this ballet, the mare slowly settled down and allowed Ezer to shoe her. Moreover, the horse became generally more tractable. We can speculate that Ferenczi intuited the significance of mirroring and that it helped him understand emotional communication via his concept of empathy. Freud, at the same time, used the metaphor of the telephone to convey how the unconscious of one person could communicate with that of the other.

Harlow (1971) studied the behavior of youngsters raised by a wire-and-cloth mother monkey. He found that in adolescence they responded with healthier behavior in the company of normal, playful adolescent monkeys. The monkeys, long deprived, imitated their more normally adjusted peers. These changes can be explained as an activation of neural mirror systems and support Panksepp's (2006) view that positive social changes caused by tactile stimulation are mediated by brain opiates.

Clinical Studies

Marshall (1995) suggests that Pinel (1806) and his assistants were the first to use mirroring and joining techniques in Parisian hospitals. Pinel describes how his assistant, Mme. Pussin, intuitively mirrored her patients:

> A maniac, reduced to extreme danger by stubborn abstinence, threw himself into a great passion, and repelled the victuals which the governess had brought him with rudeness and abuse. Dexterous by nature, and rendered still more skillful by experience, she veered about in a moment, acquiesced in his purpose, and even applauded his delirious conduct. She then skipped and danced to droll things, and at length made him laugh. Availing herself of this favorable moment, she persuaded him to eat, and thus saved his life. (p. 96)

In another instance, three patients, each claiming to be Louis XVI, hotly disputed their respective rights to regality. Concerned about the escalating argument, Mme. Pussin took aside one of the patients and questioned him with great gravity, "How happens it that you should think of disputing with such fellows as those, who are evidently out of their minds; we all know well enough that your majesty alone is Louis XVI?" That patient withdrew with "ineffable disdain." Mme. Pussin applied the same tactic with the second patient, leaving the third "in undisputed possession of his honor."

Freud (1912) considered that one of the roles of the analyst was to be a mirror to the patient. "The doctor should be opaque to his patients and, like a mirror, should show them nothing but what is shown to him" (p. 118). Freud's emphasis was on opaqueness or neutrality rather than any active and intentional mirroring of the analysand.

Anna Freud (1926 [1927]), working with a ten-year-old boy who was rejecting, mistrustful, and without "intrapsychic conflict," reports:

> At first, for a long time I did nothing but follow his moods along all their paths and bypaths. If he came to his appointment in a cheerful mood, I was cheerful too. If he were serious or depressed, I acted seriously. If he preferred to spend an hour under the table, I would treat it as the most natural thing in the world, lift the tablecloth and speak to him under it. If he came with a string in his pocket, and began to show me remarkable knots and tricks, I would let him see that I could make more complicated knots and do more remarkable tricks. If he made faces, I pulled better ones; and if he challenged me to trails of strength, I showed myself incomparably stronger. But I also followed his lead in every subject he talked about, from tales of pirates and questions of geography to stamp collections and love stories. (p. 12)

I treated a 15-year-old delinquent who chronically attempted to escape from a residential treatment center. He and I agreed that he was intelligent, but I constantly criticized him for his failures at escaping. Moreover, I suggested ploys to avoid his being apprehended. At one point the youngster asked for help in escaping. I agreed to help him formulate a foolproof scheme. During our extensive planning, he looked forward to his sessions and was a model student, to the surprise of the staff who wanted to know my "secret." The boy asked me to physically assist him in an elaborate escape plan. I refused on the grounds that my collusion might cost me my job, and I emphasized that we were talking, not acting. Despite his fury, he attended sessions, sometimes excoriating me and sometimes proceeding with alternate escape plans. Ultimately, he stayed until his sentence expired, and he was released.

The director of the institution commended me for my work with the boy, but when I revealed to him my hyper-mirroring strategy, he almost fired me. Other examples of joining resistances with delinquents are provided by Marshall (1974, 1979).

Anna Freud's (1936) technique is not only one of empathic mirroring, but a one-upmanship that, to my knowledge, she displays nowhere else in her writings. This technique of one-upping the patient may have emerged in the process of her analyzing August Aichhorn, but it is unclear who influenced whom. She referred delinquent and character-disordered children and adolescents to Aichhorn (1935) who was an early master of mirroring techniques. For example, if a youngster revealed that he was apprehended while committing a theft, Aichhorn might tell the boy that he was stupid in getting caught and suggest an ingenious manner of stealing and not being caught. The boy, finding that Aichhorn was not only a thief at heart, but a better one, would thus develop a narcissistic/idealizing transference.

Aichhorn is a pivotal clinician in the history of mirroring because of his influence on his analysands Kurt Eissler and Heinz Kohut. Eissler (1949) in the classic *Searchlights on Delinquency* acknowledges Aichhorn's contribution and in other articles gives clinical examples of his own use of mirroring. But Kohut (1971), in his voluminous work on mirroring, rarely mentions Aichhorn. Spotnitz (1978) was influenced by Aichhorn's work in that he recommended Aichhorn's schematic plan for working with delinquents: establish a narcissistic transference through mirroring and develop and analyze the object transference.

Another clinician influenced by Aichhorn was Vienna-born Rudolph Ekstein (Ekstein & Caruth, 1971). Ekstein's work underscores the fact that echoing and mirroring are techniques of choice in the treatment of children, adolescents, and patients with primitive or preverbal conditions. Ekstein was one of the first supervisors who recognized the importance of countertransference and the need to teach students how to use their patients' emotional communications in order to mirror them.

Lacan saw the "mirror stage" as one of the significant aspects of a person's life. As I tried to understand his changing views about this stage, I came to realize that I could not begin to validly represent his positions except to say that Lacan was not only fascinated by this stage, but gave it a central position. Despite the salience of the mirror stage to his theory, Lacan does not appear to have used techniques of mirroring or psychological reflection as did Spotnitz, save for a minor technique called echoing.

Milton Erickson (Ross, 1980), a medical hypnotherapist, used mirroring and joining to induce a trance state. Erickson would imitate his patient's behavior by mirroring his movements or the decibel level, pace, and accent of his speech and would even readjust his breathing and pulse rate to that of his client. Basically, Erickson believed that the mirroring stage enhanced his patients' suggestibility.

Whitaker (1980) introduced the process of "bilateral trance induction," in which "patient and therapist hypnotize each other from time to time." In their work with close-binding families, Whitaker et al. (1965) maintain that in order to develop any leverage with the family, it is necessary to join the members at an emotional level and experience their inductions and influence. Sometimes, Whitaker and his colleagues would "hyper-mirror" the family's plight in ludicrous "outcrazying" scenes. For example, given a suicidal adolescent, Whitaker and his co-therapist might discuss the contents of the obituary, the possibilities of murder-suicide, fantasies about the funeral, or the effect on the family. Regardless of Whitaker's rationale, it is clear that this highly intuitive master clinician found that mirroring his patients and families was a first step in getting their emotional attention and communicating on an unconscious level.

Chicago University-based Carl Rogers developed a powerful school of client-centered psychotherapy. At its base it is a process of empathizing with his client's feelings and reflecting these feelings back to his client. Rogers (1946) believed it was essential to identify with the client in order to understand "the client as the client seems to himself" (p. 420). Given this "as if" position, the therapist feeds back in language his understanding of the patient's affective states. While the induction of feeling states is on an emotional level, the feedback process tends to be cognitive as compared to the techniques used by clinicians such as Whitaker and Spotnitz.

At the same time in Chicago, Heinz Kohut established a very influential school of psychoanalysis that stressed the analyst's ability to empathize deeply with the patient. Kohut (1971) took great pains in describing the different mirror transferences and sought to reestablish the early good mother-child relationship in the treatment: "the listening, perceiving, and echo-mirroring of the analyst now reinforces the psychological forces which maintain the cohesiveness of this self-image—archaic and (by adult standards) unrealistic though it may be" (p. 125). Kohut correctly noted that that level of nurturing could not be long maintained and at some point the analyst would break that empathic bond in a way similar to that of the original disruption of the bond. He surmised that when the analyst recognized the nature of the disruption and took reparative steps, self-structure would be enhanced. From the point of view of this paper, Kohut's efforts to empathize with the patient are similar to mirroring the patient at an affective level.

Other master clinicians have used mirroring techniques, but not in a systematic, integrated manner. Frieda Fromm-Reichmann, Harry Stack Sullivan, Robert Lindner, and Harold Searles give examples in their clinical descriptions. John Rosen (1962), in his work with schizophrenics, would "confirm" the delusional system of a paranoid patient. Moreover, he would "re-enact an aspect of the psychosis" and shape his interventions to outrageously mimic and exaggerate the patient's irrationality. The "paradoxical intentions" of Victor Frankl (1959) may be considered emotional mirroring as he tried to replace his patients' fears with their unconscious wishes. Joining techniques were also crucial to the school of strategic therapy developed by Don Jackson, Jay Haley, and the Palo Alto group.

The scope of the clinicians who systematically used mirroring techniques strongly suggests that mirroring is a significant psychoanalytic concept across theoretical persuasions, patient populations, and geographic locations. As I review the work of these clinicians, I see several commonalities. One is that those clinicians worked with patients who evidenced primitive mental states or narcissistic disorders—the most difficult patients. Virtually all of these clinicians were trained in the use of traditional psychoanalytic interventions, but their traditional techniques were insufficient. The clinicians did not rely on textbook solutions, but on something that spontaneously and surprisingly emerged from themselves in the interaction. For example, in working with an autistic, mute youngster who was throwing objects about the room, I blurted out, "Stop throwing things, or I'll throw you out." To my amazement the boy laughed and began chanting repetitively, "Trow you out, trow you out." His parents reported that he began to communicate verbally to them that evening. An extensive analysis of this incident with my supervisors revealed that I had unconsciously mirrored his core fear—being thrown out of his house and abandoned. Yet, I had communicated to him that my nonverbal communication of staying with him was more significant than my words. My words did not mean I would go into action.

In discussing transmuting interventions, Joyce McDougall (1992) revealed that she inadvertently shouted at a patient who was threatening suicide, "If you commit suicide, I'll kill you!" This outburst precipitated mutual laughter and a temporary resolution of the crisis.

The foregoing interventions were precipitated by a desperation in the therapist when all else had failed. Essentially, the analysts were forced into a situation that called for a special response that mirrored an important aspect of the patient's psyche. The reason for this special response was suggested to me by Richard Sterba (1970). When he was asked about mirroring techniques, he replied, "Mirroring is something an analyst does when he doesn't know what to do." Although Sterba meant to demean mirroring, there may be more validity in his statement than he realized as evidenced in mother-infant interactions and by social scientists who believe that mirroring may be a "default" mechanism (Dijksterhuis & Bargh, 2001). Dijksterhuis (2005) clarifies, "We do not choose to imitate at some times and not others. Rather, we are wired to imitate and we do it all the time, except when other psychological processes inhibit imitation" (pp. 218–219). This theme of the ubiquitous use of mirroring techniques will be readdressed in the section on "Mirroring as a Potential Defensive and Survival Mechanism for the Analyst."

Developmental and Mother-Child Studies

In order to more fully understand the implications of mirror neuron studies as well as the significance of Spotnitz's concept of mirroring let us consider some of the clinical research on mother-child interactions.

One of the early psychoanalytic investigators, Spitz (1957), spotted the interactional aspect of mirroring in mother and child. "We may note here that few of us are aware of the fact that it is not only the child who imitates the grownup, but that the obverse is also the case" (p. 41). Anticipating the direction of the field, Spitz announced, "Yet [being imitated] plays a significant role in the formation and development of object relations both from the standpoint of the parent and from that of the child" (p. 41).

Piaget (1962), in studying the mutual reciprocal imitation of child and adult, indicated that being imitated was a necessary stage in learning to imitate. Moreover, the monumental shift from sensorimotor to representational behavior can only occur as a result of the mother's imitating the child.

Winnicott (1971) was a leading proponent of the importance of mirroring in mother-child relations. His observation that "The precursor of the mirror is the mother's face" (p. 111) indicates that the mother's face is the first object differentiated from the self. Moreover, in order for the infant to mature, the "good-enough" mother must look like what she sees in the baby. Winnicott argues that there is a need to be mirrored, which, if not satisfied, leads to "chaos, and the baby will organize withdrawal, or will not look up except to perceive, as a defense. A baby so treated will grow up puzzled about mirrors and what the mirror has to offer. If the mother's face is unresponsive, then a mirror is a thing to be looked at, but not to be looked into" (p. 113). He also advocated that "giving back what the patient brings" (p. 17) is a *sine qua non* in psychotherapy. It seems likely that one's ability to mirror is a function of one's being mirrored.

Recent studies by Beebe and Lachman (2002) and Stern (1985) in which a mother is spoon-feeding her young child show that baby and mother open their mouths in virtual synchronicity as the spoon nears the baby's mouth. These studies reveal that there are mutual reciprocal interchanges where the shifts in the mirror and the mirrored occur in milliseconds. In fact, Cohn and Beebe (1990) in their split image studies could not detect some of the facial changes unless they slowed their video to 1/12 second per frame. These shifts are automatic and unconscious just as in the mirror neuron studies. The rhythm in the rise and fall of intensity and duration of contact between mother and baby is reminiscent of Spotnitz's (2004) "contact function," which, in turn, may bear on the timing and intensity of mirroring by the analyst.

Social Cognition Studies

Some theorists suggest that imitation is a major "hard-wired default mechanism." Social cognition researchers have documented that the ability to imitate is inherited. Meltzoff and Moore (1989) found that newborns who were on average 32 hours old imitated facial acts. The youngest imitator was only 42 minutes old. In later studies Meltzoff concluded that infants possessed a neural system that was activated when they saw an action and when they performed that action.

Another series of experiments conducted by Dijksterhuis (2005) promotes the idea that imitation is the "social glue" that binds people together. Several experiments demonstrated high correlations between imitation and liking. For example, Bernieri (1988) found that subjects whose actions were imitated felt more positively about and in greater rapport with the mirroring persons. Chartrand and Bargh (1999) conducted a study wherein a confederate purposefully imitated the body posture of the subject. The surreptitiously mirrored subjects liked the mirroring confederate rather than a confederate who did not mirror. Subjects who worked with a confederate demonstrated considerable imitation of certain behaviors such as foot-shaking and nose-rubbing. Furthermore, subjects who wanted affiliation with another person tended to imitate that person. The researchers have considered that liking facilitates imitation. But the preponderance of evidence suggests that imitation leads to liking. Dijksterhuis (2005) summarizes,

> The "social glue" function of imitation is well documented. Imitation of postures, speech, and facial expression leads to greater rapport and liking, to smoother interactions, to mood contagion, which can lead to more satisfactory relationship, and even to a higher income. (p. 212)

The reference to higher income refers to a study in which waitresses were instructed to imitate the verbal behavior of customers when they ordered. Under mirroring conditions, waitresses received significantly higher tips.

These experiments reinforce the idea that mirroring enhances the positive narcissistic transference. Clearly, the data can be translated as reinforcing Spotnitz's characterization of the effects of mirroring: "If he is like me, he likes me."

Spotnitz consciously acted on his identification with Freud for he declared, "I followed in his footsteps, pretty intentionally, and to the extent to which I knew what he did, I did the same" (Sheftel, 1991, p. 30). Spotnitz emphasized the point by saying he even learned how to smoke cigars.

The Neuroscience Correlates of Mirroring: Mirror Neurons

An important trend in psychoanalysis is to correlate psychoanalytic phenomena with neurological events as evidenced by the journal *Neuro-Psychoanalysis* and by Shepard's (2005) examination of the convergence of psychoanalysis and neuroscience. Noted neuroscientists believe that the research may demand a change in our thinking about mind-brain issues. However, a substantial relationship is apparent between Spotnitz's concept of mirroring and the research on mirror neurons. The following discussion cites only a sample of a large array of studies that herald the beginning of an exploration that may lend more meaning and credence to Spotnitz's clinical insights and to psychoanalytic practice in general.

The vast majority of studies about mirror neurons have been conducted by non-clinicians. Similarly, many analysts (including the author) have a very limited understanding of the anatomy and biological processes of the brain. Therefore, the bridges between psychological mirroring and mirror neurons are fragmentary, fragile, and temporary—

perhaps like Bailey bridges built by army engineers during World War II until more lasting structures could be constructed.

Spotnitz's early training in Berlin and at the New York State Psychiatric Institute was largely in neurology. Like Freud, he frequently thought about the neurological bases of psychological phenomena. For example, Spotnitz (1977) hypothesized a communication bridge between group cohesion and brain functions that he labeled "intra-cerebral synchronization." As group patients bond and attune to each other, "Neurons form an infinite number of connections and get into step" (p. 100). He goes on to make an observation that anticipates some results of neuronal research:

> Everything known about the electrical activity of the brain justifies the assumption that, as each group member develops ties with the other members and communicates with them on the same wave-length, a special pattern of rhythmic activity among interconnected neurons sets up in his brain, through the process of mutual stimulation. (p. 100)

Beginning in 1987, with a serendipitous finding in an experiment with monkeys, the research on mirror neurons has been expanded to include research on humans and human interaction. The original research provides the simplest introduction to mirror neurons. In a project designed to "map the brain," an electrode, planted in a neuron of the precortex of a macaque monkey, fired when the monkey moved his hand to grab food. By chance, a technician reached for a morsel and noted that the implanted neuron was activated. After replicating the experiment and installing controls for alternate causes, the experimenters concluded that a given neuron fires under two conditions: when the monkey performs an act and when the monkey observes a person performing the same act. Because electrodes cannot be implanted in human subjects' brains to study individual neurons, researchers have relied on technology such as EEG and fMRI. These studies reveal that groups of neurons or "mirror neural systems" exist in the brain that are activated when a motor act is performed *and* when that act is perceived. Moreover, in the mirroring process, the neurons in the observer are fired when *intention* is perceived. That is, if the experimenter waves his hand over the banana, no mirror neurons are fired, but if the experimenter's hand is about to grasp the banana, the neurons fire. Thus, we can say that the corresponding mirror neurons of two people resonate with each other when intention is perceived. There is one caveat: In order for the behavior to trigger the analogous mirror neurons in another person, that behavior must be in the repertoire of the observer. For example, in my treatment of Lisa, perhaps one would say that the "right feelings" she yearned for were not in my repertoire or were not of sufficient strength.

Subsequent research that identified audiovisual neurons indicates that different sensory modalities can be involved in the neuronal mirroring. Moreover, affect systems are involved as indicated by Wicker et al. (2003) who demonstrated that experiencing disgust and witnessing disgust in another person's face fires the same neural system. Mirror neural systems have been shown to be involved in emotions such as shame, lust, guilt, and pride. Other studies indicate that the same neuronal systems fire when a person reads about certain motor activities and when the person views the same activities on a videotape. When a person observes another being stuck with a pin, the observer's pain neurons are activated. In general, there seems to be parallel neural processes regardless of the type of sensory stimulation. That is, visual or auditory stimuli can trigger motor neurons in another person. The pattern of excitation of the mirror neurons in the dyad are approximately the same. An important finding, which has implications for "the talking cure," is that mirror neuronal systems seem to be found near Broca's area, a section of the brain involved in speech production and comprehension. Similarly, an area of study relevant to psychoanalysis pertains to the evolution of mirror neurons in animals and man, that is, when and why in the evolutionary process did mirror neurons and systems evolve and what are the links to the development of language.

It seems clear that we have identified some of the neurological correlates of emotional communication. Clinicians like Laquercia (2005) and Laub (2006), who write about intuition, and those who question the seemingly mystical concepts of induced countertransference and projective identification can breathe easier and feel on more solid ground. In classes, as I discussed projective identification, especially the model espoused by Ogden (1982), students always, and rightfully so, asked, "How do drives, feelings, etc. get projected *into* another person?" The students intuitively understood that unconscious communication did occur, but they were not satisfied with my feeble explanations. The mystery is being solved. Freud and his cohorts who hesitantly discussed telepathy, mind reading, and other forms of nonverbal communication would appreciate the current findings.

The Paradigm and Some Implications

One may consider that there is a feedback loop wherein one person's behavior triggers mirror neurons in another that may prompt some behavior that in turn triggers mirror neurons in the first person—and so on in an infinite loop as in a servomechanism. A possible conclusion of this formulation is that a new configuration is constantly being created. Ogden (2003) conceptualizes a "third" being produced continually. Wolstein (Hirsch, 2000) focuses on the ever-changing "here-and-now" interaction and experience of the psychoanalytic dyad.

I theorize a continuous feedback loop of two sets of interacting mirror neurons. That is, something new is being created at every nanosecond. The new configuration then changes the reciprocal neuronal functioning until the interaction is broken off. It is helpful to put the data into a systems or field-theory framework. The earliest and simplest systems phenomenon I encountered was during World War II when scientists developed an anti-aircraft shell containing a proximity fuse. The fuse contained a radar/sonar device that changed the distance at which the shell would be exploded to disable an aircraft without a direct hit. This simple model is vastly expanded in the current missile systems that constantly observe targets and change direction according to the movements of the target. The target plane, in turn, adjusts its trajectory to avoid impact.

Another analogy may clarify the complexities of interacting human mirror systems. Imagine two opposing electronic devices that can videotape and record each other. Also imagine the fact that being video-taped by one machine changes what will be videotaped by the other. There is constant interactive and synchronous change in each machine.

I am suggesting that the mirror neuron research, albeit at an early stage, can help us develop a model of the mind and of the interactions of minds. We cannot abandon our hard-earned knowledge of the unconscious and intrapsychic processes. Yet, the data pleads for an interactive, reciprocal systems model to accommodate our understanding of human communication. Perhaps Winnicott intuitively sensed the process when he declared that there is neither infant nor mother, but a virtually synchronous unit that changes in microseconds, as demonstrated by the programmatic work of infant researchers. Moreover, the data provides a neuro-physiological basis for processes such as identification, introjection, projective identification, enactments, countertransference, and perhaps for any interactive process.

Mirroring as a Potential Defensive and Survival Mechanism for the Analyst

Strengthening defenses through mirroring has had a long history in modern psychoanalysis. Given that mirroring achieves certain goals for the patient, let us consider how mirroring may provide reinforcement of the analyst's defensive structure.

The discovery of mirror neurons has sparked meaningful speculation about their survival and adaptive functions in the ontogeny and phylogeny of virtually all species. That is, the abilities to imitate, to anticipate others' moves, and to empathize have great survival value. Imitation is more than the highest form of flattery. At perhaps a deeper phylogenetic level, and not necessarily a function of mirror neurons, mimicking has survival value. For example, Ratcliffe and Fullard (2005) report that moth's ears are tuned to receive the radar-like emissions of a predatory bat. Upon receipt of these signals, the flying moth can emit the same sound, which confuses the bat. Many animals also use camouflaging or mimicking in order to fend off predators. One is reminded of Erickson and Rossi's (1975) confusion techniques (essentially imitating the person) and also Spotnitz's (2004) reference to the effects of confusing the patient through mirroring. Spotnitz and learning specialists believe that this period of confusion not only "neutralizes" the patient, but may move him from one belief system to another.

In this "impossible profession," analysts frequently cannot "be themselves" in that they cannot necessarily act on their thoughts and feelings. Spotnitz has advised that an analyst "save" her vindictive feeling so it may be used at a time when the patient needs that feeling, but this suppression may extract an unknown emotional and somatic toll on the analyst. I recall Katherine Wolf (1951), herself a child analyst, saying that child analysts had the lowest life expectancy in the medical profession. Holmes (2006) acknowledges that Phyllis Meadow taught her that "becoming an analyst" involves "learning to live with madness, aggression, and the unknown."

Rarely are analysts mirrored by their patients, especially when the analyst tends to be a blank screen. Langs and Searles (1980) provide the exceptions to this rule by suggesting that the analysand assists and even analyzes the analyst—a scenario that is feasible in the mirror neuron paradigm.

Analysts, by virtue of allowing transferences to develop, expose themselves to the intense emotionality of their patients and develop countertransferences. Inexperienced analysts are often devastated by feelings that are induced by patients. In some instances, the analyst has grave difficulty in understanding, using, and shaking off feeling incompetent, confused, lustful, or like a "bad analyst" as discussed by Epstein (1999). Mirror neuron research suggests that there is virtually no escape from the stimulation of patients. The burgeoning literature on countertransference attests to clinicians' necessary interest in differentiating between objective and subjective countertransferences. Spotnitz's extensive discussions on induced feelings and countertransference have helped to identify the source and meaning of analysts' feelings.

The question I pose is how can an analyst survive given the constant emotional barrage from patients and, at the same time, be connected with patients' primitive emotional states. Analysts have used many defenses and coping mechanisms. Perhaps the most time honored is the "everything is transference" defense, wherein the analyst can dismiss her contribution to the patient's reactions. Terms such as "neutrality," "evenly hovering attention," and "blank screen" all legitimize the need to maintain a certain distance from the analysand. Freud contributed to this position, especially in his rationale for the use of the couch and in his wariness of countertransferences. Klein reinforced the emphasis on labeling phenomena as transference and then interpreting. But to her credit, she eventually did recognize that projective identification informs the analyst. Ferenczi, in his later work, broke the mold (as well as his relationship with Freud) by emphasizing the effects of the unrecognized mutual feelings of analyst and patient. Kohut was another more contemporary and controversial voice that cautioned that resistances could be augmented by the analyst's lapses in understanding. However, labeling a clinical event as, for example, transference, resistance, or projective identification may have a more or less cognitive defensive edge to it.

Other less desirable defenses of the analyst include terminating the treatment, referring the patient for medication, prematurely putting the patient in group therapy, interpretation, self-disclosure, and appealing to theory and authority. Of course, there is the old psychoanalytic joke whose punch line is, "Who listens?"

There is an established need for maintaining a certain cautious distance between patient and analyst in order to allow the transferences to develop and to protect the analysis, the patient, and the analyst. On the other hand, there are exaggerated and inappropriate defenses against the affective vitality and turmoil of the analytic interchange. How does one arrive at a healthy homeostasis? Is there a distancing process that allows analysts to "be in touch" without jeopardizing the participants and the analysis? Meadow advocates "being with the patient"—but for how long and with what intensity? Perhaps Levenson (1972) was correct in saying that the analyst allows himself to be emotionally entangled and then "works himself out." Was he amplifying Harry Stack Sullivan's concept of the participant-observer? Whitaker, far from being an interpersonalist, also advocated being drawn into and becoming a part of the group or family system and then separating.

Decety and Chaminade (2003), in a series of experiments, provide an experimental basis for achieving an optimal stance in the analytic process. They found that their subjects reported less distress in experiencing another person's pain when the subject believed that the pain was in the service of cure. For example, a mother's anguish is apt to be ameliorated when she knows that her child's cry of pain is produced by a flu shot. The attitude is perhaps too close to the old saw It's for your own good.

Decety and Chaminade's studies also indicate that the mirroring process does not imply a one-to-one correspondence in brain firings in a dyad. For example, when a person views the pain of another, overlapping or adjacent areas of the brain will fire. Therefore, the emotional experience will not be entirely syntonic. There are wide variations in the ability to experience the feelings of others.

Another solution derives from an experiment by Frable et al. (1998). Students with "concealable stigmas" (homosexuality, bulimia, and impoverished financial backgrounds) experienced a heightened self-esteem and mood when in the company of those with similar stigmata. Similarly, group supervision with peers who have hidden their feelings about their work can stabilize an insecure therapist.

An answer I propose for maintaining a clinical balance is in the direction of the analyst's mirroring the patient. In a consultation with Spotnitz (2003), I asked how I could protect myself from a patient who, in spite of the supervision, was driving me out of control with his unremitting narcissism. His advice was, "Talk about yourself. Become an egomaniac like he is." Essentially, he was not telling me to self-disclose, but to mirror the patient's self-preoccupation. Initially, my self-directed talk enraged the patient, who mounted devastating attacks on me and the therapy. I was dismayed until, in the midst of his fury, he began to scream about the offensive dismissive behavior of his father.

When mirror neurons interact, as described above, it behooves the analyst to consider Bion's well-known aphorism about beginning the analytic session without memory or desire. It is better to have the patient's mirror system lead the analyst, than the analyst lead the patient. For example, if for some reason the analyst is looking forward to seeing a particular patient, the analyst should silently examine that countertransference feeling and try not to communicate those feelings until the analyst knows where the patient is coming from. Also, going into a session with a theory about sexuality, aggression, inferiority, etc. may compromise the patient's mood and his neural functioning. There are exceptions to that rule especially when treatment-destructive resistances prevail. For example, if a patient fails to pay regularly, is chronically late, or signals premature termination, the analyst may address these resistances at the beginning of a session.

The last part of maintaining a clinical balance is to take our own medicine. That is, maintain ourselves in a supervisory/therapeutic relationship in an individual and/or group setting. We know from our own experience and from outcome studies that the "talking cure" helps. Recent brain studies support this view. For example, Winerman (2006) reports that "verbalizing an emotion may activate the right ventral lateral prefrontal cortex, which then suppresses the areas of the brain that produce emotional pain" (p. 35). The modern psychoanalytic emphasis on "saying everything" is reinforced because mirror neuronal activity, while present in many parts of the brain, seems to be concentrated near Broca's (speech) area. The evidence from varied fields may allow psychoanalysts to feel assured that mirroring techniques are not simply "default" techniques, but constitute an array of interventions that have powerful effects on people. The conditions under which mirroring techniques are employed for the benefit of the patient *and* the analyst deserve considerable exploration, expansion, and research.

Summary

Evidence from several realms of knowledge, scholarship, and psychoanalytic practice inform us that emotional communication is a function of mirror neurons and the processes of mirroring. Major psychoanalytic constructs such as transference, countertransference, projective identification, and induced feelings take on additional validity in the light of these studies. Therefore, we are encouraged to expand and refine Spotnitz's mirroring theory and techniques to enhance the analyst's ability to meet the unconscious and emotional aspects of the analytic situation, to allow the analyst to maintain an optimal analytic equilibrium, and to make ours a "possible profession."

REFERENCES

Aichhorn, A. (1935), *Wayward Youth*. New York: Viking Press.
Bateson, G. (1972), *Steps to an Ecology of Mind: Collected Essays in Anthropology, Psychiatry, Evolution, and Epistemology*. San Francisco: Chandler Publishing Co.

Beebe, B. & F. M. Lachman (2002), *Infant Research and Adult Treatment: Co-constructing Interactions.* New York: The Analytic Press.

Bernieri, F. (1988), Coordinated movement and rapport in teacher-student actions. *Journal of Nonverbal Behavior,* 12:120–138.

Chartrand, T. L. & J. A. Bargh (1999), The chameleon effect: the perception-behavior link and social interaction. *Journal of Personality and Social Psychology,* 76:893–910.

Cohn, J. R. & B. Beebe (1990), Sampling interval affects time-series regression estimates of mother-infant influence. *International Conference on Infant Studies,* Montreal.

Decety, J. & T. Chaminade (2003), When the self represents the other: a new cognitive neuroscience view on psychological definition. *Consciousness and Cognition,* 12:577–596.

Dijksterhuis, A. (2005), Why we are social animals: the high road to imitation as social glue. *Perspectives on Imitation: From Neuroscience to Social Science.* Vol. II. S. Hurley & N. Carter, eds. Cambridge, MA: MIT Press.

Dijksterhuis, A. & J. Bargh (2001), The perception-behavior expressway: automatic effects of social perception and social behavior. *Advances in Experimental Social Psychology.* Vol. 30. M. Zanna, ed. New York: Academic Press.

Eissler, K. R. (1949), Some possible problems of delinquency. *Searchlights on Delinquency.* K. R. Eissler, ed. New York: International Universities Press.

Ekstein, R. & E. Caruth (1971), Certain phenomenological aspects of countertransference in the treatment of schizophrenic children. *The Challenge: Despair and Hope in the Conquest of Inner Space.* R. Ekstein, ed. New York: Brunner/Mazel.

Epstein, L. (1999), The analyst's "bad-analyst" feelings: a counterpart to the process of resolving implosive defenses. *Contemporary Psychoanalysis,* 35:311–326.

Erickson, M. H. & E. L. Rossi (1975), Varieties of double bind. *Collected Papers of Milton H. Erickson on Hypnosis.* New York: Irvington.

Ferenczi, S. (1955), Taming of a wild horse. *The Selected Papers of Sándor Ferenczi.* Vol III. New York: Basic Books.

Fossey, D. (1970), Making friends with mountain gorillas. *National Geographic,* 137:48–67.

Fossey, D. (1971), More years with mountain gorillas. *National Geographic,* 140:574–585.

Frable, D. E., L. Platt & S. Hoey (1998), Concealable stigmas and positive self-perceptions: feeling better around similar others. *Journal of Personality and Social Psychology,* 74:909–922.

Frankl, V. E. (1959), *Man's Search for Meaning: An Introduction to Logotherapy.* Boston: Beacon Press.

Freud, A. (1926[1927]), Preparation for child analysis. *The Writings of Anna Freud.* New York: International Universities Press.

Freud, A. (1936), *The Ego and the Mechanisms of Defense.* New York: International Universities Press.

Freud, S. (1912), Recommendations on analytic technique. *Standard Edition.* London: Hogarth Press, 12:111–120.

Freud, S. (1913), The disposition to obsessional neurosis. *Standard Edition.* London: Hogarth Press, 12:313–326.

Gilhooley, D. (2005), Aspects of disintegration and integration in patient speech. *Modern Psychoanalysis*, 30:20–42.

Harlow, H. (1971), *Learning to Love.* San Francisco: Albion.

Hirsch, I. (2000), An interview with Benjamin Wolstein. *Contemporary Psychoanalysis,* 36:187–232.

Holmes, L. (2006), Becoming an analyst: learning to live with madness, aggression, and the unknown. *Modern Psychoanalysis*, 31:113–118.

Hume, D. (1739–1740), *A Treatise of Human Nature.* New York: Oxford University Press, 2000.

Kohut, H. (1971), *The Analysis of the Self.* New York: International Universities Press.

Langs, R. & H. S. Searles (1980), *Intrapsychic and Interpersonal Dimensions of Treatment: A Clinical Dialogue.* New York: Jason Aronson.

Laquercia, T. (2005), Listening with the intuitive ear. *Modern Psychoanalysis*, 30:60–72.

Laub, L. (2006), Intuitive listening. *Modern Psychoanalysis,* 31:88–101.

Levenson, E. A. (1972), *The Fallacy of Understanding.* New York: Basic Books.

Margolis, B. (1986), Joining, mirroring, psychological reflection: terminology, definitions, theoretical considerations. *Modern Psychoanalysis,* 11:19–36.

Marshall, R. J. (1974), Meeting the resistances of delinquents. *The Psychoanalytic Review,* 61:295–304.

Marshall, R. J. (1979), Antisocial youth. *Basic Handbook of Child Psychiatry.* Vol. III. J. D. Noshpitz, ed. New York: Basic Books.

Marshall, R. J. (1995), Pinel: the first modern psychoanalyst? *Modern Psychoanalysis,* 20:175–182.

McDougall, J. (1992), Personal communication.

Meadow, P. W. (1991), Resonating with the psychotic patient. *Modern Psychoanalysis,* 20:87–104.

Meltzoff, A. & M. Moore (1989), Imitation in new born infants: exploring the range of gestures imitated and the underlying mechanisms. *Developmental Psychology,* 25:954–962.

Ogden, T. H. (1982), *Projective Identification and Psychotherapeutic Technique.* New York: Aronson.

Ogden, T. H. (2003), What's true and whose idea was it? *International Journal of Psychoanalysis,* 84:593–606.

Panksepp, J. (2006), *Affective Neuroscience: The Foundations of Human and Animal Emotions.* New York: Oxford.

Piaget, J. (1962), *Play, Dreams and Imitation.* New York: Norton.

Pinel, P. (1806), *A Treatise on Insanity.* New York: Hafner, 1962.

Ramachandran, V. S. (2000), Mirror neurons and imitation learning as the driving force behind "the great leap forward" in human evolution. *The Edge.* http://www.edgeorg/3rd_culture/ramachandran/ramachandran_pl.html.

Ratcliffe, J. M. & J. H. Fullard (2005), The adaptive function of tiger moth clicks against echolating bats: an experimental and synthetic approach. *Journal of Experimental Biology,* 208:4689–98.

Rogers, C. (1946), Significant aspects of client-centered therapy. *American Psychologist,* 1:415–422.

Rosen, J. N. (1962), *Direct Psychoanalytic Psychiatry.* New York: Grune & Stratton.

Ross, E. L., ed. (1980), *The Collected Papers of Milton H. Erickson on Hypnosis.* New York: Irvington.

Sheftel, S. (1991), *Just Say Everything: A Festschrift in Honor of Hyman Spotnitz.* New York: Association for Modern Psychoanalysis.

Shepard, M. (2005), Toward a psychobiology of desire: drive theory in the time of neuroscience. *Modern Psychoanalysis,* 30:43–59.

Spitz, R. A. (1957), *No and Yes: On the Genesis of Human Communication.* New York: International Universities Press.

Spotnitz, H. (1977), Group cohesion and cerebral synchronization. *Group Therapy.* L. R. Wolberg, ed. New York: Stratton Intercontinental Medical.

Spotnitz, H. (1978), Personal communication.

Spotnitz, H. (1981), Ethical issues in the treatment of psychotics and borderline psychotics. *Psychotics, Ethics and Values in Psychotherapy.* M. Rosenbaum, ed. New York: Free Press.

Spotnitz, H. (2003), Personal communication.

Spotnitz, H. (2004), *Modern Psychoanalysis of the Schizophrenic Patient: Theory of the Technique.* 2nd Ed. New York: YBK Publishers.

Sterba, R. (1970), Address to Postgraduate Center for Mental Health, New York, NY.

Stern, D. N. (1985), *The Interpersonal World of the Infant: A View from Psychoanalysis and Developmental Psychology*. New York: Basic Books.

Whitaker, C. A. (1980), Hypnosis and depth therapy. *International Congress on Ericksonian Hypnosis and Psychotherapy*. Tape 50. Garden Grove, CA: Audio-Stats Infomedix.

Whitaker, C. A., R. E. Felder & J. Warkentin (1965), Countertransference in the family treatment of schizophrenia. *From Psyche to System: The Evolving Therapy of Carl Whittaker*. J. R. Neill & P. Knisken, eds. New York: Guilford Press, 1995.

Wicker, B., C. Keysers, J. Plailly, J. P. Royet, J. Gallese & G. Rizzolatti (2003), Both of us disgusted in *My* insula: the common neural basis of seeing and feeling disgust. *Neuron,* 40:655–664.

Winnicott, D. W. (1971), *Playing and Reality*. New York: Basic Books.

Winerman, L. (2006), Talking the pain away. *Monitor on Psychology,* 37:35.

Wolf, K. M. (1951), Personal communication.

300 East 74th Street
New York, NY 10021
simmbob@aol.com

Modern Psychoanalysis
Vol. XXXI, No. 2, 2006

Book Reviews

THE EGO AND ANALYSIS OF DEFENSE. 2nd ed. Paul Gray. Northvale, NJ: Jason Aronson, 2005. 325 pp.

It is a pleasant surprise to find a "landmark" book by a highly respected psychoanalyst, one who has received an American Psychoanalytic Association Outstanding Contribution award for his contributions on technique; a book that contains ideas familiar to modern psychoanalysis: "analysts [should] facilitate verbal expressions of increasingly specific undisplaced derivatives of aggression" or "analyze resistances rather than overcome them." While there is no mention of Spotnitz directly, either in the text or reference list, there appears to be a clear relationship to ideas that emanate from his work. As Spotnitz (1985) has communicated, what is of utmost importance is that the ideas have found their way into the main body of psychoanalysis. The book by Paul Gray, who died in 2002, contains many interesting and valuable ideas and is well worth reading, especially for students of modern analysis. Gray's work will provide a contrast between modern analysis and more traditional ego-psychoanalytic approaches to treatment. It reinforces how important it is for the analyst to focus on the patient's mind, rather than the patient's life outside the room. Many chapters have been previously published, but a few are published here for the first time.

Gray attributes his ideas about technique to the discrepancy between analytic techniques in theory, which emphasizes the importance of following the patient's mind, and those discussed in clinical conferences, case presentations, and supervision, where interest is often shown in the patient's behavior outside the analytic situation (p. 223). He says, "I've

© 2006 CMPS/*Modern Psychoanalysis*, Vol. 31, No. 2

tried to develop a technique of defense analysis that would attain the most effective access to drive derivatives and in that way facilitate analytic progress. I believe that focusing attention consistently on what happens 'inside' the analytic hours helps patients become aware of the many unconscious activities they use to resolve conflict *at the time they're using them*" (pp. 223–224).

Gray says he got support for his ideas from Anna Freud and others. He tells a charming personal anecdote about an interaction with Anna Freud. In an early paper, Gray says Anna Freud's 1936 paper

> tactfully perpetuated a myth when she claimed that her monograph only summarized Freud's ideas at the time . . . but she had reached beyond him and his implications. She had dared to apply his ideas to the structure of the ego and its inclusion in the analytic method, going further than anyone had gone before. For decades she loyally did not include this. In my paper I disputed her discrete position in the matter by suggesting a limitation in Freud's scope of comprehension of the defense alterations of the ego as compared with Anna Freud's own elaborations on the subject. In her reply, she did not at all dispute my stand regarding her father. (p. xxii)

In his first chapter, Gray focuses on the analyst's "listening perspective." He recommends observing data limited essentially to that inside the analytic situation. This is in the interest of improving the analysand's eventual capacity for self-analysis. When "the patient's unbypassed ego functions have become involved in a consciously and increasingly voluntary co-partnership with the analyst, the therapeutic results of the analytic treatment last the longest" (p. 32). He calls this technique "defense analysis using close process attention" (pp. 239–240). He enumerates ten aspects of close process attention analysis that can be taught, compared with more traditional analysis, which relies on interpretations often emanating from the analyst's own unconscious and from "free-floating attention." Close process analysis involves consistent focus on the patient's verbal/vocal flow of material and the analyst's comprehension and memory of what he is observing.

Gray emphasizes that he applies this technique only with patients whose psychological potential permits a consistent and extensive focus on the analysis of resistance. For patients who are unable to allow increasing ego participation, even though given an extended opportunity to do so, he recommends "reverting to a more traditional interpretative approach or using dynamically oriented psychotherapy" (p. 229).

Gray does not, as Spotnitz does, have a concept of providing schizophrenics (i.e., all patients according to Spotnitz) "with the kind of object relationship that they need to sustain the more turbulent emotions they induce." Nor does Gray have a concept that sanctions a wider range of interventions—ego-reinforcing, emotional, and symbolic (Spotnitz, 1985, p. 37). In fact, Gray's stress on defense analysis using close process attention risks stimulating iatrogenic narcissistic regression through an extreme routinization of technique. However, for patients who are amenable to cooperating in the tasks of observation and can develop understanding of the manifestations of involuntary solutions to unconscious conflicts, this approach seems like an excellent technique. When I used the technique briefly in a few long-term cases, for example in a group analysis situation, it appeared to result in movement that was not present before.

In order to clarify Gray's technique, I will provide an example described by him:

> During the early hours of an analysis, an analyst told a female patient, in very clear and appropriately spoken terms, that something the patient had just expressed had interrupted and replaced an uncomfortable preceding thought. The analysand, quiet for a few seconds, then responded in a serious and thoughtfully unprovoking tone, "What is it that I am supposed to do with that?" The analyst dealt with this by replying, also in a thoughtful tone, that the patient wished the analyst to do the thinking for her. Although there eventually would be times in the analysis for such an interpretation, it was not helpful at this point; for, in fact, the patient did *not* know how to make use of what the analyst had said. In a subsequent hour, following similar remarks by her analyst, the analysand, now more cautious, did manage to say she "really" did not know what to do with his observation. This time, the analyst was able to say that by his comments he was trying to provide an opportunity for her to notice that in attempting to be spontaneous and candid in expressing her thoughts and feelings, she had reached a specific place that became difficult—there was some conflict—and suddenly she had turned to another line of thought, as if she had taken refuge in it. He added that if in retrospect she could confirm this, then she might be free, by "going back" to that difficult place, to try to understand with the analyst's help what sort of "risk" had inhibited her. If she could do this, she might not have to avoid such conflicted thoughts or feelings. Within the bounds of what her resistance permitted, she was subsequently able to begin the task of gradually bringing into her awareness how currently unnecessary were her ego's unconscious, reflexive, defensive activities. (p. 77)

A modern analyst can see from this example that the goal of these remarks by the analyst is to stimulate insight in the patient and encourage identification with the analyst. It requires a high level of maturation for a patient to become capable of this degree of cooperation. I don't doubt that the technique can be valuable. In my brief experience with Gray's technique, though limited to a few long-term cases, I have observed positive changes.

However, it also seems to me that the close process attention defense analysis could lead to heightened intellectual and obsessional defenses on the patient's part. This is a criticism classical analysts have leveled at Gray. Gray gives this argument consideration in one of his papers. He says:

> The purpose of focusing attention on the moment-to-moment events in the hour is to hold the analytic process close to what the patient is actually experiencing. If that leads to *increased* unconscious defense ("obsessional thinking"), then the method is being misused. *Any* analytic technique can lend itself to intellectualization if the analyst is so inclined. The whole point of focusing on the immediate moment is to help the patient know how, when, and why he uses defenses. In this way, the patient can eventually choose whether or not he still will use these (formerly unconscious) means to ward off affect-laden mental contents. (p. 228)

Gray goes on to discuss the role of suggestion in analytic techniques (of which he disapproves), his possible overemphasis on transference, the role of the superego as an ego defense, and the reporting of memories and dreams as defense. These are defenses used as resistance and are important subjects for analysts committed to the close process attention defense analysis.

A major aspect of Gray's thinking involves the task of analyzing conflict over aggression. He traces a short history of the lag in technique involving analyzing aggression as an instinctual drive on a par with the sexual drive. "This failure," Gray says, "prevents analysands from developing incrementally the strength necessary to find adequate or sublimated outlets in a real world for their aggression. . . . Nonetheless some patients with severe pathology may actually need to establish this capacity for unconscious control as part of their therapeutic outcome, especially impulse ridden or borderline individuals who lack the capacity for conscious volitional management of excessive degrees of aggression" (pp. 253–254). To emphasize the importance of dealing with aggression Gray refers to Wangh (1996) and says that "psychoanalysis is necessary to civilized human survival. Among such individuals, [as decision makers and leaders in various fields,] an experiential, not merely intellectual, awareness of the ubiquity of instinctual drive derivatives of aggression is vital if indeed our civilization is to survive" (p. 267). In light of the violence extant in our world today, the complaint of many analysts about the dearth of patients may be an ominous portent.

REFERENCES

Spotnitz, H. (1985), *Modern Psychoanalysis of the Schizophrenic Patient.* 2nd ed. New York: Human Sciences Press.
Wangh, M. (1996), Has psychoanalysis a future? It had better, for all our sakes. *The American Psychoanalyst,* 30(1):38–39.

*Gerald Fishbein**

THE SPHINX ON THE TABLE: SIGMUND FREUD'S ART COLLECTION AND THE DEVELOPMENT OF PSYCHOANALYSIS. Janine Burke. New York: Walker and Company, 2006. 384 pp.

This is a valuable contribution to what has come to be termed "Freud Studies," the field of theory and research that explores and illuminates aspects of Freud's work and thought but is not an examination or discussion per se of the clinical aspects of psychoanalysis. Ms. Burke's extraordinary publication can be enjoyed both for the pleasure of finding new knowledge created through research and analysis and the pleasure of reading an original and lively study that goes beyond the expected range of most biographies.

A slim oddity of a volume that appeared in 1976 was, I believe, the germinal work that made *The Sphinx on the Table* possible. This was Edmund Engelman's (1976) *Berggasse 19: Sigmund Freud's Home and Offices, Vienna 1938.* Engelman was a photographer and friend of August Aichorn, a psychoanalyst doing pioneering psychoanalytic work with delinquent adolescents and a close associate of Freud.

It was May of 1938; the Nazis had already arrested Anna Freud once, taken her in for interrogation, and, thankfully, released her. Princess Marie Bonaparte had convinced the Freuds to leave quickly, and she had just made arrangements for them to move with all of their possessions to London. Aichhorn felt that this historic place where Freud lived and worked must be recorded on film. The result was a series of photos, made without lights or flashbulbs so as not to attract the attention of the SS, that revealed what was previously known only to Freud's associates and patients. Freud's offices were filled with Greek, Roman,

*The author appreciates the assistance and support of Linda Gochfeld, Denise Hall, Risha Handlers, Robert Mehlman, Jennifer Troobnick, and Joan White.

Egyptian, and Asian antiquities—thousands of them, a private museum of the highest caliber. Concealed from the Nazis, the negatives changed hands several times, ending up with Anna Freud.

When Engelman's book was published in 1976, Anna Freud still lived in the family's London home; the Freud Museum in London came into existence after her death in 1982. These were the first images of Freud's art collection revealed to the public, a visual recording of Freud's inner sanctum where he sat among those gods who had been at the center of his writings for so many years. This was a most private collection, and before this Freud's extensive holdings, the fruits of what he called his "addiction" to collecting, were little known. This slim volume contained a memoir by Engelman, some descriptions of the artworks written by Rita Ransohoff (1975), and a wonderful introductory essay by Peter Gay that can be seen as the inspiration for Ms. Burke's new work.

Prior to the publication of Engelman's book, there were only a few writings about Freud's life or any scholarly nonpsychoanalytic discussions of his thought or his work. Gay (1998) had not yet written his *Freud: A Life for Our Time*. Ernest Jones's (1953–57) three-volume work was the most widely available biography. Paul Ricoeur's *Freud and Philosophy: An Essay on Interpretation* was published in 1970, setting the stage for discussion of Freud's thought outside the clinical, case-history context. Others by Sachs (1945), Schur (1972), Roazen (1975), and Zweig (1933) had also been published. Ransohoff (1975) had published her piece about his art collection in *Archeology* magazine the year before. But it was most notably Peter Gay's introductory essay in Engelman's work that presented the range of approaches that we see in *The Sphinx on the Table*. Another recent book of importance is *The Compulsion for Antiquity: Freud and the Ancient World* by Armstrong (2005)—a brilliant and inspiring work. It does not discuss Freud's art collection, but rather his conceptual relationship with the ancient world and how this influenced his life and works. Freud, in a way, invited these sorts of approaches to his ideas; his study (1907) of Jensen's *Gradiva* showed how literature ("dreams that had not been dreamed") could be analyzed. "Civilization and Its Discontents" (Freud, 1930) was a work of cultural criticism; his writings on Michelangelo and Leonardo and those on Dostoyevsky and on folktales, among others, showed the ways in which it was not only the patient lying on the couch that could be analyzed.

The places and the gods of mythology were a constant presence and often became references for core concepts in his theories. One cannot imagine studying Freud without Oedipus, Narcissus, Pompeii, or ancient Egypt. It is important to recall that Freud did not see psycho-analysis solely as a form of therapy. He made it quite clear that psycho-analysis was a tripartite undertaking: a means to do scientific research, a framework for study of the human mind, and an evolving methodology for therapeutic treatment.

Everyone who studies Freud's writing feels that they know him in some way. In his works he often discussed his personal experiences and inner world directly, and "The Interpretation of Dreams" (1900) is centrally autobiographical. His correspondences with numerous colleagues found their way into print, whether among his own volumes of writing or those that were published many years later, such as those with Lou Andreas-Salomé (Pfeiffer, 1972) or Arnold Zweig (Pfeiffer, 1970). In 1985 Masson's complete translations of the Fliess letters opened a door into another dimension of Freud's early work, in which we found, interwoven with talk of his travels and his art collection, more personal details than had ever been published before. But to actually see in Engelman's images the setting in which Freud worked was to leap to another level of understanding. All around Freud were objects that *looked* at him—objects of great antiquity and value, yes, but even more, objects that represented a narrative of the human condition, of human nature. Perhaps they did not see him, but it was clear their gaze had to have been a source of his energy, inspiration, and perhaps his grandiosity. Hundreds of pairs of eyes were fixed on him from every direction.

I am reminded of Lacan's (1977) story about his trip on a commercial fishing boat. The fisherman, laughing, pointed at a tin can floating in the water and asked Lacan, "Do you see that can? Well, it doesn't see you!" Lacan reported that he was very disturbed by this, and the feeling, as he analyzed it, arose from the fisherman's message that Lacan had no significance there, no place in the fishing and canning business, no significance on the boat; he was just an invisible piece of flotsam, not even important enough to matter to a tin can. If Freud wanted to be sure that he had a place in history, as we know he did, then he would at every moment need to confront the gaze of the gods, his own mortality, and the need to make what he did of great importance.

Considering "The Interpretation of Dreams" (Freud, 1900), we must remember the multiplicity of meanings and the overdetermination of manifestations in the human psyche. This also applies to his art collection: they are not *only* mythical figures. His dream of his mother's falcon-headed pallbearers, for example, revealed to him a boyish pleasure at a pun on the slang word for copulation: "The German slang term referred to is '*vögeln*', from '*Vogel*' the ordinary word for 'bird'" (583n). And in his office a falcon-headed figure gazed at him. It surely reminded him, every day, of this overdetermination. Nonetheless, it still took him many years to understand that both Eros and Thanatos, as he later came to understand the dual drive theory, were expressed in that dream. *The Sphinx on the Table* never makes the mistake of simplifying Freud. Although Burke misses the connection of the falcon-headed figure to the important dream of his mother's death and his memory of childhood sexuality, she manages, like a good patient, to talk about very interesting details such as this in language that lets us know that she does, in some way, unconsciously understand that it is "something":

> A strange, ungainly work made of gessoed and painted wood, *Falcon-headed Figure* looks less a work of art and more a child's ancient, ugly, cherished toy. (p. 22)

For in several respects, that's exactly what it was.

Ms. Burke has published more than 15 volumes of art history, criticism, and biography. She is from Australia, where the book was published under the title *The Gods of Freud*. Like *The Sphinx on the Table*, that title, too, is something of a mystery. Freud made no secret of the fact that he was an atheist—so who are his "gods"? In every depiction of the Sphinx, from Ingres' painting, which has become such an emblem, to the great Sphinx at Giza, it is represented as too massive to be sitting on a table. And we must also remember that the Sphinx was considered dangerous. So, from the start, we are presented with a Sphinx-like riddle, and here, confronting the myths of Freud the father of psychoanalysis, we find ourselves in the role of Oedipus himself. We can solve the riddles easily enough (mythical gods are no longer objects of worship, but rather literary figures; small, silent statuettes of sphinxes are created as artworks for decoration and ritual), but what does the dangerous Sphinx really have in store for us? When we learn from the Fliess letters that Freud had even personally packed and taken these little figures with him on vacation (where many of his works were written) and that he had arranged them exactly as they were situated in his office, something deeper seems to present itself for consideration. Is this Freud as the small boy taking his "action figures" with him everywhere he goes, the grandiose aspirant to history who needs to be looked at by the gods, the art collector literally in love with his collection, the frightened child with his collection of transitional objects, or . . . ? I think one of the central strengths of Ms. Burke's work is that she does not attempt to hypothesize an answer to a question and then go about proving it. She lays out all of the many interwoven threads, lets them mingle with our own interpretations, offers her own vivid insights based on art history, and lets Freud stew, tasty or otherwise, in his own juices. She respects her readers' intelligence, and her interpretations are never didactic, for example:

> Freud's *Eros* is depicted as a handsome adolescent, with the same sublime, enigmatic smile that attracted Freud to Leonardo's angelic studies of youths and madonnas. *Eros'* charm is seductive, referring to love's illusions, its blindness. But his joyful vitality, conveyed by his light stance, raised arms and wings stretched full flight, symbolises the rapture and energy of love's awakening. Freud respected Eros, "the preserver of all things", though recognising that he was also a mischief-maker. Eros aroused desire, for people and for objects. Plato suggested love and desire are directed at "what you don't have, what isn't there, and what you need." Freud, lover of beautiful things, recognised the urge. The statue of *Eros* was an object of desire he had to possess. Not only did it epitomise classical civilization and the brave new ideas Freud developed in relation to it but, equally, *Eros* was an item of pure aesthetic pleasure. (pp. 48-49)

Here, she uses Freud's self-interpretation to help us understand his passion for collecting:

> Having lost his father, his need for consolation was immediately expressed by surrounding himself with sculptures that constituted "a defense mechanism against anguish and the experience of loss, a bulwark against the fear of abandonment and the dread of being alone and defenceless". Not long before he acquired his first antiquities, Freud declared that a collector was engaged in a game of substitution, in which the objects involved—whether the amorous adventures of a Don Juan or the daredevil exploits of a mountaineer—were "erotic equivalents", items of conquest and desire offering relief, love tokens designed to soothe and heal. (p. 143)

In the paragraph above, she first references a book on collecting by Patrick Mauries (2002), *Cabinets of Curiosities*, and then the Fliess letters. Throughout the book, there are extensive endnotes and, looking at her bibliography, I cannot but be astounded at the range and extent of her sources. The research for the work had to have been an extraordinary effort of art scholarship, delving into Freud's material, others' writing on Freud, mythology, the ancient world and its art, the social and political era prior to World War II in Vienna, the history of late nineteenth-century and early twentieth-century archeology and museology, travel . . . and it continues. Yet, this is no postmodern mashup that has at its center the author's own narcissistic adventures in academia.

One feels that the sources make sense and that the new knowledge she gives life to in this work arises from the ways she has understood the connections among these diverse fields. As in many important biographies and art histories, she helps us feel as if we understand something about the subjects—in this case, a collector and his collection in his time, pursuing his work. But what a collector, what a collection, what a time, and what work! Yet, the writing often feels effortless, not weighed down by the gravity of historical importance nor by an agenda that seeks either to reify or to discredit Freud. But she does not shy away from interpretation, nor from interpreting Freud. Her writing reveals her to be quite skillful, though perhaps a bit out on a limb at times:

> Freud drew divisions. Moses could not be both Egyptian *and* Jew, as other scholars had suggested. He had to be one or the other. Nor could Freud allow his collection to extend beyond his rooms. It must be contained . . . Images of Isis, Osiris, and Horus were not empty idols but redolent metaphors for sexuality and family relationships, areas that proved fruitful for Freud. . . . To prove that Moses "civilised" the Jews by converting them to a superior form of worship, one that reviled images, Freud repressed his collection's importance to him. Why does the ego repress what is deep and instinctual? "Either because it is paralysed by the magnitude of the demand or because it recognises it as a danger." God the Father was deemed of greater historical significance than Freud's old and grubby gods . . . As Freud argued the case for the significance of monotheism, he continued to surround himself with the artifacts of polytheism, just as the repressed drive, despite the ego's attempts to block it, returns as strongly as ever because it has "either regained its forces, or collects them again, or it is reawakened by some new precipitating cause." (pp. 248–249)

But going out on a limb is by no means alien to psychoanalysis, and Burke has written a provocative book because she has not shown a resistance to taking chances. In *Freud and Philosophy*, Ricoeur (1970) wrote:

> There is no doubt that psychoanalysis is a hermeneutics: it is not by accident but by intention that it aims at giving an interpretation of culture in its entirety. But works of art, ideals, and illusions are various modes of representation. And if we move from the periphery to the center, from a theory of culture to the theory of dreams and neuroses, which form the hard core of psychoanalysis, we are constantly led back to interpretation, to the act of interpreting, to the work of interpretation. It was in the work of dream interpretation . . . that the Freudian method was forged. (p. 66)

Burke relates and interprets, for example, Freud's addictions to cigars and to collecting, his insecurities, and his reactions to the reception of his work in his time. We learn about the group of early psychoanalysts who gathered around Freud, the Vienna Psychoanalytic Society, his relationships with dealers of antiquities and with visiting writers, and his fascination with the great archeological exploits of his day. One feels swept along by the ease with which she evokes Freud's world. It never feels gratuitously gossipy—just gossipy enough. She suggests possible connections but never overdoes it; her interpretations are worth thinking about.

One of the wonderful things about this book is its form. Its structure is more like the unconscious, more like what we experience clinically in free association than a sequential narrative biography. It is more like what we hear as we listen to a patient talking on the couch than the usual exposition on someone's life we might hear at a lecture. It is diachronic, rather than synchronic; its narratives emanate from subjects she identifies, and these allow her to follow threads that might not have otherwise been allowed to emerge. For example, in talking about the evolution of psychoanalysis she discusses Freud's idea of keeping patients on the couch, and this takes her to the subject of why Freud used the couch, of the actual couch itself and how he obtained it (a gift from a patient), and then of the carpet he laid upon it. This then leads to a discussion of carpet collecting in Vienna, the particular carpet he had there (a Persian Qashqai), the culture of the Qashqai women who wove it, and because it had been written in Persian, she thinks about *The Arabian Nights*, the story of Scheherazade and her thousand and one nights of storytelling.

> On a rug created by women, Freud's patients, who were mostly women, captivated him with their tales, woven from the fabric of dreams and fears. The roles of storyteller and audience, like those of Scheherazade and the emperor, involve a compact of trust and commitment. Freud regarded psychoanalysis as a shared endeavor: "It is left to the patient in all essentials to determine the course of the analysis." (p. 136)

With equal ease, she lets us follow her train of thought and her scholarship and brings us back to the point, over and over, that all this stuff he had collected makes sense in the context of Freud, his ideas, his life, and his work. By observing the fundamental psychoanalytic rule of saying everything that comes to mind, she allows what she sees and understands to unfold in a way that we too can understand. The book is organized in such a way that, in a suitably psychoanalytic fashion, we can observe repetitions and symmetries. As in the unconscious, time itself is not a factor, and she can move from one period to another and back, revisiting events from a variety of perspectives. It is a biography that is informed by an essentially nonclinical understanding of psychoanalysis as much as it is by recent developments in art theory. It shows how she can as an art historian—as have others such as Konald Kuspit, P. Adams Sitney, and Christian Metz—use a deep understanding of psychoanalytic literautre to help others apprehend art in a different way, thus validating Freud's belief that psychoanalysis can also be a general study of the human mind.

Some may be disappointed to learn that Freud not only had no interest in the emerging art of his time, which is now generally seen as one of the most fertile and revolutionary periods in art history, but that he even disdained it. Again, the impulse for his interest in art is seemingly his need to connect himself to weighty narratives of the past, not esthetic research, speculation, experimentation, or the modernist undertakings of medium-specific, self-referential art for art's sake. But what we learn from the earlier example of overdetermination, and considered in the light of such important new insights as those offered in Armstrong's (2005) work, leads me to stop short of being too sure of the real reasons for Freud's aversion to contemporary art. He had no interest in abstraction of any sort, nor in Surrealism, which claimed him and the discovery of the unconscious as its inspiration. Impressionism, Cubism, Futurism, Constructivism, Dada—none of it attracted him. Perhaps had he known about Picasso's collection of African and Oceanic art, his eyebrows may have lifted for a moment, but apparently the two never met. Freud met André Breton and found him foolish. Salvador Dali managed to get to know Freud a bit, but it seems that it was Dali's penchant for manic flamboyance that attracted Freud, not his artwork. When he visited other cities, it was always the collections of artifacts, such as those at the British Museum or the Vatican, that Freud pored over. Freud gravitated toward that which was either representational or functional, and he gave no attention to abstraction, except to the degree, of course, that all representation is conceptually an abstraction of something else. Images, figures, things with names: these were his familiars. A pattern on a carpet was not an abstraction, rather simply a pattern, a property of a thing that was a carpet or a fabric. Such objects were not, as claimed by many of the emerging new forms of art, new ways of representing the world, which, for example, might represent a subjective mode of perception. As for the pure painting, nonobjective work of Kasimir Malevich, I have to wonder if Freud even knew that it existed.

I will venture an interpretation of my own in the face of the question, Why did Freud claim utter disinterest in modern art? I do not believe that it was about his taste in objects, his bourgeois sensibility, or his artistic conservatism. Burke ascribes it to a kind of *horror vacuui*—an art-critical term meaning pretty much what it looks like. But I think that, for him, modern art occupied a similar territory as did psychosis. He *decided* that it was off-limits for his work. Like narcissism, whose "stone wall" he believed psychoanalysis could not tear down, modern art appeared to have emerged from madness, while ancient art seemed to have emerged like Athena born from the head of Zeus—beautiful, whole, and "like us"—human in form, aesthetically pleasing, and embodying a story. I take my cue here from Michel Foucault (1965) who wrote, at the conclusion of his *Madness and Civilization,*

> The frequency in the modern world of works of art that explode out of madness no doubt proves nothing about the reason of that world, about the meaning of such works, or even about the relations formed and broken between the real world and the artists who produced such works. And yet this frequency must be taken seriously, as if it were the insistence of a question . . . but let us make no mistake here; between madness and the work of art, there has been no accommodation, no more constant exchange, no communication of languages; their opposition is much more dangerous than formerly; and their competition now allows no quarter; theirs is the game of life and death. Artaud's madness does not slip through the fissures of the work of art; his madness is precisely the *absence of the work of art*; the reiterated presence of that absence, its central void experienced and measured in all its endless dimensions. . . . Madness is an absolute break with the work of art; it forms the constitutive moment of abolition, which dissolves in time the truth of the work of art; it draws the exterior edge, the line of dissolution, the contour against the void. (pp. 286–287)

Freud, like many psychoanalysts today, was convinced that the treatment of psychosis with psychoanalysis was futile. And so, to have attempted to understand and to interpret art that appeared to come out of madness itself was to attempt to use psychoanalysis to interpret psychosis. But this is the conception of modern art with which Foucault disagrees. Foucault was able to identify that it is exactly in psychosis, the other side of the "the contour against the void," that art no longer exists. He is saying that art can only exist on this side of the stone wall of narcissism. What Foucault describes as the "reiterated presence of that absence" seemed close enough to psychosis that it presented an insurmountable obstacle to Freud. Modern psycho-

analysis describes these psychic states as being established in preverbal stages of development and expressed by the psychotic as a regression to this preverbal (preoedipal) period, a time Freud believed outside the range of psychoanalytic work. If Burke is onto something in
discussing Freud's *horror vacuui*, as I believe she often is in this book
by virtue of the free associative method she apparently used to write
it, perhaps she is pointing at his desire to "a-*void*" the dangerous territory of psychosis that led his resistance. Freud's unwillingness is, in
a way, understandable, even if disappointing. Freud already encountered enough problems having his work accepted in his own time, and
as things were, he certainly did not need to subject such a new field
of study to so much additional pressure. In addition, his methods of
psychoanalysis worked quite well in curing patients of phobias, neuroses, and obsessions. This work, in itself, took an immense amount
of research and theoretical development. Since his time, a new body
of clinical research and theorization has helped to develop new under-
standings; many of us now believe, based on clinical experience, that
psychoanalysis *can be* a valuable tool in the treatment of psychosis
and the borderline conditions.

I highly recommend that anyone who has an interest in Sigmund
Freud and his work read Janine Burke's new book. It is a striking example of how much can be gained when research into the life story and the
life work of a creative person is woven with openness and imagination
in the mind of a creative writer who understands her subject and can
communicate her insights with verve and originality.

REFERENCES

Armstrong, R. H. (2005), *The Compulsion for Antiquity: Freud and the
    Ancient World*. Ithaca, NY: Cornell University Press.
Engleman, E. (1976), *Berggasse19: Sigmund Freud's Home and Offices,
    Vienna 1938*. Chicago: The University of Chicago Press.
Foucault, M. (1965), *Madness and Civilization: A History of Insanity in the
    Age of Reason*. R. Howard, trans. New York: Random House.
Freud, S. (1900), The interpretation of dreams. *Standard Edition*. London:
    Hogarth Press, 4–5.
Freud, S. (1907), Delusions and dreams in Jensen's *Gradiva*. *Standard
    Edition*. London: Hogarth Press, 9:1–96.
Freud, S. (1930), Civilization and its discontents. *Standard Edition*.
    London: Hogarth Press, 21:59–145.

Gay, P. (1998), *Freud: A Life for Our Time*. New York: W. W. Norton & Co.

Jones, E. (1953-57), *The Life and Work of Sigmund Freud*, 3 vols. New York: Basic Books.

Lacan, J. (1977), *The Four Fundamental Concepts of Psychoanalysis*. A. Sheridan, trans. New York: W. W. Norton & Co.

Masson, J. M., trans. & ed. (1985), *The Complete Letters of Sigmund Freud to Wilhelm Fliess 1887–1904*. Cambridge, MA: The Belknap Press of Harvard University Press.

Mauries, P. (2002), *Cabinets of Curiosities*. London: Thames & Hudson.

Pfeiffer, E., ed. (1970), The *Letters of Sigmund Freud and Arnold Zweig*. London: Hogarth Press and the Institute of Psycho-analysis.

Pfeiffer, E., ed. (1972), *Sigmund Freud and Lou Andreas-Salomé: Letters*. London: Hogarth Press and the Institute of Psycho-analysis.

Ransohoff, R. (1975), Sigmund Freud: collector of antiquities. *Archaeology*. April.

Ricoeur, P. (1970), *Freud and Philosophy: An Essay on Interpretation*. D. Savage, trans. New Haven, CT: Yale University Press.

Roazen, P. (1975), *Freud and His Followers*. New York: Alfred A. Knopf.

Sachs, H. (1945), *Freud: Master and Friend*. Cambridge, MA: Harvard University Press.

Schur, M. (1972), *Freud: Living and Dying*. London: Hogarth Press and the Institute of Psycho-analysis.

Zweig, S. (1933), *Mental Healers: Franz Anton Mesmer, Mary Baker Eddy, Sigmund Freud*. London: Cassell.

Kenneth Feingold

Books Received

Araoz, Daniel. *The Symptom Is Not the Whole Story: Psychoanalysis for Non-Psychoanalysts.* New York: The Other Press, 2006. 265 pp. softcover.

Barbanell, Les. *Removing the Mask of Kindness: Diagnosis and Treatment of the Caretaker Personality Disorder.* New York: Jason Aronson, 2006. 195 pp. softcover.

Cramer, Phebe. *Protecting the Self: Defense Mechanisms in Action.* New York: Guilford, 2006. 384 pp.

Farber, Barry A. *Self-Disclosure in Psychotherapy.* New York: Guilford, 2006. 242 pp.

Golan, Ruth. *Loving Psychoanalysis: Looking at Culture with Freud and Lacan.* New York: Karnac, 2006. 238 pp. softcover.

Goodheart, Carol D., Alan E. Kazdin, & Robert J. Sternberg. *Evidence-Based Psychotherapy: Where Practice and Research Meet.* Washington, DC: American Psychological Association, 2006. 296 pp.

Hopkins, Linda. *False Self: The Life of Masud Khan.* New York: Other Press, 2006. 525 pp.

Kantrowitz, Judy Leopold. *Writing about Patients: Responsibilities, Risks, and Ramifications.* New York: Other Press, 2006. 335 pp. softcover.

Kramer, Peter D. *Freud: The Inventor of the Modern Mind.* New York: HarperCollins, 2006. 214 pp.

MacKinnon, Roger A., Robert Michels, & Peter J. Buckley. *The Psychiatric Interview in Clinical Practice.* Second Edition. Washington, DC: American Psychiatric Association, 2006. 661 pp.

Morrison, James. *Diagnosis Made Easier: Principles and Techniques for Mental Health Clinicians.* New York: Guilford, 2006. 318 pp.

Nobus, Dany & Lisa Downing, eds. *Perversion: Psychoanalytic Perspectives/Perspectives on Psychoanalysis.* New York: Karnac, 2006. 350 pp. softcover.

Petrucelli, Jean, ed. *Longing: Psychoanalytic Musings on Desire*. London: Karnac, 2006. 253 pp. softcover.

Prochnik, George. *Putnam Camp: Sigmund Freud, James Jackson Putnam, and The Purpose of American Psychology*. New York: Other Press, 2006. 471 pp.

Raubolt, Richard, ed. *Power Games: Influence, Persuasion, and Indoctrination in Psychotherapy Training*. New York: Other Press, 2006. 352 pp. softcover.

Renick, Owen. *Practical Psychoanalysis for Therapists and Patients*. New York: Other Press, 2006. 179 pp. softcover.

Rosenfeld, David. *The Soul, The Mind, and the Psychoanalyst: The Creation of the Psychoanalytic Setting in Patients with Psychotic Aspects*. New York: Karnac, 2006. 264 pp. softcover.

Shengold, Leonard. *Haunted by Patients*. New Haven, CT: Yale University Press, 2006. 255 pp.

Symington, Neville. *The Blind Man Sees: Freud's Awakening and Other Essays*. New York: Karnac, 2004. 226 pp. softcover.

Williams, Meg Harris. *The Vale of Soulmaking: The Post-Kleininan Model of the Mind*. New York: Karnac, 2005. 252 pp. softcover.

About the Authors

GUTTMAN, STEPHEN R., M.A., graduated with a master's degree in psychoanalysis from Boston Graduate School of Psychoanalysis-NY and holds a certificate in psychoanalysis from the Center for Modern Psychoanalytic Studies. He is a New York State licensed psychoanalyst in private practice in New York City.

LUIZ, CLAUDIA, Ed.M., received her graduate degree from Harvard University and trained at the Boston Graduate School of Psychoanalysis. She is in practice in Brookline and Westwood, MA.

MARSHALL, ROBERT J., Ph.D., is a faculty member, training analyst, and supervisor at the Center for Modern Psychoanalytic Studies. He is a diplomate in clinical psychology from the American Board of Professional Psychology and was chair of the Publications Committee, Division 39 of the American Psychological Association. He has authored more than 30 professional chapters and articles. His books include *Resistant Interactions: Child, Family, and Psychotherapist* and *The Transference-Countertransference Matrix: The Cognitive-Emotional Dialogue in Psychotherapy, Psychoanalysis, and Supervision.* He is in private practice in New York City.

MILLER, PATRICK LEE, Ph.D., is assistant professor of philosophy at Duquesne University in Pittsburgh. He holds a Ph.D. in philosophy and an M.A. in Greek, both from the University of North Carolina at Chapel Hill. He also holds a didactic academic associate degree from the Psychoanalytic Institute of the Carolinas.

SCHELLEKES, ALINA, M.A., is a psychoanalyst who also teaches at the Israeli Psychoanalytic Society, the University of Haifa, and the Tel Aviv University School of Psychotherapy, where she is chair of a new program of advanced studies on primitive mental states. She is also a senior clinical psychologist at the Brull Mental Health Center, Ramat Chen, Israel.

WADE, JENNIFER, M.S.W., is coordinatior of the Phyllis W. Meadow Award for Excellence in Psychoanalytic Writing and a licensed and certified psychoanalyst with a private practice in New York City.

Printed in the United States
83098LV00003B/157-555/A

9 780979 097256